Let the

# CRAZY CHILD

Write!

# Let the
# CRAZY
# CHILD
# Write!

## Finding Your Creative
## Writing Voice

### Clive Matson

New World Library
Novato, California

New World Library
14 Pamaron Way
Novato, California 94949

© 1998 Clive Matson

Editorial: Tona Pearce Myers
Cover design: Alexandra Honig
Text layout and design: Margaret Copeland, Terragraphics

Permission acknowledgments on page 263 are an
extension of the copyright page.

Library of Congress Cataloging-in-Publication Data
Matson, Clive, 1941–
Let the crazy child write! : finding your creative writing voice /
by Clive Matson
p. cm.
ISBN 978-1-880032-35-0 (alk. paper)
1. Authorship.   I. Title.
PN153.M38  1998
808' .02—dc21
98-21570
CIP

First Printing, November 1998
ISBN 978-1-880032-35-0
10  9  8  7  6  5  4  3  2  1

*This book is dedicated to the creative spirit in all of us*

# Contents

# Acknowledgments

In 1978 I was touring the Northwest on a shoestring, giving poetry readings, when I was asked to lead a class at Peninsula College in Port Angeles. My host, Jack Estes, must not have minded that I dressed at a local gas station out of a suitcase thrown in the back of my battered '55 Chevy, or that I had no classroom experience. I asked what he wanted me to teach, and he suggested an exercise, designed by David Wagoner, that names the Editor, Writer, and Child as voices in the writing process.

I gave the exercise to twenty earnest students the next afternoon, and every one of our comments suddenly had an identity. One of those three voices was speaking, and we could also recognize whether it was being helpful or not helpful — on the spot. Our excitement was visceral. The classroom transformed into a living laboratory, and I became custodian of its creative energy.

I took the exercise to the Bay Area and several times across the country; over ten years the "child" evolved to "Inner Voice" and "Crazy Person" and finally to "Crazy Child." Students everywhere taught me how to lead workshops. Norine Radaikin, Renée June, and Skip Robinson gave of their expertise early on as did Ruth Gendler, Karyn Mazo, and Paul Mariah later, and more recently Sharman Murphy, Erin Donahue, and Jeff Karon. Money didn't matter much to me, and I never made enough to fix the torn front fender of that car.

I learned that workshops work best when they foster honesty and power, and I would miss three-fourths of it if I weren't looking to find beauty — or at least interest — in unsuspected places. For this ready openness I have models in my mother, Evelyn Matson, who enjoys talking to strangers, and in Herbert Huncke, who made a career of it.

But this book could not exist without the excitement of workshop participants. Novices, discovering creative writing, and seasoned writers, struggling with its perennial snarls, both contribute to the elevated mood — and to my wonderment. The workshops display, magically, how skills are picked up in the flow of a need to speak. Learning a technique at an urgent moment is inspiring, and teaching thus becomes a dance.

I gained much over the years from attending workshops led by others, notably Josephine Miles, Robert Bly, and Thaisa Frank, and also from classes at Columbia University: the playwrighting workshop of Robert Montgomery, the nonfiction workshops of Frank MacShane, and the fiction analysis of Robert Towers. Few of the sayings and exercises here have originated with me; much of this book issues from the generosity of the writing community. I took from the ideas of Nelson Bentley, Barbara Robertson, Ron Schreiber, Richard Silberg, Will Dunne, and others; essential research was conducted by Kate St. Clair, Gayle Staehle, Jack Schiemann, Jo Lynn Milardovich, and others; David Wagoner provided the seed.

The dance of teaching the exercise created unusual procedures, and these were enlivened and tested in a range of venues. The East Bay Socialist School offered a room for my class; John Oliver Simon left me his Open Exchange poetry workshop; my older sister, Judith Matson, opened doors for courses at Pacific Oaks College in Pasadena. Lower Columbia College in Washington sponsored me, as did Rockland Center for the Arts in West Nyack, New York, the National Organization for Changing Men, St. John's University Continuing Education, Buffalo's Poets and Writers, Wilbur Hot Springs, Moonwhistle Daycare, and many others. The University of California at Berkeley Extension offers my class, through the offices of Liz McDonough and, originally, Sue Smith.

It seemed natural to make the procedures available in a book, and in this I was encouraged by Peter Beren, Robert Fuller, and

Patrick Miller. Organizing the material was an arduous task, especially since I wished to capture the spirit of the workshops accurately. I could not have done this without the urging and support of many students, and especially of my wife, the poet Gail Ford, who, besides putting up with this writer's moods, became one of the manuscript's best readers.

Many readers, among them Lin Carlson, Susan Ito, and Celia Cuomo, provided valuable feedback. If I could remember and name all those who helped over the last twenty years, the list would fill the trunk of that old Chevy. The final form of this book owes much to Marc Allen and Tona Pearce Myers at New World Library.

Now as ever, in whatever venue, the journey into the workshop is fascinating — I never know what will happen when the dance begins. I sold that turquoise-and-white Chevy a few years ago for a fair price, $250, resisting the urge to mount it on boards and glue it to the side of a garage.

# Preface
## The Crazy Child

*Beginning my studies the first step pleas'd me so much . . .*
*I have hardly gone and hardly wish'd to go any farther,*
*But stop and loiter all the time to sing it in ecstatic songs.*
WALT WHITMAN, from "Beginning My Studies,"
*Leaves of Grass*

The Crazy Child is an aspect of your personality that is directly linked to your creative unconscious. It is the place in your body that wants to express things. It may want to tell jokes, to throw rocks, to give a flower to someone, to watch the sunset, to make up insults, to sit quietly — or to play video games. All these impulses, all the thrilling, scary, or ordinary ones, come from your Crazy Child.

The Crazy Child is also your connection to the past. Everything in your genetic history, your cultural history, your familial history, and your personal history is recorded in your body — in your nervous system. Your Crazy Child has direct access to it all. Everything you have done, and everything that has been done to you, is in its domain.

I experience my Crazy Child as energy coming up from my feet, through my torso, and up the back of my neck. It connects me to the Goddess, to God, to the earth, to space, to darkness, to my senses, to my dreams, and to sex. All the exciting and all the dark stuff simmering or roaring through my body is the Crazy Child.

Your "creative unconscious," your "creative source," and your "Crazy Child" are close cousins. I often use the terms interchangeably, but "Crazy Child" has the virtue of sounding playful and wild. When you address it as your Crazy Child, your creative unconscious may feel invited to come out, make itself comfortable, and start writing.

## The Crazy Child's Goal

The Crazy Child's goal is to express itself — to have some kind of existence in the world. We spend so much of our lives telling it to behave, or to shut up and go away, that it probably feels unappreciated. The Crazy Child would like to be heard.

Writing is a safe way for this part of you to be in the world — or a relatively safe way. If your Crazy Child wants to rob a bank, writing about a robbery is more prudent than doing the robbing. If your creative unconscious has an insight that makes you feel vulnerable, you can write it in a private diary.

When the Crazy Child writes, it's a raw, truthful part of you that reveals itself. It has not been civilized. My Crazy Child knows what is happening, in spite of all contrary messages. It knows what it's like to live in my neighborhood, in this culture, in this time, and in my body. My Crazy Child is the real me — or at least an essential, energetic part of me.

The Crazy Child coils tension into a story, loads a poem with gripping images, unfurls a play's or novel's plot ratchet by ratchet, and punches up an essay's most dramatic point. The other voices, the Writer and Editor described below, are valuable aids to writing. But the Crazy Child — your creative unconscious — is the source.

## Crazy Child, Writer, Editor

The Crazy Child has two companions: the "Writer" and the "Editor." These three voices are much the same as the Freudian id, ego, and superego, and much the same as the child, adult, and parent of Transactional Analysis. Sometimes the voices get along well, and sometimes they are unruly antagonists.

The Crazy Child is equivalent to the child or the id. The id, literally, means "it" — but the word has a darker flavor. Some German parents, when they want to discourage their children from going out at night, say the "id" is outside, just as we would say "bogeyman." The Crazy Child has some of that forbidden aura.

The Editor is the superego or the parent — the "should" voice. It analyzes and criticizes our writing, and is intelligent, well-read, and thinks it is civilized. Its judgments can be helpful, harsh, or anywhere in between. The Editor might say you are right on schedule and doing well, or it might tell you to get a real job.

The Writer is the voice that negotiates and plans, and it strives for coherence and reason. The part I am thinking with now is the Writer, which is the same as my ego or my adult. I use it to organize this book, to plan my writing life, and to schedule my lunch breaks.

If you are reading this with your Writer, you are probably absorbing it carefully. Your Editor could be assessing it at the same time, and possibly deciding that you're not good enough for this book, or that *Let the Crazy Child Write!* is too elementary or far too strange — or it's a perfect match. Your Crazy Child will have its own feelings: it might be scared, irritated, awed, or delighted.

All aspects of writing are expressed in these voices. One of them — Crazy Child, Writer, Editor, or some combination — is chattering at every moment. When they quarrel, the Editor often tells the Crazy Child it's stupid or shy or sappy. These quarrels can stop your writing cold.

*Let the Crazy Child Write!* will help your Editor and Writer understand how your Crazy Child is the vital force behind your creativity. They will learn to honor and tune in to your creative source. When they are all getting along, the Editor and the Writer respond warmly to the Crazy Child.

## All You Need Is the Urge to Write

*Let the Crazy Child Write!* is for anyone who wants to write. You may have no experience whatsoever, or you may have written as a child and are interested in trying it again. Perhaps you keep a journal or have begun stories, poems, plays, or essays on your own.

Your job might involve some writing, such as preparing technical manuals or reports or briefs, and you are curious about creative writing. You may even have taken a class or read an inspirational guide, and now you want to explore the nuts and bolts.

All you need is the urge. *Let the Crazy Child Write!* will help you develop a connection between writing techniques and your unique creative source. You will learn, step by step, how to tap into your creative unconscious — your Crazy Child — and its indispensable, dynamic feel for writing.

## HOW TO USE THIS BOOK

*Let the Crazy Child Write!* is meant to be read on your own or with a writing group — either way. The chapters build one upon another, so it's useful to read them in sequence. But you don't need to; you might learn as much by following your nose and skipping around.

Each chapter introduces a writing technique. A discussion explores the technique, an exercise gives you a taste of it, and a workshop section, which is optional, suggests how to give and receive feedback. Each chapter closes with a short writing practice that gives you experience with the technique.

### Discussion

Every chapter begins by discussing a technique of creative writing. The focus is on how that technique works in conjunction with the nervous system, and why it is important to creative writing — both to writers and to readers.

Examples show how the technique functions in stories, poems, plays, and essays, and how the energy and pungency of the technique arises automatically and naturally from our creative unconscious. That mischievous Crazy Child heightens our skills because it already wields them.

The discussion will indicate what you know, but don't understand that you know. Learning creative writing is first a matter of bringing writing techniques into awareness. They are alive and thriving in the realm of the Crazy Child.

## Exercise

Every chapter presents an exercise that gives you hands-on experience with its topic. You can do the exercise on your own or, if you have a workshop, do it during a workshop meeting. Do it quickly and with as much exuberance as you can muster. Don't worry about how well you are writing. There is no wrong way to do any of the exercises — except not to write at all.

You can do the exercise in a half hour. You can lie on your bed, prop yourself on the stairs, lean against a tree, or sit in a cafe with other people or by yourself, however you are comfortable. My favorite spot is at my local daycare center, in a tiny room painted like a magic forest.

In general, follow the method suggested by Natalie Goldberg in her book *Writing Down the Bones:* keep the ink flowing. If you use a computer, keep those fingers wiggling. If you use a pen, keep that pen on the page, and keep it moving.

It doesn't matter how good the writing is. It matters only that you are writing. You're retrieving some of the natural writing skill your creative unconscious has, and acquiring a feel for it. That's the goal.

## Workshop

You may want to wait until you feel confident as a writer before you join a workshop. You can read this book on your own and ignore the workshop sections, or you can peruse them for more information about writing.

If you've already written pieces you like, or if you just feel daring, consider starting a group. A workshop consists of two or more like-minded people who give each other feedback on their writing. This can be done in person, by mail, or by electronic mail. Workshops generally function best, however, when everyone is physically present.

You find out two things in workshops: how well your writing is going, and what steps to take next. These are surprisingly difficult to learn on your own. Your Editor often has too many suggestions or too many hostile judgments. A workshop will provide you with constructive insights in a way that you'll be able to hear — even if your Editor and Writer are being contentious.

When you are ready, suggest to a suitable friend that the two of you start a workshop. If a friend doesn't come to mind, post a note on a community bulletin board, advertise in a local paper, or make an announcement at a reading. Once you find someone, you can both invite friends.

You may be surprised how many people want to write. Decide on a regular meeting schedule and ask that members commit for a specific number of sessions. At each meeting, plan to hear everyone's practice piece, written since the last meeting, and plan to write and listen to the exercise for the chapter you are reading.

It may take several sessions before your group gels, so be patient; the ideal is for each person to feel engaged and encouraged about writing. A workshop's first concern is to establish a safe atmosphere. When it's well on track everyone gets excited and stimulates better and better writing in each other. You have then created a "fermenting brew."

Several ground rules, outlined on page 17, help generate this brew. I call the guidelines "kindergarten rules" and indeed they seem childlike, but they have a complex history. They have evolved over twenty years in my workshops and in other workshops around the country. The underlying concepts were first presented in 1973 by Peter Elbow in his book *Writing Without Teachers*.

The kindergarten rules constrain the Editor from giving heavy criticism that can stop people from writing. The ground rules establish a "syngenetic" workshop that focuses on understanding the writer's primary impulse. The syngenetic workshop supports what each person is doing well, and cultivates each person's unique strengths.

## Practice

The practice section gives suggestions for a longer written piece that develops each chapter's technique. The exercise gives you a quick hit and the practice expands your skill. Often the practice is an extension of the exercise. I will present several alternatives, and you should choose whichever one excites you.

The point of writing a practice piece is to solidify what you have learned before you go on to the next topic. It could take two to three hours. You might write more quickly, or you might take ten hours or more. There is nothing wrong with either.

As you write, follow the spirit of the guidelines — whether you choose one of the alternatives or devise something on your own. If you write three to five double-spaced pages, or the equivalent, you are doing enough to benefit. More is not harmful.

We need to practice a new skill many times before we can do it well. The human nervous system needs to repeat a technique some two thousand times before the skill can be performed without thought. The practice gives you a start on those two thousand repetitions.

## Work Hard and Have Fun

Working with *Let the Crazy Child Write!* is a win-win situation. No matter how small or immense your writing career becomes, you will benefit from this book. You will discover how very interesting writing can be, and you will learn about creating detail, characters, dialogue, action, and more.

*Let the Crazy Child Write!* will also help you in writing letters, memoirs for your family, school papers, and even with the writing you do at your job. You will be able to write more clearly and more vividly, and enjoy doing it far more than you did before. You might also discover that you want to make creative writing an important part of your life.

Since *Let the Crazy Child Write!* develops basic skills and nourishes your creative source, it gives you a solid foundation for a writing career. You will discover the unique power in your own psyche and body. You will find out how well your Crazy Child can write.

# Chapter 1
## Image Detail

*Without . . . playing with fantasy no creative work has
ever yet come to birth. The debt we owe to the play of
imagination is incalculable.*

CARL JUNG, *Psychological Types*

We begin with "image detail" because it's essential for strong writing, and because it's fun. Every moment of our lives we are surrounded by sensory information — the stuff of image detail. Your Crazy Child delights in it.

An image detail is that small part of an image that sticks in our minds. The worn green fabric on the end of a diving board, the pearly scar on a lover's neck, a piece of chewed gum in the boss's ashtray — these are image details. We remember the object, or the person, or the feeling of an entire scene from one detail.

The details that catch your attention in life are the same ones that catch your attention as a reader, and the same ones that work for you as a writer. Much of the adventure of writing is discovering which details are most gripping for you, the observer. As you look around, some details will strike your eye, and some of these will tug at your breastbone.

You are starting a journey and it is filled with fascinating images. What about that boy leaning out of a car window with a green carnation in his teeth? What about that peculiar interview

1

with your boss? Maybe her eyes teared up, and at the same time she unwrapped a fresh piece of gum.

Writing is largely a matter of paying attention. You need to see, hear, taste, feel, and smell details in order to write them. You might notice them instantly and choose them in a snap — because they rise unbidden from your unconscious. Or you might turn a scene over and over in your mind, getting to know it well, before you find the appropriate detail.

Either way is fine. Whether you write slowly or rapidly is simply a signal of how your Crazy Child works. It's the part of you that feels. Those twinges and gasps are from your creative unconscious, from your Crazy Child. So are the sharp, brittle facts that come from deep inside with an utter clarity, the ones you know must be true.

The goal of *Let the Crazy Child Write!* is to help you establish a working relationship with your creative source. In this chapter you will be introduced to your Crazy Child, and you will become familiar with the kinds of details it sees.

## How Image Detail Works

Small details provoke our minds to fill in the entire picture. Especially effective are odd or dissonant details. We remember the experience of diving when we remember the worn fabric of the diving board under our toes. We see the entire blue plate when we remember a shell-shaped chip on its edge.

These small, odd, or dissonant details work because of the close attention that is required to see them. You need to be quite near the plate to notice that shell-shaped chip in the first place. You can do this by moving close physically, or by zooming in with your imagination. The reader, by taking in your words, comes as close to the object as you are.

If you write that you had your elbow on the boss's table when you saw that gum in the ashtray, the reader imagines being in that same position. If you write that you see a pearly scar when your cheek is on your lover's shoulder, the reader's cheek is there too. The reader's nervous system is automatically present, and fills in the scene as the words are read.

This picture-making might sound rare or exotic, but it is neither. Picture-making is automatic in every human being. It is the job of the human imagination to make images. By "imagination" I mean more than simply dreaming something up willfully. I mean the automatic imaging process that goes on beneath our awareness.

Creating and processing images — sensations, feelings, thoughts, observations, memories — goes on all day and all night. We might notice images only a few times during the day or in the morning when we remember a striking scene from a dream. But our imagination is always busy.

An old saw about a three-legged dog states, "You can't imagine a three-legged dog running." But as soon as you read that sentence, your nervous system contradicts it — you do see that three-legged dog. And it's running. The dog is ridiculous, clumsy, endearing, inspiring, or even oddly graceful.

You have at this moment demonstrated how the human nervous system works. Your nervous system began to register the three-legged dog, and your Crazy Child made an exact picture. Your nervous system and your Crazy Child did their everyday job. You were stimulated by an odd detail — the dog with a missing leg — and your imagination filled in the picture.

## Powerful Image Details

I have already talked about small and odd details. "Small," however, does not necessarily mean physically small. An image may be small only in comparison to the larger picture. On the roof of a Los Angeles nightclub is a neon martini, and in the martini is a blinking pink olive. That olive may be two feet across, but it is small compared to the cocktail glass.

Any picture that the reader can complete by imagining part of the body is also powerful. One writer uses hands to convey an image when she says the afterglow of lightning "looks like fingers poking down from the sky." I instantly imagine my fingers hanging down.

The shape and motion of the fingers mimics the shape and motion of the lightning. The technical word for this comparison, using the word "like" or implying its use, is "simile" (pronounced *sim*-i-lee). A simile works when the image and reality both contain a similar feature. Both "simile" and "similar" come from the Latin *similis,* meaning "like."

Homer's "rosy-fingered dawn" is almost a cliché because it has been quoted so often. It's widely quoted in the first place because it's so appropriate. Long, thin clouds stretched across the dawn sky do look like fingers tinted with a rosy color, and the fingers reach into the day. The image fits the event.

We feel anything strongly that relates to the body. The body is, after all, where the nervous system resides, and any detail that in some way touches the body becomes vivid. When we hear of children in our cities moving their beds out of the line of gunfire, we see this clearly — very clearly. We do not have to be there.

We imagine the scene. We move the bed, with the child, in terror or in a nightly numbness. We imagine the bullets angling through the window, we hear the thudding sound and see the shards of glass — our nervous system makes sure we do this. We see the entire scene, just as we see that three-legged dog, loping awkwardly down the street.

## Images Other Than Pictures

The term "image" applies to any sensory impression, and every sense receives and creates images. A particular smell is an image, a sound is an image, a taste is an image, and so is any particular touch. There is also an important sixth sense — the kinetic sense

— that gives us images of motion and momentum.

So far I have discussed images as visual impressions — images that we see with our eyes or imagine with our mind's eye. Images from other senses work in the same way. Small, odd, and dissonant details are vivid, and so are details that relate to the body.

> *What is there, then, about place that is transferable to the pages of a novel? The best things — the explicit things: physical texture. [Stories] . . . need the warm hard earth underfoot, the light and lift of air, the stir and play of mood, the softening bath of atmosphere that give the likeness-to-life. . . .*
>
> EUDORA WELTY, *Place in Fiction*

## Repeated Image Detail

It may be powerful to repeat an image detail. This is especially true if the detail is changed slightly when it reappears; it has a way of adding meaning to itself.

I have already repeated a few details, on pages 1, 2, and 3. That chewing gum in the boss's ashtray might mean more on page 2 than when you first read it. It might be disgusting, instead of a curiosity — it has accrued feeling with repetition. You can forge a unique sensation by repeating a detail in a story, poem, play, or essay.

## Image Detail in Stories

Linda Cohen uses image details in the following excerpts from her novel-in-progress about early twentieth-century immigrants. We can read how revealing her details are, and also, when she repeats them, how they gain power. Her main character, Rose, has just met Sal in the restaurant where Rose is waitressing:

She finally looked up into the man's broad face. He smiled at her and a reddish-brown scar formed a little diamond under one of his eyes.

She looked away as she spoke, outside the front door as it opened again. "We have very good hamburgers here." All that hair he has is frightening, she thought. I've never seen anyone look so much like he came right from the animals. Darwin was right. Except this man came direct from a bear.

Rose pushed past the cook's station through the swinging doors and into the bathroom. She put down the toilet seat and sat on top of it.

The reddish-brown scar that makes a diamond is an excellent detail — small and odd. It brings me right next to Sal's face. Cohen also shows us Sal's hairiness, and, in the last sentence, shows an odd detail about Rose. When Rose sits on the toilet seat, it's a purposeful action: she is using the bathroom as a place to be alone and think.

. . . it's so hard to be a waitress and think at the same time. She put up their orders, then rushed over to where the cereal was and poured out two bowlfuls and a pitcher of milk. She carried it all on a tray to Sal. His legs were stretched out onto the seat of the chair across from him, and he was reading the newspaper again.

"I'm sorry I took so long with your cereal." Rose extended her neck to see the newspaper open to the business section, with a banner at the top of the page that read: "Coolidge Prosperity: Unemployment Way Down/Production and Consumption at an All-Time High."

Notice how the phrase "extended her neck" gives a precise feeling about Rose and about her relationship to Sal. It's a small, odd, physical action, and others will follow:

. . . Sal sat up straight and confident as he poured milk into his second bowl of cornflakes. He took a spoonful of cereal and watched it move toward his mouth. The scar under his eye formed a little diamond again. . . .

There's the scar again, and in the next excerpt two new details appear. The reader is becoming acquainted with Sal one detail at a time, just as you do in life. Both the reader and Rose get to know Sal at an equivalent pace:

A sharply chipped tooth peeked out from the side of Sal's mouth. He was smiling at her with wide open eyes, his long eyelashes nearly touching the eyebrows on his low forehead. . . .

He took Rose's hand, wrapping his big fingers around her smaller ones. . . . With her free hand Rose fidgeted with the narrow brim of her hat. She let her other hand hang limp in Sal's, unsure of what to do next. His hand felt bumpy and hairy, like a paw.

Sal's hairiness has become a singular attraction and it comes up again, bearlike and sexy. The next image gives another detail we can relate to our bodies:

. . . Rose's bloomers and waitress skirt were hidden underneath her coat as it flapped against her calves. . . .

The reader gains a sense of the styles of that time. As we stand with Rose, we can feel the wind on bare calves. Rose and Sal then go to a social meeting:

"How do you do, all of you." Sal gave a little salute with his hand and took a slurp of coffee.

Edmund, the college graduate, took a sip of black coffee from his cup, then set it down so loudly and casually on the saucer it nearly spilled.

Sal's wariness and Edmund's uneasiness are displayed as they drink coffee. Next Rose and Sal are outdoors, and we read details about their bodies, shadows, the air, and a leaf:

> "But you embarrassed me." The breezes were coming out of nowhere, finding the only bare skin on Rose's neck.
>
> "Your mama doesn't go for Italians?" Sal grinned and glanced over at Rose's house, then he moved away from the streetlamp until he was under a tree. The shadows of leaves bounced around his face and coat.
>
> "Rose, you're a beauty. I saw it right away. I've gotta tell you that." Sal reached up and pulled a leaf off the tree. He began ripping it apart.

We see a new facet of Sal as he tears up the leaf and we see the tree anew, just as we would in life. Throughout these excerpts Cohen brings us next to the characters and directly into the scenes. Her details have this effect because they are small, odd, and dissonant.

## Imaginary Image Detail

Image details that you imagine work just as well as those you see. Cohen was born after the days of Rose and Sal, so she could not have seen the details she writes. They are from her imagination, but that doesn't make the process of finding them any different.

Cohen must imagine the scene so deeply that the details come alive, and then she must write them down. Or she could have gone to a restaurant in present time, seen someone remarkable, and given his characteristics to Sal. In both cases, writing vivid details is a matter of seeing.

## Image Detail in Poems

Image detail is basic. It works at the automatic level of the nervous system — in any form of writing. It works in poems, plays, and essays just as it does in Cohen's novel. The only difference is in the play of the imagination: you might go to a more inventive place when you write poems.

An example is on page 69 of this book. When Mary Oliver writes, "the clear pebbles of the rain / are moving across the landscapes," she creates a fanciful image. It conveys a magical, bell-like sense of the scene.

On pages 81–82 Christopher Russell recounts that the poet "becomes brittle and suddenly / collapses in a pile of shards, / like a Ming vase dropped on a garage floor." We feel the poet's disintegration with all the impact of a precious object hitting cement.

When Sharman Murphy observes on page 31 that she "cracked my elbow / scraped my arm / I ripped my shorts," we get an ample sense of the event. This works especially well because these details come after she has averted the accident. She didn't have time, earlier, to notice her abrasions or her torn clothes.

In the love poem on page 32, when Michael McClure writes "your backbone line," I am drawn into the special state of mind which saw that detail. It's a detail that would be seen with an attentive, appreciative eye — a lover's eye.

Image detail, in these examples, has filled in the scene, brought us deeper into each piece, and made the poet's point more lucid.

## Image Detail in Plays

Plays benefit from image detail in two important ways. As a playwright, you can describe your scenes and your characters in a detailed fashion. You can dress your characters, give them mannerisms or funny tics — whatever you like — and you can give them revealing things to do as they speak.

If Cohen's novel were a play, for instance, Sal could tear up that leaf on stage. The playwright could set it up quite simply:

*Sal:* Rose, you're a beauty. I saw it right away. I've gotta tell you
   that.

*[Sal reaches up and pulls a leaf off the tree. He begins ripping it apart.]*

The audience gets to see, live on stage, what Cohen presents to our imagination. I am using the same words she uses, changing them to present tense.

A second important place for image detail is in the speeches. Almost any character's speech can be expanded to include sensory details that are natural to that character's style. You have a lot of leeway; audiences are hungry for detail. As you include image detail, the audience will find the scene enriched and the characters deepened.

Image detail can make a story powerful, and your characters probably know this. In these speeches from Sam Shepard's play *Buried Child,* physical details add texture and impact:

> *Vince:* . . . What is this anyway? Am I in a time warp or something? Have I committed an unpardonable offence? It's true, I'm not married. . . . But I'm also not divorced. I have been known to plunge into sinful infatuation with the Alto Saxophone. Sucking on number 5 reeds deep into the wee, wee hours. . . .
>
> *Halie's Voice:* Good hard rain. Takes everything straight down deep to the roots. The rest takes care of itself. You can't force a thing to grow. You can't interfere with it. It's all hidden. It's all unseen. You just gotta wait 'til it pops up out of the ground. Tiny little shoot. Tiny little white shoot. All hairy and fragile. Strong though. Strong enough to break the earth even. It's a miracle. . . .

The image of sucking on those reeds lets the reader imagine Vince late at night. And Halie's description of those hairy roots, in their various aspects, conveys a feeling of mystery and power.

## Image Detail in Essays

This chapter is an essay. The first details I used were the fabric on the diving board, the scar on the lover's neck, the gum in the ashtray, and the green carnation in the boy's mouth. They illustrate how we fill in a scene from a single detail.

My intent is to present a scattershot of images, hoping one will hook you. I'm concerned specifically with words and their relationship to our nervous system and to the Crazy Child. The beauty of this topic is — since you're reading words — the dynamic can be demonstrated as you read. Perhaps the scar or the gum aroused your interest.

Not all topics provide an arena so rich in relevant details. You may have to search for useful ones. Minor points may be easy to illustrate, as in the next paragraphs. I use cat scratches on a couch, a Naugahyde cushion, a penknife, ions on a light bulb — and ask which of these details are the most powerful.

My broader point is to demonstrate that your Crazy Child knows instinctively about seeing and writing. Choosing the three-legged dog and the blue plate with the shell-shaped chip on its edge took considerable thought. They were tried out in classes and workshops, too, before I was confident that they work. The underlying principle of an essay becomes clear to the reader — and the reader's nervous system — if you give precise, physical examples.

Every essay has a topic, and almost every topic has a component in the real world. You have the potential to notice crucial image detail when the real world is involved. Once you start seeing the details, there will be a profusion of them. It's up to you and your Crazy Child to pick ones that work for your purpose.

## Image Detail and the Crazy Child

In any scene there are almost an infinite number of details. You could capture them all with a camera — all the visuals, small, odd, and dissonant. But such a photograph would be cluttered with useless and ineffective details.

If you want to convey the feeling of being in a room, you might start by describing the furniture. But where would you stop? Should you stop at the cat's claw marks on the back of the couch? Should you stop at the fatty-acid molecules that have penetrated the Naugahyde cushion? The small penknife that slipped out of someone's pocket and is hidden in the crease of the easy chair? The radioactive ions sticking to the surface of a light bulb?

You need include only the details that do effective work. If you are writing a mystery novel, you might want to include the penknife, but not the cat scratches. An essay about cats, in contrast, could include those scratch marks. A science fiction story might use either the fatty acids or the ions. So might an essay on indoor pollution.

> *Even if I could put down accurately the thing I saw and enjoyed, it would not give the observer the kind of feeling it gave me. I had to create an equivalent for what I felt about what I was looking at, not copy it.*
>
> GEORGIA O'KEEFFE

Perhaps Georgia O'Keeffe was talking about her painting of a poppy. She did not take a snapshot with her brushes. She probably listened into her body and saw with her eye at the same time — and painted a poppy flamboyant enough to convey what she felt as she looked at those orange petals.

Of course, only O'Keeffe knows what she did. But my experience suggests that a feeling in the body, a Crazy Child sensation, directs the eye in choosing the detail. The two actions — listening to the Crazy Child and observing with our senses — occur at the same time.

The most vivid details are those most deeply felt by the creative unconscious. This is the thesis of *Let the Crazy Child Write!* and it puts image detail squarely in the province of the Crazy Child. We may not know, consciously, what our most deeply felt images are. We may find them by watching our subject closely, or we may find them by getting into a zone and letting them flow out our fingers.

> *It may be going too far to say that the exactness and concreteness and solidity of the real world achieved in a story correspond to the intensity of feeling in the author's mind and to the very turn of his heart; but there lies the secret of our confidence in him.*
>
> EUDORA WELTY, *Place in Fiction*

Small, odd, and dissonant details work the same way in all creative writing — stories, poems, plays, and essays. Finding those that work best for you is an interesting journey. Your Crazy Child will pick details different from anyone else's.

## EXERCISE

You do not need any particular skills to do this exercise. You need only be able to write words. You can be a through-and-through beginner otherwise, and do it very well. And, if you are a beginner, you have the advantage of approaching *Let the Crazy Child Write!* with an open mind.

You may be more practiced than you realize. Many people who think of themselves as beginners are, in fact, quite experienced. Any kind of writing is invaluable experience, including brochures and business letters. You have to push words out your body and onto paper, and you cannot do this without learning how words work together.

If you are an absolute beginner, you have a fresh mind. You may have a few ideas about what constitutes powerful writing, but those ideas are preconceptions that can restrict the Crazy Child and your creative flow. The fewer preconceptions you have, the more you may learn from *Let the Crazy Child Write!*

In the next section I will describe an exercise and present several ways to approach it. Read the entire section before you begin. An idea or a phrase in it somewhere could be what you should start with, because it excites your Crazy Child. You stand to write powerfully anytime your creative unconscious is engaged. And you'll have fun in the process.

## Interview

An effective way to practice seeing and writing image details is to interview someone. A relative or a stranger will do, as well as a friend, or someone in your workshop — while it is meeting. You can also pretend to interview yourself.

For fifteen minutes or so, ask questions and take notes, copious notes, even if they don't seem to go anywhere. Watch for details that snag your attention. People will always manifest something interesting. They will say something appealing, or there will be something arresting on their person like their earrings, the design of a T-shirt, a hairstyle, some highly articulated muscles, an object in a pocket, or a mannerism — something.

You and your Crazy Child are on a treasure hunt. This hunt is special, because you do not know what the treasure is. You may not recognize it even when you stumble upon it. You will likely not know until you read the exercise later and realize that some detail has brought your subject clearly back to mind.

The trail to the treasure could start anywhere. It may start with

something the person says, or a piece of jewelry, or the gum that
your interviewee is chewing — follow whatever trail you find yourself on. Write a lot of details, especially those that are odd, novel,
or intriguing.

## Truth or Fiction

In this exercise it does not matter if you write falsehoods or truth,
and it does not matter where you find the details. They may be
entirely in your imagination, or they may be in front of you wav-
ing flags. Your task is to notice vivid details and to write them.

You could write exactly what your interviewee says. All of it
might be very interesting. Or you could change a detail here and
there as you go along or later, when you write up your notes. Or
you may add a plethora of new details — either way. You can be as
extreme as you like.

If your interviewee is chewing gum, and that reminds you of
your boss, follow that thought. Why not make your subject the
boss, or the boss's secretary? Or if your interviewee's green bracelet
reminds you of the jade-colored carnation in the boy's mouth, follow that trail. What did the boy do next? Or what did you want
him to do?

## Writing Your Notes

When you're done, look over your notes. You will discover, hidden
or obvious, the trail you were following. Take another fifteen
minutes to flesh it out. Be free, wild, and extravagant as you write.
Do a portrait, or, if the spirit moves you, write a story, poem, play,
or essay.

Relax and write whatever you like. It's best if you don't try to
write a perfect piece — or anything near perfect. This is an exercise, meaning you are developing a skill, not necessarily creating a

product. You also don't have to be accurate to your interviewee.

Write whatever truth or fiction you find most interesting. "Interesting" does not have to mean upbeat or exciting. It may be most interesting that the interviewee reminds you of your wacky aunt. Perhaps they both have car parts in the living room, and one day a weird thing happened on the way to the kitchen sink.

This exercise provides practice in seeing details. You are letting your Crazy Child do much of that seeing, and every Crazy Child has its own unique way. But there is no telling in advance what your way is. Put those image details on paper, lots of them. You are venturing into new territory.

## WORKSHOP

A workshop consists of two or more like-minded people who give each other feedback. You read your exercise to them, and they give their responses. They read their exercises in turn, and the rest of you respond.

On pages xvii–xix I outlined several ways to start a workshop. Three is a good number of people for beginning a workshop, and five or six is ideal. But you can also do a workshop with just one other person.

### The Syngenetic Workshop

"Syngenetic" means having the same origin. When the feedback has the same origin, as nearly as possible, as the impulse of the writing, then it can assist in improving the writing. Workshops are most successful when writers understand each other, and respect the thrust of each other's writing.

This understanding may be achieved by following a few simple ground rules. I call them "kindergarten rules," because they seem childlike, but they are deceptively difficult to follow.

1. Author hands out copies and reads the work. Workshop members listen and take notes.

2. Workshop reads over copies a second time, quietly, and makes further notes. Author is silent.

3. Each member of the workshop says what lines are memorable, repeats the words verbatim, and says why they are effective. Author takes notes.

4. Workshop discusses the dynamics of the piece: What happens? What is the conclusion? What does a particular image convey? Author does not speak. Author listens and takes notes.

5. Workshop makes one or two rewrite suggestions, three at most. Author takes notes.

6. Author speaks. Workshop responds.

The dynamic of the syngenetic workshop keeps everyone's attention on the writing itself — and on feeling the writing to its roots. If you follow the rules precisely, you will be guided into the writing with a clear mind. You need to discover what the writing is about. The goal of the syngenetic workshop is to further the primary impulse of the writing.

Since the Crazy Child or creative unconscious is largely unknown, by definition, you may not have a clue how to hear someone else's writing. The group may be equally clueless about your writing. These are reasons why the rules should be respected. Groups also lose the ability to comprehend someone's writing because — without anyone wishing it — they develop an exclusive aesthetic.

For this first session, since you have written a rough-draft interview during the meeting, it is necessary to give only positive feedback. Guard against subtle criticisms that masquerade as compliments, such as, "I like this, but something didn't work." You will benefit if you practice giving — and receiving — clear, positive feedback with no "buts."

## Read Out Loud and Take Notes

Read to your workshop, slowly and clearly, what you have written. If the piece is short, read it a second time. The workshop will not have copies of what you wrote a few minutes ago, so they must hold the piece in their minds. Reading it a second time will give them a chance to understand it more fully. When you are finished, the workshop should take a few moments to absorb what you have written.

The workshop then identifies which image details are most vivid. This is positive feedback, and following the syngenetic model, they should repeat your words back to you. Take careful notes, indicating each detail they point out. You might underline the words, or use exclamation points in the margins, or squiggles, or stars — whatever makes sense to you.

While the workshop is talking about your piece, you should remain silent. This is an essential kindergarten rule. You should remain silent until they are completely finished, and they might need as much as ten minutes. It is absolutely not useful to discuss or counter their feedback. The workshop's attention and yours should stay — entirely — on what others get from your writing. If someone raises a question about the text, let others provide the answer, or try to. You take notes.

There are, however, two cases when asking questions is fair. The first case is if you do not understand the words that are being spoken. You should ask that those words be repeated or be explained. The feedback should naturally be expressed in words you can understand.

The second case is when the feedback is vague. It is only slightly useful to hear that your details are effective. For example, someone might say, "Your description of the boyfriend is interesting," but this doesn't tell you which phrases are working. Was it the description of his face, or of his jacket, or of how he was moving? It's to your advantage to ask for verbatim feedback. The workshop should try to recall your exact words.

## The Author's Job

You have an important job as you listen to the workshop. Your job is to believe the praise. The workshop is being honest, and their positive feedback is probably accurate. As you work with *Let the Crazy Child Write!* trusting the workshop's positive feedback may be the single most important thing you do. When someone says an image detail is vivid or gripping, indicate that with a note on your copy, and believe it. Do not leave this crucial task to your memory.

The workshop is a mirror for your writing. Their praise reflects what you are doing well, and it is valuable information about your Crazy Child. You find out in the workshop how effective your Crazy Child is. This is not something you can learn on your own.

Often we have banished the Crazy Child from our minds. We may even have forgotten that we have a creative unconscious. This is no surprise, for we are trained from an early age to hide it. The Crazy Child does not help us in school or with our parents, and it does not go over well at work — quite the opposite.

We also train ourselves to discount the Crazy Child. You may think the details you write are dull, or boring, or simply not of interest to anyone — and these judgments may be totally inaccurate. Most likely they are ways of discrediting the Crazy Child. If the workshop likes those same details, it is a lead-pipe cinch your negative judgments are in error.

The exercise puts you in a positive relationship with your Crazy Child. And when you believe the praise of the workshop, you counter the negative thoughts of your internal Editor. You are joining in honoring your creative unconscious and you are giving yourself access to its energy. You are encouraging your Crazy Child to come out and play.

## The Listener's Job

When another workshop member is reading, your job is to listen. Listen carefully for image details that snag your attention. When one does, a picture will form itself in your mind, and you may find yourself dwelling on the detail even after the author has gone on.

Listening is an art. To do it effectively, you must clear your mind, because any preconception will get in the way — any preconception whatsoever. You are not to judge whether the writing is up to par, and it is a good idea to forget that writing is supposed to do anything. You should report the effect of what you hear — nothing else.

Make your mind a blank slate or imagine your mind is an empty screen. As words are read, the image details will light up on the screen. Remember those images that are clear or striking or hold your attention for a while. All you have are words, and the responses of your nervous system.

Another way to listen is with your body. Listen inwardly for little twinges or small intakes of breath or slightly nervous feelings. You could imagine your entire nervous system is a clean plate, and report what sticks to it. Just as some food will remain on a plate tipped at an angle, only those strong or forceful images will stay in your mind.

However you do it, listening is not easy, and there are no rules for predicting vivid details. No one knows in advance what details will be the most vivid. This is especially true when a person is reading for the first time. Each reader is a new entity, each reader sets up a different context, and each set of image details is new territory.

The main thing is to notice, as you hear them, which image details are the most powerful. These details were probably chosen by the Crazy Child, and they are likely to feel strange to the author

— which is why the listener's job is important. The most powerful details could be impulsive, wacky, bizarre, finely textured, perfect, or ethereal. There is no formula for what the Crazy Child does well.

Once you identify the vivid details, repeat them to the writer. It's ideal if you repeat the words verbatim. Then it will be obvious to everyone, even to the author, that those words are powerful — because you remember them. It is also valuable to take notes. This is not cheating. You are reminding yourself which details are vivid, and when the author is finished, you can refer to your notes to repeat the author's exact words.

## PRACTICE

This writing practice is a suggestion for developing your familiarity with image detail. Read the entire section before you start writing, just as you did with the exercise section. The practice isn't designed to be done on the spot. You might want to spend an hour or two doing the practice, or several hours over several days.

As practice, write a second interview, and this time select someone with an interesting hobby or job. Spend more time with your interviewee, look closely at the hobby or job, and write five pages or so — you can write more, of course.

The type of person you choose to interview is important. It could be the person from your exercise, especially if that person's hobby or job deals with physical objects. The more tactile elements your senses have to feed on, the more material you will have for making vivid details. A weaver, a microbiologist, or a car mechanic are all good subjects. So are a dancer or a farmer or a stamp collector. There are millions of good subjects.

Take the reader on the same journey you take for the interview. Give the reader a picture of the front door, the person, the workbench, the sounds, the smells — anything that strikes your senses. Proceed through the interview showing details in the same order that you notice them, or in the same order that they happen. Include what the person says in greeting — and include any odd things the person says.

## New Journalism

When you write those odd details, you give the reader the feel of the person, the place, and the work — even the joy or the adventure or the agony of it all. This is "new journalism," also known as "literary journalism."

Technically, new journalism is journalism that uses story techniques. Old-style journalism simply lists the information. For purposes of *Let the Crazy Child Write!* new journalism takes the reader on the same journey the writer makes to find the information.

> *Take the reader on the same journey*
> *you make to find the information.*

Barry Newman does just that in his article "Fisherman." We see the farm, its surroundings, and the man coming out to greet us, just as he does:

> Leigh, England — Kevin Ashurst's maggot farm — a cinder block shed attached to an air scrubber — is a mile outside this old mill town, in a field of pink wildflowers.
>
> "Looking for work?" a tattooed man calls when a visitor drives up on a hot morning. In the yard, some dead sheep nourish a new generation of bluebottle flies. Two workers, bent over the carcasses, scoop the maggots into plastic tubs. The smell is about as bad as a smell can get.
>
> Ashurst, a meaty man of 43, wipes his hand on his dungarees to clean off the offal, and extends the same hand in greeting. Then he reaches into a tub and brings up a sample of his

finest produce — moist, white and writhing.

"See, that's the size of 'em, like," he says. "Them's good maggots, quality maggots. They'll keep like this for a week in the 'fridge."

Who keeps maggots in the 'fridge? Coarse fishermen do. Kevin Ashurst sells maggots to coarse fishermen. He's a coarse fisherman himself, and a good one. Coarse fishermen bait their hooks with maggots to catch coarse fish — like barble, dace, bleak and roach. Coarse fish live in murky waters, are mostly tiny and make awful eating. Game fishermen, who catch salmon and trout, think of them as vermin. Some think the same of coarse fishermen.

Until about ten years ago, British upper-class fishermen succeeded in keeping the upper-class fish to themselves. The working class had to fish in abandoned gravel pits and industrial canals. The sport wasn't refined, but it was diverting enough, once money got involved.

The author puts the reader in his shoes as he learns about coarse fishing. Quoting the owner gives the reader a sense of who he is, and the smell brings us right into the scene. When you do your interview, however, you may choose something that smells good.

New journalism is what Newman employs in the first four paragraphs. By paragraph five, he slips into old-style journalism and simply lists information. He shows us that the line between the two genres is not rigid.

## Alternatives

There's no reason to limit your interview to a person: this practice also works when you interview a place. One writer chose to spend a night in a hospital, as part of her job, and reported what the experience was like. You could interview a restaurant, a golf course, a nightclub — you name it.

You can also pretend you are a stranger interviewing yourself.

This is a challenge because you will need to see yourself through a stranger's eyes. What would someone see when meeting you for the first time? For the same reason, interviewing a friend is complicated. You may know your friend too well, and you'll need to concentrate on imagining you are seeing your friend for the first time.

### *Show, don't tell.*

Remember to show us the details, don't simply tell us about them. This directive is universal among writers. If an author writes that someone has a handsome face, I know the face is not ugly. Since there are six billion people on the planet, the writer has described some three billion of them. That's too many! I see only a handsome blank, or something the writer did not have in mind.

But if the writer shows me a detail, I can see the face. Remember the pearly scar on the lover's neck, or the shell-shaped chip in the blue plate, or the gum in the boss's ashtray? Go for the small, the odd, and the dissonant. If you do use a general adjective, like "handsome," be sure to back it up with image detail.

As you work, follow the trail of details. Be exact, and do not worry about the effect. The more odd or dissonant or flamboyant your details are, the more freely your Crazy Child is writing. The wilder you write, the more you stand to learn about your own creative unconscious — and the more likely your writing will be truly vivid.

# Chapter 2
## Slow Motion

*Find out . . . what the action was that gave you the excitement. Then write it down making it so clear that . . . it can become a part of the experience of the person who reads it.*
ERNEST HEMINGWAY

"Slow motion" writing follows image detail naturally. Both techniques work on the same principle, so you will be able to learn slow motion without a hitch. Both techniques are also fundamental to powerful writing. And both are enticing playgrounds for the Crazy Child.

Slow motion writing springs from the nervous system's ability to make images from words. When you describe an event, the nervous system sees it. If you present the event one split second at a time, the human nervous system will duplicate the presentation. Your reader will experience that event in those same split seconds.

Most events can be slowed down. You can present momentary slices of a woman turning a lipstick tube around her lips, a girl concealing a knife behind her wrist, a man fingering the top button of his pants. When they unfold in slow motion, the events can be utterly captivating.

We see a slow motion event in much the same way as we see the three-legged dog. The instant we hear the phrase "three-legged dog," we automatically imagine the dog standing in such a way that its legs are visible. We can count the legs.

Similarly, in slow motion writing, we see the event from a slowed-down perspective. The author presents it slowly, so the reader receives it slowly. The author will typically convey the event one slice — one snapshot — at a time.

In life, our sense of time slows because of some adrenaline-producing situation — because of danger or excitement or anxiety. Time slows down in writing for the same reason. We may not know, from the clues in the first snapshot, the exact nature of that situation, but we will be ready for — something. Quickly. Our nervous system senses the probabilities in an instant.

Any change in the image, from one snapshot to the next, becomes part of the interest. We might see the three-legged dog one way at first, a different way next, and a third way the following split second. We will see these snapshots in the sequence that the author presents them.

We see the dog gathering itself lopsidedly to jump. Then it springs sideways, with its mouth open and slobber coming out between its teeth. Next we notice that the expression on the dog's face resembles a smile. And finally the dog lands in the lap of its beloved master, who hugs and pats the dog, or asks it to get down, or is angry at being interrupted — whatever the author's Crazy Child suggests.

These split-second snapshots, taken together, give us the event. The reader is in the event, and the reader feels the emotion of the event. We wonder why the dog is jumping, see slobber coming out its mouth, and pick up additional clues as they are presented. When all the clues are received, we see the entire event — or as much as the writer wishes to convey.

## Kinetic Detail

The "kinetic" sense is often called the sixth sense. It is the sense of the weight of an object, its motion, and its momentum — or its resistance to a change of motion. The kinetic sense applies to a marble or a barrette as well as to refrigerators and bulldozers.

The kinetic sense tells us we can pick up the marble easily, and unsnap a barrette with the fingers of one hand. This same sense tells us we cannot pick up a refrigerator with a shovel. The momentum of the refrigerator, to stay exactly where it is, is too great for the shovel's leverage.

Slow motion writing is ideal for conveying kinetic detail. In basketball, taking a dunk one split second at a time, we might watch the player twisting, swooping an arm around, fully extended, with the ball in a wide palm. The dynamics of the motion are displayed before the reader, one slice at a time. Slow motion writing is very much like slow motion action on television.

Kinetic detail does not have to be dramatic, large, or obvious. A bride might push the wedding band back and forth on her finger. This stimulates the sense of touch, hers and the readers — naturally. The motion will also convey the weight of the object. How firmly it moves, or does not move. How its fraction of an ounce might feel like fifty pounds to her, or like a feather.

These are kinetic details. So is the gum a woman is chewing. She rolls it between her fingers with spit and folds it up in a gum wrapper, and deposits the wad in the office ashtray with a soft click. That "click" is aural and kinetic. We hear the sound, and its particular quality registers with our kinetic sense. This sense tells us the wad is soft, sticky, and light in weight.

Because the event is divided into split seconds, the reader is in the event. Time is slowed down, and the reader will see the event just as it is presented, in slow motion. The nervous system, doing its usual job, will respond with images as the words are presented.

## Slow Motion in Stories

By focusing on the split second, fiction can be utterly gripping. Prose also has great flexibility. In his novel *Jurassic Park*, Michael

Crichton handles dramatic events by slowing the action down. He also slows the action down variably — sometimes more and sometimes less — according to the intensity of the moment. A dinosaur, in this example, has chased Tim and Lex into a darkened building:

> Tim sprinted, flinging his weight against the stainless-steel door of the locker, slamming it shut. It slammed on the tip of the tail! The door wouldn't shut! The velociraptor roared, a terrifying loud sound. Inadvertently, Tim took a step back — the tail was gone! He slammed the door shut and heard it click! Closed!
>
> "Lex! Lex!" he was screaming. He heard the raptor pounding against the door, felt it thumping the steel. He knew there was a flat steel knob inside, and if the raptor hit that, it would knock the door open. They had to get the door locked. "Lex!"
>
> Lex was by his side. "What do you want!"
>
> Tim leaned against the horizontal door handle, holding it shut. "There's a pin! A little pin! Get the pin!"
>
> The velociraptor roared like a lion, the sound muffled by the thick steel. It crashed its whole body against the door.
>
> "I can't see anything!" Lex shouted.

The tension is agonizing, because of the very real danger of Lex and Tim becoming a meal. The author throws in an element that jacks the tension even higher: Lex can't see. From here on the kinetic details have the added edge in that we have to feel them, like Lex — with our fingers:

> The pin was dangling beneath the door handle, swinging on a little metal chain. "It's right there!"
>
> "I can't see it!" she screamed, and then Tim realized she wasn't wearing the [night vision] goggles.
>
> "Feel for it!"
>
> He saw her little hand reaching up, touching his, groping for the pin, and with her so close to him he could feel how frightened she was, her breath in little panicky gasps as she felt

for the pin, and the velociraptor slammed against the door and it opened — God, *it opened* — but the animal hadn't expected that and had already turned back for another try and Tim slammed the door shut again. Lex scrambled back, reached up in the darkness.

"I have it!" Lex cried, clutching the pin in her hand, and she pushed it through the hole. It slid out again.

"From the top, put it in *from the top!*"

She held it again, lifting it on the chain, swinging it over the handle, and down. Into the hole.

*Locked.*

The velociraptor roared. Tim and Lex stepped back from the door as the dinosaur slammed into it again. With each impact, the heavy steel wall hinges creaked, but they held. Tim didn't think the animal could possibly open the door.

The raptor was locked in.

He gave a long sigh. "Let's go," he said.

He took her hand, and they ran.

The author skims the surface of the excitement through much of this excerpt. His writing darts quickly from peak to peak. But when he comes to the crucial moment, he slows down.

When Lex is trying to find the pin, the writing moves excruciatingly slowly. We are almost dying as she fumbles in the dark. These kinetic details pull us intimately close to the action. When she pokes the pin the wrong way, the game seems to be over. But the author gives her another chance. What satisfaction we feel when she finally gets the pin in the hole — and the door stays locked!

## Slow Motion in Poems

Very short events are recorded in the following poems. The authors are, in their separate styles, being accurate to the split second. Sharman Murphy's poem reports one incident when, while rock climbing, she vaults across a gap to save herself:

Three Easy Moves

and I'll arrive at knife-edge climax,
granite ridge that punctuates ascent.


How does it happen?
Four hundred feet accomplished,
and death drop no longer an issue here;
attention falters.
                    Surprised.

                              I'm off balance!

                              Falling backward

The body's instincts
flick through options:
                    Drop down here

                    and son of a gun

                    I'll still be hurt.

                              I've got to act.

                    Six feet across:

                    another granite wall

I vault, twist to face
opposing rock face

                    no scream, but only

                    my own audible command:

                              DON'T FALL

          Wham!

Hit first with vibram edges
an instant next with hands

                    (DON'T FALL)

Slam

almost flat against

      Hang on

momentum prints my body

on ungiving rock

              HANG ON

        I cling.

I down-climb sixteen feet

to where I would have landed.

Tremble,

cracked my elbow

scraped my arm

I ripped my shorts,

but shoot,

                  (hang on)

         what do you know?

        my body made a choice

                (don't fall)

        I'm still intact.

    Four easy moves. . . .

The reader is right there inside the event and can feel the
climber's balance go awry. We hear the yell "Don't fall!" and the
echoes of that yell as she re-adjusts and makes her leap to safety.
We can even feel her trembling as she climbs down.

"Three Easy Moves" reports an event that lasted five or six seconds. It is mostly external — with some internal thoughts and
commands. The following poem by Michael McClure, in contrast,
reports an event that is mostly internal, one that lasted possibly
thirty seconds. The poet conveys the sequence of emotion-laden
thoughts, one after another, as he looks at his wife:

OH WHY OH WHY THE BLASTED LOVE
THE HUGE SHAPE CHANGE? OH WHY
the tortured hand when clouds are down? I love
your lips and hands and legs. Your backbone line,
your breasts. The movement of your face and move
from them now. Oh why the words of lies above. Oh why the shape
change of movement, energy? when I will return to you
Oh awkward Love awkward, I love your
fingertips. Oh black
and sorrowed night. Oh mother and child.
Must I learn new love anew? No
choice! Are we joined forever
or is that lies! I remember
love in darkness and feel of flesh. Oh
CHANGE


No ease to truth. I half admit it.


The poet is anxious that the usual attraction he felt for his wife may have disappeared now that she is pregnant. Did you understand this?

McClure is very accurate to the feeling of the moment. He is completely inside the anxiety. He takes the reader with him, without giving an explanation of the poem's subject. While this requires some concentration on the reader's part to understand, it also makes the poem strong.

Both pieces are intensely physical. The action in "Three Easy Moves" must have etched itself in Murphy's musculature. Similarly, the emotions in "OH WHY . . . " are located in McClure's body. To write these pieces, the authors could simply have listened to the memories in their bodies. Strong writing often depends on remembering clearly.

> *In a poem the excitement has to maintain itself. I am governed by the pull of the sentence as the pull of a fabric is governed by gravity.*
>
> MARIANNE MOORE

Marianne Moore's poems are less physical than these examples, but she refers to the same process when she speaks of excitement. You can understand the flow of a poem by monitoring the excitement line by line. Poets use a variety of methods for keeping the reader involved. It's gratifying when excitement pulls us along from moment to moment.

## Slow Motion in Plays

In a play, a character portrays the action live on stage. The playwright does not have to rely on words on paper and the reader's imagination. The actor can relay an event to the audience using slow motion techniques — describing an action snapshot by snapshot. In the character's speech itself, you, the playwright, can use all your techniques for vivid writing.

The actor can even talk about an event while still feeling its effect. The actor can gasp, breathe quickly and say nothing, and then come out with what happened next. Or the actor can choke up completely and stay silent. The next words might have to be coaxed out by the other characters.

Imagine your main character is standing center stage as the curtain opens, right in front of the audience. Everyone waits for the character to speak. If the character is in the grip of that intense event, it would be natural to use slow motion techniques in the very first speech. Have the character break the event down into split seconds, and say them one at a time. This is a surefire way to get your audience to the edge of their chairs — immediately.

Since drama is live, the excitement conveyed can be instant and immense. It's also in the moment-to-moment control of the playwright. This means it's in the moment-to-moment scrutiny of the audience, too, so you need to use the technique with care. Since slow motion writing is similar in all forms, simply do what story writers and poets do. Slow the action down, divide it into split-second fragments and have your character report them precisely.

## Slow Motion in Essays

I wrote a brief essay on page 25–26, when I introduced slow motion writing. It was easy to demonstrate slow motion by simply doing it, with the three-legged dog. I started with the dog "gathering itself lopsidedly to jump. Then it springs sideways, with its mouth open and slobber coming out between its teeth. Next we notice that the expression on the dog's face resembles a smile. . . . "

If you find a physical example for your topic, you can bring it into dramatic focus by using slow motion techniques. It's best if the example is physical and can be put into motion. You can splice in comments along the way.

Since an essay is not concerned with keeping the action flowing, that flow can be stopped any time you want. It's fine to display the event one segment at a time. Each segment can be tiny. Discuss the present segment, and move on to the next.

Aldo Leopold's *Sand County Almanac*, quoted briefly on page 70, contains some fine image detail:

> I only know that a good file, vigorously wielded, makes my shovel sing as it slices the mellow loam. I am told there is music in the sharp plane, the sharp chisel, and the sharp scalpel, but I hear it best in my shovel; it hums in my wrists as I plant a pine.

That humming is vivid. If it suited his purpose, Leopold could have written about planting the pine moment by moment. He could have described the shovel snapshot by snapshot — cutting through loam, sliding deeper into the earth, slicing roots, hitting pebbles, then swinging up with a full load. He could have made us feel the humming even more.

## Reading Is a Physical Process

Have you ever gotten excited while you read? Of course you have, and the explanation is simple. Our nervous system doesn't make a great distinction between imaginary scenes and real life. Whatever excites or frightens us in life, will do the same when presented to our imagination.

When we read slow motion writing we sense excitement. Your imagination sees the scene the author is displaying as though it's happening right before your eyes, and you can feel time being slowed down. You recognize this as a sign of emergency — even before the cause is stated. Your body pumps up some adrenaline.

So, reading has a physical effect: we feel excited. Bang! The pistol shot scares us, even on the page. We flinch mentally, get ready to duck, and wonder what's going on. This is only a trick, of course, but the kind of adrenaline it stimulates is the same as in life.

You could say we are slaves to our nervous system. It is busy making images, even when we are most cynical. We may pretend nothing is happening, or persuade ourselves that the images have no effect. Make no mistake, however, the nervous system of every living person is doing its job. It is making images. You can see the edge of the knife behind the girl's wrist. You see the tears in the bride's eyes.

## Writing Is a Physical Process

Slow down the act of writing, and you will discover that writing is a physical process, too. The Crazy Child may send words up your back or whisper them in your ear. Or you may not notice words until your creative unconscious is raging, and you're jumping up and down with a snapping energy — chock full of words.

One writer gets taken over by a peculiar sensation of color, and then she finds the words in her belly. Another feels the words slide up his spine, and he thinks it's as ordinary as bread and apples. These are unusual, but your way might be unusual too. Words probably have as many ways of creating themselves in the body as there are people in the world.

Words next appear in your mind, and from here on the process of writing is manifestly physical. You corral the words, somehow. Then you push them down your arm and into your fingers. From your fingers you guide them onto a keyboard and a screen, or out a pen or pencil onto a piece of paper.

If you write at all, your nervous system obviously knows how. Doing the writing teaches you how. Writing of any kind makes you proficient at capturing words in your mind, taking them one at a time or in bunches down your arm, and nudging them out into the world.

You may have kept a journal for a few years. You may have written school reports or business memos or lawyer's briefs or case histories; if you have done any of these it means you have already practiced a lot. If you have only taken minutes for meetings for five years, you may think you can't write — but this is not true. Your body already knows how.

Words are like water. They flow down your arm onto the page or onto the screen, and they create a channel through your nerves. The more they pour through you, the more they define the channel. It gets deeper, more comfortable, and more efficient. Soon writing becomes easy.

It's novel to realize that writing is physical. It's more novel to discover how. Listen to what's happening in your body while you are in the heat of creating — when juices are flowing the fastest. Or try reviewing one of your pieces. Tinkering with the last paragraphs might put you back in that creative place.

What sensations are in your arms? Is there a tickle somewhere in your chest? In your solar plexus? Is there a flush of excitement behind your eyes? If you have to force yourself to the computer or to the pen, what sensation do you have after the words start coming?

Once you know what the sensation is, you may be able to recall it — anytime. When you want to write, try visualizing the sensation. You may find that you can recreate it full-blown. You could say, "I know that place," and possibly you are on its doorstep. Suddenly you're breezing into the house of your Crazy Child, and it's about to start talking. Get your pen.

## Slow Motion and the Crazy Child

If expressing itself is the goal, the Crazy Child can do so robustly with slow motion writing. With image detail, your creative unconscious pulls the reader into a scene. With slow motion writing, your Crazy Child pulls the reader into a dramatic movie.

Whatever spin your creative unconscious might desire, it can be emphasized with slow motion snapshots. You might draw the reader into that ring's motion on the bride's finger. You might intend to contrast the bride's mood with the groom's shyness. Or your creative unconscious might simply want to show the bride's expression as the ring slides back and forth.

Both poems on pages 30–32 are full of anxiety, and they are very different. Each author's Crazy Child has picked the feelings and the details; there must be as many ways to write these events as there are people. Your Crazy Child will want to write it one way, and mine another. Each time, using slow motion techniques, we will convince the reader.

This is the wonderful part of being alive that writers relish and exploit. Life is interactive and responsive. Slow time down, put the reader in the writer's shoes and the reader will respond. You can cause the reader to see and feel more or less what you do.

The reader is putty in your hands. Your Crazy Child is about to take the reader on a marvelous journey.

## EXERCISE

The next paragraphs present an exercise, just as in the first chapter. Before doing the exercise, I recommend you read the rest of this section. In the exercise sections, all the material is arranged to augment the exercise. It should help you understand the exercise more fully, and allow you to have more fun when you do it — and to learn more.

### Accurate to the Split Second

Pick an event and write it for twenty minutes, being accurate to the split second. Be sure to slow time down with your mind's eye so that you can see each one of those split seconds. The event can be internal, or external, or a combination of both. It can also be real or imagined. It could be something that happened to someone else.

Choosing the event can be the easiest or the most difficult part of the exercise. If your Crazy Child wants to write something that happened to you, by all means do it. This gives you access to the event. You have all your research material at hand. The event is recorded in your body, or in your musculature — as well as etched in your memory. All you need to do is retrieve it.

Even if you think you remember the event completely, listen inwardly — into your body. Listen for new or unfamiliar sensations. Dare to write unusual or bizarre details, for they may surprise you with their power. You may discover a new, exciting kind of material, or you may find yourself using techniques you hadn't thought of before.

Prose is fine for slow motion writing. You can write ordinary sentences, like those Crichton uses in *Jurassic Park*, on pages 28–29. Or you can write a poem, if you wish, and use the form of Murphy's "Three Easy Moves," on pages 30–31, in which the columns separate the external experiences from the internal.

Slowing the event down, and speeding your mind up, are the important things. You will begin to see almost everything that happens in those few seconds.

## Slow Motion and Journalism

You could argue that slow motion writing is a kind of journalism. In fact, our working definition of new journalism states, "Take the reader on the same journey you make to find the information." This sounds like what happens in slow motion writing, especially if we accept a broad definition of "information." It can be the story, or the event, or the feelings, or some combination.

Slow motion writing is like journalism in that the author is reporting. The more precisely you report that split second, the more precisely the reader will see it. As we have shown, this kind of writing is not limited to journalism. An essay might need slow motion writing. A story or a novel might use it repeatedly, and it might be essential to a poem.

Remember to show, not tell. Show the action, and be sure to include plenty of image detail.

## WORKSHOP

Print or type your image detail practice from last week and make a copy for every person in the workshop. Double-space your prose and leave wide margins. This allows space for everyone to make notes. It also makes for easier reading. A poem or a play may be single-spaced, however, because there generally is ample blank space around the words.

Your second workshop should have the same format of the first workshop, with the addition of suggestions for rewriting. From here on, the workshops in *Let the Crazy Child Write!* are to be conducted exactly as depicted on pages 16–17. This syngenetic format is the one followed in all my workshops, including the most advanced ones.

## Suggestions for Rewriting

While the workshop is giving positive feedback, each listener goes over the piece several times. This happens as a matter of course — as part of the nervous system's job. When someone makes a positive comment, your nervous system automatically brings that line into focus. You review your own response, and compare it to the other's. Your own becomes deepened and clarified.

The result, for the workshop as a whole, is to become well acquainted with its responses, and to understand the causes of those responses. The workshop thus comes to understand the piece thoroughly. Most importantly, the workshop becomes familiar with the primary intent of the piece. It's useful to give rewrite suggestions after achieving this awareness — not before.

As a listener, you have taken inventory of your responses, including places in the piece that did not seem clear. Is something missing somewhere? Are there places in the writing that are hazy, where you are not sure what is happening? These responses can be subtle and fleeting, but they are important. Taking notes as you listen can be very useful.

Many listeners will ask for something more from the author. Perhaps there could be more dialogue or perhaps more details about the physical surroundings would make the scene more vivid. Sometimes the author is so familiar with the interviewee that the author forgets to say what the person looks like. Perhaps the main character could be shown with more detail. Or perhaps more could be added to the ending.

These comments, suggesting that the author has left something out, are usual in workshops. The listeners, however, should be accepting of whatever style the author's Crazy Child has chosen. The choice of style is not in the province of the listener's analysis — that is the author's business.

Style is a complex business that includes attitude and life experience and intent and much more. It is far too complex for someone other than the author to tinker with. As a listener, you should take the style as a given. From within the author's style, you can listen for what can be improved.

Two or perhaps three rewrite suggestions, in total, are sufficient. The author should try only one of them, anyway. If you are the author and the workshop gives you several suggestions, try the one that seems most relevant. Or try one that your Crazy Child thinks would be the most fun. You will find that following one suggestion is plenty of work, and usually involves important learning.

Nevertheless, when you are the author, write down all the suggestions for rewrites clearly. Write them down even if you don't agree with them. The feedback is information, and you may find some of it useful in the future. You might realize, when you do your next piece, that some of the feedback could apply to it.

Be sure to notice what you have done well. Writing is about knowing how strong you are, and how real, and how you can accomplish what you want. Take in the feedback that affirms your Crazy Child. Use your strengths. Relish them. You can repeat your strengths, or expand on them, in the next practice piece.

## Who Is Correct?

Say you have written a piece about a high dive that went awry. One person in the workshop might be sure the diver's foot slipped off the diving board, and another might be equally sure someone's remark distracted the diver. You, the author, know which one happened — or perhaps both did. But do not say anything. If you are to learn from this workshop, you must follow the kindergarten rule. Be silent and listen attentively.

The job for the listeners is to state clearly why they have their responses. If you are one of the listeners, be succinct. State your position once, or at most twice. Say, for instance, "I thought the diver slipped on the edge of the board because of this sentence . . ." and then read the exact words. Or say, "For me it was obvious her boyfriend's comment was responsible, because right here the writer says . . . " and then repeat the words.

Do not get into a discussion. Neither you nor the workshop is supposed to decide which listener is correct. The workshop's function is to display to the author what the writing conveys. If the writing conveys two different things to two different readers, this is important information for the author. The author's job is to listen, and to believe both people. Most likely they both have valid points.

You, the author, may then decide how to change the piece. You are the boss. You can make clear what happened. You can make it clear which one of the possibilities was crucial, or equally clear that they both were.

Or perhaps you realize that you want something entirely different to happen. Your Crazy Child might have entered the arena and has a new interpretation it's hot to present.

## PRACTICE

Either expand your twenty-minute slow motion exercise or choose a new event. By now you should have a feel for which would be most interesting. If you expand the exercise, look to include new details. There might have been another person at the scene, and if so, including that person could give the writing extra punch.

In that short exercise it's easy, also, to overlook image details. You might have included kinetic and visual details, but left out the aural ones, the ones you hear. Was someone saying something, or shouting?

If you choose a new event, write one that is completely different. It doesn't have to be a disaster. It can be watching a sunrise, hearing a great song, or meeting someone you find very attractive. Or you could repeat the event from the exercise but make some part of it very different. Perhaps your Crazy Child is itching to present a radically different ending.

Your creative unconscious picks the emotion of the event. Remember the wedding vow on page 27, and how that ring might feel heavy or light? There are as many possible feelings as there are people. Let your Crazy Child choose whatever feeling it likes. If your creative unconscious picks an emotion that makes you feel vulnerable, or frightened, or even stupid — go with it. Go with the feeling your creative source chooses. Whatever it is, it will have a way of becoming something unique, human, and powerful.

However you do your practice, remember to include kinetic details. The motion and momentum of objects will help your writing mimic life, in vivid and unexpected ways. Kinetic details let the reader experience the event in the same way that you did, or that you imagine one would. Include those usual details, too, from the five senses: sight, smell, taste, hearing, and touch. You are making the scene come alive for yourself and for the reader.

# Chapter 3
## Hook

*No tears for the writer, no tears in the reader. No surprise for the writer, no surprise for the reader.*

ROBERT FROST

The "hook" is what grabs the reader's attention. We sit up and take notice when we read an effective hook. We might feel intrigue, tension, excitement, or even shock. The hook is what stimulates us to read further. The hook is anything that makes the reader curious — the more curious, the better.

It is best if the hook is in the first sentence. Certainly the hook needs to be in effect in the first paragraph. Even in a novel that unfolds slowly, the tip of the hook should prick us early on the first page. If it does not, the reader may put that book down, and pick up another — or do something else. Most modern novels have a hook that works quickly. So do poems, plays, and essays.

"Hook" is an apt metaphor for what the first sentence or first paragraph can do. It grabs us like a meat hook. It arcs in like a curved, sharp piece of metal, pierces our thoughts and yanks us out of our everyday routines. It pulls the reader into the story, poem, play, novel, or essay. We suddenly become absorbed in the writer's creation.

We could rephrase Robert Frost's statement and say, "No

curiosity for the writer, no curiosity for the reader." The principle is the same. What you are curious about will create curiosity in the reader. What the Crazy Child is drawn to will also draw in the reader.

Consider those first examples of slow motion writing on page 25: "A woman turning a lipstick tube around her lips, a girl concealing a knife behind her wrist, a man fingering the top button of his pants." These phrases work as hooks.

They are hooks because each one is part of a larger picture. Each one suggests some other significant action, or several other actions. Each phrase is a small piece of a jigsaw puzzle. We are curious what will happen next and our imagination instantly tries to picture the entire scene.

As a reader, you cannot help but be curious about the rest of the picture. It is the job of the human nervous system to make images. The corner of a picture provokes us into completing the picture. Our nervous system works in the same way with hooks as it does with image detail. When we are shown the shell-shaped chip on the blue plate, we imagine the entire plate. When we see a piece of the action, we start imagining what happens next.

We wonder — instantly — why the girl is hiding the knife. Is she in danger? Is someone else in danger? And why is the woman putting on her lipstick so slowly? Is someone watching? Or is she getting ready for a big event, and she is mulling over a strategy? And why is the man unbuttoning his pants? Is he going swimming, or is his lover before him?

## Crazy Child Hooks

The Crazy Child is interested in hooks. A Crazy Child hook is no different from the hooks I am discussing — it is designed to snag attention. The creative unconscious has expertise in hooks that comes from long experience.

The creative unconscious has been using hooks since the beginning of its existence. The youngest Crazy Child part of you is an infant. That infant learns right away how to hook its parent's attention — using a hook is essential to any infant's survival. If a parent's attention should wander, the infant does not get fed. If the infant becomes ill or is in danger, it must let its caretaker know instantly.

Later, the child learns how to grab attention — with words. When it is no longer an infant, it cannot rely on chortling or crying. If it wants anything — a cookie, a new toy, a trip to the bathroom, a Band-Aid for a hurt spot — it must choose words that elicit attention. At times, the child's wish is for its world to be seen and responded to by others. Isn't that the writer's wish also, to have our world seen and responded to?

Even if all you remember from childhood is wanting to avoid attention, you know about hooks. Perhaps you did not want to mow the lawn or wash dishes, or perhaps you were trying to avoid a sneering sibling or random swats from a disturbed adult. Then your Crazy Child's effort was to avoid attention — which, like seeking attention, requires instinctive knowledge of how attention works.

We have been experts at using hooks since the dawn of language. A Neanderthal parent needed its children's attention when a pack of wolves approached. The scout who met a saber-toothed tiger on the prowl needed to attract the attention of the tribe, and yet not attract the tiger. A shout of "Tiger!" would not work, not in this case. You can bet your ancestors needed quick facility with hooks — subtle and effective ones — in order to survive. This knowledge is in your genes.

Remind yourself that your nervous system does indeed know about hooks. As a species, we have 35,000 years or so of practice with the hook. All you need to do is call up that instinct — the same one you practiced as a child.

## Plot and the Hook

The hook is the first element of plot. The image I use for the engine that powers the plot is a magnet. That magnet pulls the reader through the entire story, poem, play, or essay — it is what keeps the pages turning. A forceful hook produces the same result. The hook captures our interest and makes us start turning pages.

The hook becomes the first scene of the plot — the first event in a chain of events, and the rest of the action will follow. As we think about hooks, it does not help to worry about the entire plot. We do not need to know what follows. To start the plot well, we need only to think of an effective hook.

An effective hook may describe a situation that is tilted somehow — out of balance and moving. That motion may flow by itself into the plot. It could involve a person who is mystified, or joyous, or very upset. It could even involve someone who is simply not paying very much attention. That lack of attention could lead to a very strange occurrence.

Often, in poems or essays, the message is something the author knows well. The author has a point to make, and the hook is the first statement in a chain of logic. That chain of logic is the plot. A simple, strong statement can get the plot moving. The author is on a mission, and sets up a first line to excite our curiosity.

## Hooks in Stories

Consider the first sentence of Flannery O'Conner's story *Wise Blood:*

> Hazel Moses sat at a forward angle on the green plush train seat, looking one minute at the window as if he might want to jump out of it, and the next down the aisle at the other end of the car.

Why is this man acting like he might jump out of the train? Is someone coming after him? Is he watching the end of the car to spot someone evil through the sliding door — before that person spots him? Or are these dramatics only in his mind, and he is fighting psychological demons? The reader does not know.

Notice how the odd and dissonant setup works here. Just as in image detail, the odd and the dissonant pique our curiosity. Moses might be a very strange person or perhaps he is simply in a difficult situation. This doubt, created by the setup, makes the reader curious. We definitely want to find out what is happening. To do that, we must read on.

In the first paragraph of her story "An Interest in Life," Grace Paley also uses dissonance:

> My husband gave me a broom one Christmas. This wasn't right. No one can tell me it was meant kindly.

This gift has a double message, and that creates dissonance. A gift, by definition, conveys honor and love to the person receiving it. But this gift is a broom; it seems to say, "Sweep the floor!" That's a very different message.

This opening paragraph hooks me in two ways. One, I am curious why the husband would give such a mean gift. Two, I am curious what the wife will do in response. I expect it to be something interesting — maybe something drastic. When she says, "No one can tell me it was meant kindly," the wife sounds like she will take action.

"Call me Ishmael" is the opening sentence of Herman Melville's novel *Moby Dick*. The readers of his time, who were steeped in biblical lore, understood that "Ishmael" means bastard. As soon as we know this, we are hooked. Why is the narrator calling himself a bastard?

Here's another example, from the novel *The Bean Trees* by Barbara Kingsolver:

> I have been afraid of putting air in a tire ever since I saw a tractor tire blow up and throw Newt Hardbine's father over the top of the Standard Oil sign. I'm not lying.

What in the world is next? Is the narrator about to fix a tire, without help, in a strange place? Do wild events follow this narrator around, or is she telling tall tales? This hook has us wondering about the flat tire, about Newt Hardbine's father's story, and about the narrator.

## Hooks in Poems

A hook works in poetry much the same as it does in prose. If there is a difference, it may be that the hook needs to grab the reader even more quickly in poetry. Consider the beginning of Allen Ginsberg's "Howl":

> I saw the best minds of my generation destroyed by
> madness, starving hysterical naked.

This is a marvelous hook. Ginsberg describes a generation of social trauma and change. He also suggests that he knows the causes, or at least the stories of that generation, and the reader is interested to hear more.

The opening lines of Walt Whitman's "Song of Myself" make a provocative statement:

> I celebrate myself, and sing myself,
> And what I assume you shall assume,
> For every atom belonging to me as good belongs to you.

These lines assert that the author's celebration is so basic, it is as common as atoms. This is a bold statement. I don't fully understand it, but such a possibility makes me curious, and I also sense great conviction in Whitman's words. I am curious about the vision behind them, so I read on.

We have looked at a number of hooks using oddities and dissonance. Can there be a joyous hook? Read the beginning of "The Passionate Shepherd to His Love" by Christopher Marlowe:

Come live with me and be my love,

and we will all the pleasures prove

This hook works as well as the others. We want to know what those pleasures are, and we read on.

## Slow Hooks

So far we have looked at hooks that work rapidly. Hooks can work slowly, also — but not too slowly. In his story "The Ticket," Mark Peterson uses a fair-sized paragraph:

A teenage boy crosses a street. He walks ten yards and stops in front of a video game store; he expected his best friend would be here by now. Beginning to pace, he rotates on his heel and discovers a policeman rolling his motorcycle onto the sidewalk. The motor is off, the cop's left leg swings through the air, taps the ground and pushes, while the wheels roll. The boy freezes.

The first sentence is so quiet and understated, I ask "So what?" with some curiosity. In the second sentence a touch of suspense is added. Why is the friend late? More suspense is created when the motorcycle appears — something is about to happen. When I get to "The boy freezes," I am hooked.

Did you notice the slow motion in that paragraph? The third and fourth sentences are powerful slow motion writing. They draw us into the scene. The reader can see and feel that foot tapping the sidewalk, and the motorcycle is right there next to us.

*We read five words on the first page of a really good novel and we begin to forget that we are reading printed words on a page; we begin to see images. . . . We recreate . . . the vivid and continuous dream the writer worked out in his mind (revising and revising until he got it right) and captured in language so that other human beings, whenever they feel like it, may open his book and dream that dream again.*

JOHN GARDNER

## Hooks in Plays

The curtain opens, the audience is sitting in their seats, and you, the playwright, want everyone to start leaning forward. Beginning a play with a situation that is out of kilter is a good way to start. Notice how William Shakespeare's three witches elicit our interest at the beginning of *MacBeth:*

*First Witch:* When shall we three meet again, in
      thunder, lightning, or in rain?
*Second Witch:* When the hurlyburly's done, when the
      battle's lost and won.
*Third Witch:* That will be ere the set of sun.
*First Witch:* Where the place?
*Second Witch:* Upon the heath.
*Third Witch:* There to meet with Macbeth.

He could not have told us more quickly that there is trouble brewing. We know instantly that something is up, some kind of a battle. What's more, we know it will be over before the sun sets, and that it will involve Macbeth. We might even suspect the witches are embroiled.

Shakespeare's play *Hamlet* opens as someone approaches the castle's watchman:

*Bernardo:* Who's there?
*Francisco:* Nay, answer me: stand, and unfold yourself.
*Bernardo:* Long live the King!
*Francisco:* Bernardo?
*Bernardo:* He.
*Francisco:* You come most carefully upon your hour.

Bernardo is Francisco's replacement, and someone he knows. But tension in both men is running at a high pitch — they do not recognize each other. The audience can feel that tension. We wonder what will happen next.

In the opening of Arthur Miller's play *Death of a Salesman* the husband says to his wife, "It's all right, I came back" and we learn right away that something is wrong. His trip hasn't worked out as planned. In Will Dunne's play *Hotel Desperado* one character says he knows what the other is thinking. But the other simply wants a room and isn't thinking anything devious, so he stares back blankly.

These are all provocative, engrossing beginnings. They work as hooks — I am on the edge of my chair.

## Hooks in Essays

The hook in an essay differs from the hook in a story. In a story the action is of first importance, and in an essay the topic is primary. The hook in an essay draws the reader toward its topic. The writer may use a bald statement or tilt a provocative corner of the topic toward the reader.

Barbara Robertson's personal essay, excerpted on page 98, has an interesting hook: "Did you see my ad? I'm the 'package deal'. . . ." The first sentence of the book review "One Step Beyond Black Holes," by Frederic Golden, also has an engaging hook:

If the baffling and mind-boggling ideas — alternate universes, imaginary time, the big crunch — described in Stephen Hawking's surprising 1988 best-seller, *A Brief History of Time*, left you feeling as though you had plunged into a black hole, here's a second chance at enlightenment.

This is an efficient sentence. First the author mentions the subject and reminds us of its difficulty, then the promise of "enlightenment" is dangled before us — or at least the possibility of climbing out of confusion. How this might be done, both in the review and in the book, becomes a draw for the reader.

Anyone who picks up a book of essays, or the review section of a paper, has some intellectual interest. The author can assume that the reader's mind is hungry for something to chew on. The author can do nothing better than to oblige. Throw that hook at the reader — like a Crazy Child.

## EXERCISE

Write one-sentence hooks on index cards or scraps of paper. Do them quickly, and do not worry about how effective they are. Entertain yourself. You are practicing how to write hooks. If you do them fast and allow them to be silly or stupid, this is fine. You are giving your Crazy Child a better chance to participate.

Write for fifteen minutes or so, folding the cards and throwing them in a basket. You can do this alone or with someone else. Doing this exercise with others can be fun because when you choose hooks to expand, you may choose one written by someone else. That can lead to interesting surprises.

This is Crazy Child territory. The hooks appeal to the playful or unconscious parts of our minds. Why you write a particular hook may be a complete mystery, but there is no such thing as an incorrect hook. This exercise is for exploring which sorts of hooks you, as an author, find exciting. Your creative unconscious has everything to say about that.

## Germs

These first-sentence hooks are "seeds" for more writing, but I like the name "germs" better. Both words mean about the same thing, but germs has the further implication of something dangerous or out of our control. By definition, Crazy Child material is not under the control of our conscious minds. It is new, or frightening, or exciting — and endowed with strange power.

Remember, on page xv in the preface, how the Crazy Child is like the id, the German folktale word for "bogeyman?" "Germs" have a similar scary feeling. The sentences you write may not be in your control. You write one down, and when you follow it with another, you may not know why.

Other forces can take over — maybe the bogeyman himself. Something else is most likely present, at least in the undercurrents. As you write, you may just be following along. The germ may turn into something unexpected, perhaps strange, perhaps powerful and gripping.

## Silly Hooks

As you start writing germs, do not worry if they are any good. In fact, starting with silly hooks is a fine idea. Anything stupid or cornball or obvious will serve as well as anything else. There is every reason to play with this exercise. Have fun doing it, and don't hold back. Don't let your Editor make any negative comments.

By definition, we do not know what hooks are going to work. Not in advance. In a short while you may know which ones work well for you, but at the time you write your hooks, your Editor or Writer will not know. Do this exercise in a Crazy Child manner.

We could write the phrases from page 25 as germs:

A woman slowly turned a tube of pink lipstick around her lips.
A girl concealed a small knife behind her wrist.
The man fingered the top button of his pants.

Let's do some fancier ones:

> When the sun became a thin crescent over the water, the crew raised an extra sail.
>
> If I'm not in by sundown, that whole acre of corn could go up in flames.

What about silly germs?

> "Whoops!" she said, and tried to pull her finger out of the cookie jar.
>
> Give me the fullest slice of your orange ear, and we'll see how much happy juice I can squeeze out of it.
>
> Was that really Grandma's nose? George asked himself, and looked at the poster again.
>
> Jane watched in a daze as the headlight rolled down the off-ramp.

## Expanding the Germs

When you have a basket full of germs, you are ready for the second part of the exercise. Spend fifteen or twenty minutes expanding a germ. Using one of the germs as your first sentence, start writing a story, poem, play, or essay. Pick one from the basket and run with it.

Picking one at random puts you on the spot. Sifting through the basket until you find one you like may have the same effect. You will have to work with little preparation. Your Crazy Child will have no choice but to fire up and write spontaneously. Get that pen on paper and keep it moving. What your creative unconscious comes up with may surprise you.

## WORKSHOP

When it is your turn, you have the choice of which piece to read. You can read the slow motion practice from the last chapter or read your expanded germ — which you have just written during the workshop meeting. If you bring copies of your slow motion piece, you have an advantage. You will get more detailed feedback if the workshop can look at copies. Perhaps you will have time to do both.

If you read an expanded germ, remember that you wrote for only fifteen minutes or so. A powerful piece written in such a short time deserves quite a lot of praise. Write the praise down. Or, if you are giving feedback, be sure to take the time limit into consideration.

Feedback on an unfinished draft can be very useful. The reader may want more image detail, or more dialogue, or more physical action. The writer will be able to incorporate these changes in the rest of the draft.

## Something Extra

If there is enough time, you might start by reading all the germs in the basket, and talk about them. Notice why the successful hooks work. You can usually state their appeal with one sentence, such as, "I want to know what happens next because . . ." or "This paragraph makes me curious about the officer because . . ." or, as with Ginsberg's poem "Howl," "I am curious what the poet will tell me about that madness."

It is useful to do this with all the germs, just to extend your sense of how hooks work. Of course, this chapter is designed to give you that knowledge. But the examples I mention are hooks that work for me, and the ones that work best for you may be more instructive. It's most useful to figure out why the hooks that you like work — hooks that you write and hooks that you read.

## Listen for Hooks

When you hear the slow motion practices, listen for hooks. There will be a natural hook in each piece. But the writer may not have put it in the first sentence. This is true in the first paragraphs of my slow motion piece:

Marvin had come out to the track to get some exercise, and the running bug had bit him. He had the coach watching him every afternoon, and when I asked him how things were going, he didn't talk about his girlfriend, or his classes. He would start telling me about his last workout. The 200-meter dash and what he was doing, and now he was trying to get his body at the correct lean on the long curve.

He was a forthright sort of guy with a big voice. That voice did me a good turn, and I was glad I paid attention to it one day, or I was going to hurt myself. If you've ever had a strained Achilles tendon, you know I am not talking Band-Aids and scraped knees. There was some rasping in that booming voice, when he stared at me and lay down the riot act.

My workshop knew, from the rest of the draft, that the piece is about an accident on the track. It's not primarily about running, or about Marvin, as the first paragraph implies. But the second paragraph gets the ball rolling. The workshop pointed out that the last three sentences in the second paragraph could all be hooks. They introduce the accident — or at least the possibility of one.

## Clunky Suggestions

A rewrite suggestion that is poorly worded on purpose is a "clunky suggestion." By "poorly worded" I mean a suggestion that is deliberately not polished. The reason for making the suggestion is to point out a defect, or point toward an improvement — without doing the final writing. It is not the workshop's job to make up the author's words.

In my track piece, the workshop made several clunky suggestions for a new first sentence:

Marvin had a booming voice, and I was glad I heard it that day, or I was going to hurt myself.

If you've ever had a strained Achilles tendon, you know I am not talking Band-Aids and scraped knees.

Marvin's voice was rasping, when he stared at me and lay down the riot act.

These are sentences from the second paragraph, moved to the beginning, with a few words changed for clarity. Any of them could work. More importantly, these clunky suggestions gave me ideas about how to begin the piece more strongly.

I chose a different sentence. The author, ultimately, knows best what to write:

Right when the tendons along the backs of my heels started tightening like coat hangers, Marvin read me the riot act.

I took the suggestions as prods to find words that match the intent of the story. The clunky suggestions made me choose the words — ones that match my own intent and my own style.

This is the value of a clunky suggestion. The point comes across, but the author is not tempted to use those same words. The author and the author's Crazy Child must step in. They are the ones who will come up with the exact phrase. Who else?

## PRACTICE

Imagine you are in the main post office, and you happen to glance at the "Missing" or "Wanted" posters. To your great surprise, the top poster is of an intimate or a blood relative — a parent, child, sibling, ex-lover, or spouse. What do you do now? Write the story of your reactions and how you proceed.

Notice that this setup is a launch point for a line of action. You are going to do something about this poster. Or you are going to come to terms with it, as you stand in line. All the action might be psychological and take place only in the protagonist's mind. But it is a loaded situation. Something will happen.

This setup does not give you a hook sentence. You have to create that yourself. You should make the hook work rapidly. Don't worry, however, if it does not come automatically. You will have plenty of chances to rewrite the story, and to sharpen the beginning.

***Start one heartbeat after the action has begun.***

## Beginning the Action

"Start one heartbeat after the action has begun" is a guideline that writers often use. It is an effective way to create a powerful hook. The reader wonders immediately what the rest of the action is. The author cannot give much of the action, in any case, in only one sentence. That sentence is the first brush stroke of the larger picture or the first scratch in a cougar fight.

One of the silly hooks is an example: "Jane watched in a daze as the headlight rolled down the on-ramp." We are curious about the accident that just happened, and equally curious about what might happen next. This example is meant as a clunky suggestion — as an example for understanding the hook technique. You can use the example as a starting point for writing something in your own words.

Suppose someone is selling you something on the street. How did that person get your attention? "The floating bubble burst into tiny, bright diamonds all over my coat, and there was a boy leaning over and saying, 'Want a watch?' " Substitute whatever you like for that watch. The reader is immediately curious, probably having been in that situation. Why not surprise the reader with your response?

For the missing person setup, you could try: "Was that really Grandma's nose? George asked himself, and looked at the poster again." As we read that sentence, we wonder what has happened and what will happen next. Take this sentence, too, as a clunky suggestion. You can write the same sort of thing — in your own words.

Or we could use that headlight again. "All George could think of, when he saw his uncle's photograph, was how his busted headlight rolled down the on-ramp. His uncle had smashed the Z straight into the guard rail last August, and took off through the cornfield on foot." Then what? the reader wonders.

There is no need to set the scene or to give background information. No need to warm up. With that first sentence, your piece is already hot. From the get-go, the reader is hooked into the situation, and directions are not necessary.

You can flesh out the background or fill in important details as the action proceeds. We might not know, for instance, that the photograph was in a post office until your character runs out the door.

## Alternative

Expand one of the germs into a complete story, poem, play, or essay. Deciding which germ is an easy problem. If the one you chose at random has you excited — by all means stick with it. Or perhaps you heard someone read a sentence that you liked. Or perhaps you will be most happy picking another germ at random. Why not?

However you choose your germ, look for a feeling of intrigue or mystery. It is not important to understand exactly why a germ is an effective hook. Having a feeling of intrigue makes it fine. In fact, any funny feeling about a germ is a sign that it is an effective hook. Your Crazy Child is giving you a tweak. That tweak means a story is hiding in the germ. You will find out what the story is as you write it.

## Not Knowing Where You Are Going

You do not have to know where your writing is going in order to write well. You can do the practice very well without knowing where it will end. You can even write a fine story, poem, play, or essay that way. Certainly for the first draft, you do not need to know. It may even be to your advantage not to know.

> *Art is a mystery.*
> *A mystery is something immeasurable.*
> *In so far as every child and woman and man may be immeasur-*
> *able, art is the mystery of every man and woman and child. In so*
> *far as a human being is an artist, skies and mountains and oceans*
> *and thunderbolts and butterflies are immeasurable; and art is*
> *every mystery of nature. Nothing measurable can be alive; noth-*
> *ing which is not alive can be art; nothing which cannot be art is*
> *true: and everything untrue doesn't matter a very good God*
> *damn. . . .*
>
>                                                   e.e. cummings

If you do not know where you are going, then you need to be alert for the next idea or the next sentence. It could come from anywhere. Your Crazy Child may hop around like a rabbit, and suddenly you are chasing a wild rabbit through the woods. You have no idea where your creative unconscious is going to jump next. The alertness you must have — to make the next leap after that rabbit — will transmit itself to the reader. When you feel suspense about where you are going, the reader will also.

We could rephrase Frost's words again: "No suspense for the writer, no suspense for the reader." The principle is the same. Following a sense of mystery is an excellent way to begin your writing. It's an excellent way to do an entire first draft.

Go for it. Whether you choose to expand a germ or the missing person story — or make up something on your own — you might as well let loose. The wilder and more bizarre your writing is, the more interesting a time you will have, and the more you stand to learn. Let your Crazy Child have some fun. Make fantastic leaps after that fast-moving rabbit.

# Chapter 4
## Persona Writing

*I hold a beast, an angel and a madman in me, and my enquiry is as to their working, and my problem is their subjugation and victory, downthrow and upheaval, and my effort is their self-expression.*

DYLAN THOMAS

The "persona" is the personality the writer assumes. The persona is the storyteller, or the character revealing inner thoughts, or the poet laying out a string of images, or the essayist following a chain of logic. In the first words of a piece the persona reaches out and says, "Hello."

We may think the author is speaking. But the person speaking in a story, poem, essay, or play is not exactly the author. It is a construct — someone the writer makes up. The writer creates a persona, and the persona does the talking.

As readers, we identify that persona just as we would a live person. Attitude, sex, age, race, culture, and interests — we pick up a huge amount of information about a person almost instantly. Most of it is unconscious. The reader does the same thing on the first page of a story: the reader identifies the person talking.

We identify the persona as soon as, or sooner than, we feel the hook. In the book *Diary of Ann Frank* a young Jewish girl is speaking. An old man in a wheel chair tells the story in Wallace

Stegner's *Angle of Repose*. In Margaret Atwood's novel *Surfacing* a thirtyish WASP woman is looking for her father and for her power. Floyd Salas's book *Tattoo of the Wicked Cross* is narrated by a Latino gang member. These are all personas.

It is the job of the nervous system to identify the persona. The words may convey the persona explicitly or we may discover who the persona is through tiny clues. With image detail we see an entire object from one small part and with hooks we imagine the action from one hint. With persona we sense an entire person from a few words.

Are we attracted to the persona? Is the persona intriguing? Does the persona have something to teach us? Could the persona be a friend, or is the persona frightening? There are zillions of possibilities. We want to know who is guiding us into the next page, and we feel out the persona quickly.

## Persona and Author

Even if you write as openly as possible, you cannot be totally successful — you can't put your whole self on the page. You are too complex. If you try, you may write a brave, true, wonderful piece. But it won't quite be you. There is more going on, with anyone, than words can express.

A writer uses a persona even in an autobiography. At root, "persona" means "mask," which is how psychology defines the term. It is our outside person — our mask — who greets our relatives, the children in our neighborhood, our teachers, and even our friends. We greet the world with our persona.

You may put on any mask as an author. You may pretend you are an expert in your topic or you may write as if you are a beginner. You may present yourself as cool or excited or bewildered or crazed. You can write in these personas, even if they are not accurate. You can write as if you are someone very different — on purpose.

You can be whoever you like. This is one of the great adventures of creative writing. You can be a space explorer. You can be a mother. You can be a warrior or a slave in ancient Crete, an Indian in the Amazon, a computer hacker, a revolutionary, a witch, a thief, a politician, or even your own self as a two year old. There are no limits.

What suits your Crazy Child? You can be a very rich person living in a hilltop mansion that is hidden by trees. You can be a child living in the ghetto. You can be the first woman President, and you can have fourteen tattoos. You can be an animal. Why not?

There is much persona writing in literature. The overwhelming evidence is that this role taking is not only possible, it makes for fine writing. George Sand wrote as a man, and her classic book *Silas Mariner* is written from the man's point of view. Joseph Conrad, an immigrant from Hungary, took on the role of an English explorer in *Heart of Darkness*. James Joyce wrote part of *Ulysses* from a woman's standpoint. Sappho's poems can be read with a gay or straight perspective.

## Persona in Stories

You can take pleasure in being a little different. It might give you a thrill to pretend being someone else. It is like eavesdropping or being a voyeur — with the difference that writing is legal and healthy. Read this excerpt from Jonathan Austin's story "Vines and the Quarter Moon":

> I part the leaves of the raspberry to get at the morning glory. The damned morning glory has invaded. It is everywhere. Wrapped around the long raspberry vine, twisted through its leaves, crawling along the soil beds of the vegetable garden.
>
> When Roxie was here, she would work on this. But she left me two years ago. People came and expressed their sympathies, but they could hardly say that her end was untimely. I found her here in the garden. A stroke. She was 76. I always

told her to lay off the bacon, but she had to have bacon and eggs. She lived for bacon and eggs.

He goes on to write that he is eighty and in good shape. Do you believe him? The author could be twenty-five, might hate gardening, and might not be a man.

Whatever is true about this author, I believe the persona. Jonathan Austin has me believing that his persona is eighty years old and is out gardening. When you write, it is important to deliver a believable presentation. The spell the writer weaves needs only to be convincing.

Your words create a kind of trance for the reader, and the reader is a willing participant. It is in the writer's power to influence what the reader thinks, down to the smallest detail. You control what assumptions the reader makes, entirely. The reader is putty in the writer's hands.

Your Crazy Child might think the most intriguing thing in the world is to be a child of another sex. Or a schizophrenic. Or maybe your Crazy Child has a ball pretending to be less urbane than you are. Read the beginning of Lillian Almeida's story "Eric's Come to Live on the Farm":

> Geezus Christ.
>
> Just two months past we were practically falling down the big hill out back. Just runnin' as fast and as fast as we could to keep from tumbling straight down, bodies over our own feet. Him screamin' "Jack and Jill! Jack and Jill!" Overgrown half-dressed babes fresh from our first fuck together up on the meadow. Shaken, happy, damp and reborn, laughin' like escapin' baboons. His flyin' hair showing a salting of gray. And me, well, old enough to feel younger for it all, I guess.
>
> "Just another sweet one," I'd been telling myself since. "Just another piece of ecstasy pie come and gone. Can't have 'em and keep 'em too, huh? But thank God for them at least." Two damned months seemed like a year since he'd left, and I s'pose

I was working on forgetting for my own good.

Then — geezus! — he really did what he's been sayin' on the phone! Spattered red truck comin' out of nowhere up that muddy drive again. We'd just been blowin' spun sugar up Ma Bell's dress all these weeks, is what I'd figured.

Almeida might be a sophisticated city person, pretending to be country — or she could be exactly as country as her persona. She might be even more country; she could be creating the most sophisticated persona she can imagine. The reader has no way of knowing which is accurate. We know only that the trance is convincing.

It truly does not matter what your Crazy Child chooses to be. That last image, "blowing spun sugar up Ma Bell's dress" is powerful and gripping. No matter what Almeida's background is in life, her persona is convincing.

## Talent and Persona

Talent has nothing to do with class or sophistication. It has nothing to do with whatever persona you choose, either. Instead, your Crazy Child will choose a persona through which your talent can express itself. That persona is working if your Crazy Child energy comes romping through. If your creative unconscious can do something it likes — be colorful or have a party or be very exacting — you are choosing an effective persona.

> *Everyone has talent. What is rare is the courage to follow the talent to the dark place where it leads.*
>
> ERICA JONG

Your persona does not have to be what other people like. It especially does not have to be what other writers like. In fact, it may be stronger if literary people do not like it. It's a common misconception that successful writers must appear cool or sophisticated. This is bullshit of the purest ray serene.

Talent is what is in your unconscious, and every person has plenty of talent. Consider your dreams, the beautiful, wild, extravagant, mysterious things that go careening through your psyche at night. Even if you don't remember them, you know your dreams are there. Some mornings we wake up exhausted because of our long and complicated journeys through dreamland — too much talent. Our talent has taken us for a ride.

> . . . the brain in REM sleep is working even harder than when it is awake. . . . The neurophysical activity . . . gives rise to a dream world indistinguishable from the real world — except analytically and retrospectively, from the vantage point of wakefulness.
>
> WILLIAM DEMENT, M.D.

## Persona in Poems

Just as in prose, we meet the persona in the first words of a poem. Remember the beginning of Allen Ginsberg's "Howl"? "I saw the best minds of my generation destroyed by madness, starving hysterical naked." This persona seems to be on a podium, giving the reader an overview. The open, rabbinical tone and long rhythms suggest gesticulating arms and a confident, no-nonsense manner.

In her poem "The Emotional Con Meets a Virgin Ideal" from *African Sleeping Sickness*, Wanda Coleman portrays a worldly-wise and tired persona very directly — one who has known much trouble, maybe too much trouble:

don't ask me where i've been
places dark and bloody
you wouldn't want to journey there
and i'm too tired

Notice how well these lines work as a hook. By saying "don't ask me where i've been" she provokes our curiosity instantly.

Mary Oliver shows us a different persona in this poem from her collection *Dream Work:*

### Wild Geese

You do not have to be good.
You do not have to walk on your knees
for a hundred miles through the desert, repenting.
You only have to let the soft animal of your body
    love what it loves.
Tell me about despair, yours, and I will tell you mine.
Meanwhile the world goes on.
Meanwhile the sun and the clear pebbles of the rain
are moving across the landscapes,
over the prairies and the deep trees,
the mountains and the rivers.
Meanwhile the wild geese, high in the clean blue air,
are heading home again.
Whoever you are, no matter how lonely,
the world offers itself to your imagination,
calls to you like the wild geese, harsh and exciting —
over and over announcing your place
in the family of things.

This persona is motherly and caring. She is in touch with her body, and in touch with personal feelings, and she loves nature. She is talking quietly, and I imagine her sitting with a view of the sky.

## Persona in Essays

Persona works the same in the essay as it does in poems and stories. Read this excerpt from Aldo Leopold's book *Sand County Almanac:*

> Why is the shovel regarded as a symbol of drudgery? Perhaps because most shovels are dull. Certainly all drudges have dull shovels, but I am uncertain which of these two facts is cause and which effect. I only know that a good file, vigorously wielded, makes my shovel sing as it slices the mellow loam. I am told there is music in the sharp plane, the sharp chisel, and the sharp scalpel, but I hear it best in my shovel; it hums in my wrists as I plant a pine. I suspect that the fellow who tried so hard to strike one clear note upon the harp of time chose too difficult an instrument.

This persona is questioning, independent, and lives the life of a farmer or outdoorsperson. He likes poking at pretensions. He lives in the moment and he is down to earth. Also, his first sentence is an effective hook.

## Persona in Plays

If you are writing a play, you already know the pleasure of putting characters on stage and having them speak. You can make them heroic or poignant or romantic or funny — or ridiculous. You can put as many people up there as your Crazy Child likes, and they can be extreme.

Each of your characters has a different persona. Your possibilities are unlimited: you can make them as wild or as strange or as subtle as you like. No matter what your experience is, your psyche knows about personas — the same as other writers' psyches do.

Technically, though, the playwright's persona is different from any character. If two people are talking on stage, neither one is the playwright's persona — though sometimes one may speak for the author. The gestalt of all the characters is the playwright's persona. So both characters contribute.

The easiest way to understand persona in drama is to look at your play from a different station in life. The homeless, the crippled, and the ill in Maksim Gorky's *The Lower Depths* would look different to a well-to-do writer. The polite social drama of *The Importance of Being Earnest* might look very different to Amiri Baraka. The racist, violent subway drama of his *Dutchman* would look different to Noel Coward.

You can become aware of your persona if you imagine having a very different mind. You may also gain a sense of power by doing this. You can change your persona a little — or a lot. How would you present your drama if your sexual orientation were different? If your culture or race were different?

Try imagining that you are different — just for fun. You might find, suddenly, that you do want to take a different tack. Your creative unconscious has become inspired.

## Persona and the Crazy Child

The Crazy Child knows about persona. The Crazy Child in you has been practicing personas since you were little. As with the hook, the creation of a persona is linked to staying alive. Personas are an important part of growing up.

Whenever a child tries something new, it is trying on a persona. One of its personas can walk, even though the child may still be stumbling. Another persona can talk, even if its noises are still gibberish. The child will grow into its personas and become them, one at a time. A child must feel great delight when it graduates from rug rat to walker — just look at its face.

Dare to be extravagant. Your creative unconscious may want to be someone who will shock you. You may want to write as if you know what sex feels like in another gender and in another time. If this is your Crazy Child's wish, do it. Your writing will have all the flair and energy inhabiting your body. That power will transmit itself to the reader.

The key is not to be shy. The key is to get way into this other person, to dream into this different life, to dream the little and big details — especially the little ones. That so many writers take on unusual personas indicates that you can too. The human psyche is easily capable of knowing what being another person is like.

The Crazy Child, too, is a persona. It is different from who we think we are consciously. When we become our own Crazy Child, we are taking on a persona — the persona of the creative unconscious: the part that wants to give gifts or tell stories or throw rocks or wiggle toes in the mud or build an elaborate house of cards — whatever.

Becoming your own Crazy Child is an adventure. Your creative unconscious is right there inside you. It is full of life and full of passion, and it is also a stranger. Letting it write freely may be the greatest adventure, because you don't know who your own Crazy Child will turn out to be.

## EXERCISE

Divide your psyche into the three parts discussed on page xv — the Editor, the Writer, and the Crazy Child. Ask the Editor and the Writer to leave. They can go for a walk, play a game of Scrabble, or take a nap — anything. Then let the Crazy Child write whatever it wants.

Let that part of you speak without any negative judgments whatsoever. Hear no criticism from the Editor and entertain no expectations from the Writer. The Crazy Child may want to make a mess. So what? It may be illogical, fancy, bizarre, angry, or use clichés —

there are no restrictions. Give your Crazy Child free reign.

---

*A child's attitude toward everything is an artist's attitude.*
WILLA CATHER

---

There is no wrong way to do this exercise. If the Editor or the Writer keep poking their noses in, push them away; tell them to finish their nap. Or you can write what they say. "This is drivel!" "How can you expect anyone to be interested in this?" or whatever they espouse. Simply spell it out and put it in parentheses — then continue writing whatever your Crazy Child wants.

If you take a dislike to the exercise, let the Crazy Child express that dislike. One author rolled up the whole workshop — couches, lamps, writers and all — into a Persian rug, stuffed it in the fireplace, and set it on fire. Her creative unconscious spent the rest of the exercise cavorting with the flames. The writing was terrific.

Your Crazy Child could write about what it would like to do instead. Writing about an enthusiasm is a fine way to do the persona exercise. What is your love? Roller skating, racing cars, stamps, computer games? Or guns, crystals, meditation, rap, dancing, basketball, hiking, drugs, sex? Go for it. Start writing it down. Your judgmental parent is taking a nap, and you can write whatever you like.

## Taking-Off Points

The direction you take is best chosen by your Crazy Child. There is wisdom in its first impulse. Try the exercise without any preparation — by staring at the blank sheet of paper and letting your

Crazy Child dream up a beginning. Any route into your creative unconscious is fine, even something silly or corny.

The Crazy Child lives in your body, and this is what distinguishes Crazy Child writing. Listen down into your body for an impulse, especially for a tweak of enthusiasm — or for any bit of nasty feeling. Your creative unconscious has been hearing a lot about itself in these pages. It probably has a good idea where to start.

> *First thought, best thought.*
>
> TRUNGPA RINPOCH

## Getting Unstuck

If you are truly stuck, try one of these guides.

One, think of an event from childhood and write it in a child's voice. Use childish expressions and be honest to the child's impulses, feelings, and sense of rhythm. See things that the child would see — from the child's height. Listen into that child's body and report what it feels.

Or two, look up and write a line. Pick the first thing that strikes your eye. Any physical detail can be stimulating. As you read this sentence, you have already noticed something — at least out of the corner of your eye. What was it? Look at it, write it down, and go on from there. Another sentence wants to follow that first one, and then another. Start chasing those sentences.

Keep the pen moving on the page, or at least keep it in contact with the page. The Editor will then have less chance to intervene and you might not have to give the order, "Move down to the paper." The pen is already there, ready for the next phrase. It doesn't matter what you write.

> *Don't go outside your house to see flowers.*
> *My friend, don't bother with that excursion.*
> *Inside your body there are flowers.*
> *One flower has a thousand petals.*
> *That will do for a place to sit.*
> *Sitting there you will have a glimpse of beauty*
> *inside the body and out of it,*
> *before gardens and after gardens.*
>
> KABIR, *Poem '36'*

## Crazy Child and the Body

In every class I stand up and touch where the Editor, Writer, and Crazy Child reside in my body. On top of my head is the Editor. Around my face is the Writer. My Crazy Child lives from my neck down to the bottom of my feet.

Do this yourself. Stand up, as if you are in kindergarten, and touch your own body. Kindergarten activities are as effective for your Crazy Child as they are for little people, so this is a surefire way to find your creative unconscious. Your hands may start to buzz.

My Editor stomps down on my head with his boots. The soles of those boots are engraved with words, like rubber stamps: "Drivel. Same old shit. You're no good." I can feel them stamping into my head. "You should do what the Editor says."

My Writer is the conscious part. My Writer talks about writing and plans writing projects. My Writer tries to be efficient and keep a clean desk. My Writer feels like a clear bowl, extending from my neck up to my ears, including the whole area around my eyes.

Crazy Child energy is pushing up from my feet. It comes up through my legs, my belly, my chest, and up through my spine. It is my connection to the earth, to dreams, to the Goddess, and to God. Everything that I have done and everything that has been done to me is stuck in my muscles and nerves. Crazy Child energy courses up through this vast landscape.

I have to listen down into my body to find my creative unconscious. I might see Crazy Child images or words in the back of my head, as if they are thrown there on a screen. But I'm aware that the stream of images and energy is coming up through my body. I listen down into my body to find that energy.

When you listen into your body, notice any spots of tension. Any crick or sore spot or numb area in your body is probably hiding a story. Some event was traveling through there, took a hankering to the spot, and nestled in. Let it speak out on the page. Drag it out by the tail if you have to, and squeeze until it talks.

Remember in the image detail exercise, on pages 14–15, how you followed a trail of details — real or imagined? Do the same thing here. Follow this trail of feelings and images into your body. These feelings and images lead one to another by their own mysterious logic and no one knows where they will go. No one knows what you will find, either. You are starting a treasure hunt.

Dynamic poems and stories can come straight out of this exercise, often in fine, musical sentences, for your creative unconscious likes sounds. The Crazy Child likes squishing its toes in the mud, too, and putting anything in its mouth. Biting, chewing, eating, giving gifts, being sweet, throwing rocks, yelling, spitting, anything that has to do with the senses and the body is Crazy Child stuff — anything that feels like play.

## Crazy Child Writing Promotes Good Health

If journal writing improves the immune system, as James Pennebaker reports in *American Health* magazine for January/February 1991, then Crazy Child writing must do so even more. Pennebaker explains that health is improved in students who keep personal journals. The most scientific of several studies demonstrated that T-cell counts are significantly raised when students write in their journals every day.

The studies also showed that writing papers unrelated to the students' life had no effect on their health. The inescapable conclusion is that health is improved by writing personal experiences on a regular basis. The material does need to be important to your life — about your feelings, your issues, or your relationships.

This is the arena of the Crazy Child. Any creative writing involves your creative unconscious to a large extent, including journal writing. The Crazy Child is the container for our deepest feelings. Even if we hold the conviction that we are writing fiction, the writing will involve those feelings.

It is also intuitively correct that writing promotes health. You can feel the effect. Some authors get quite excited and happy when they write. Or you may feel clean and open after you have finished writing — even if the writing was difficult.

This clean, open feeling is usual, and we receive it as a sign of health. However, you may also feel terribly vulnerable. The Crazy Child exercise may even make you feel lousy. Perhaps in the writing process you have removed some armor, and who you really are is more known to you. This is healthy, too, even if it feels bad.

## Awful-Feeling Crazy Child Writing

You are doing the exercise well if it feels like you are doing badly. This is no contradiction, for the feeling that your writing is "awful" or "drivel" is probably a judgment of your Editor or Writer. That means you are writing excluded material — material straight from the creative unconscious. The Editor keeps such vivid material away from you with those judgments. Writing drivel is good.

You would be entertained by what other writers have called their own Crazy Child writing: "Ugly, stupid, boring, flotsam, crap, sludge," or "doodling," or "junk," or "detritus," or "vomit." All of these are good signs. If you experience any self-criticisms like these, you are doing the exercise well. You might also feel excited — so much the better.

## WORKSHOP

First, share your Crazy Child exercise with the workshop. By all means share your hook practice piece too, but do that second.

The Crazy Child exercise sometimes seems chaotic, and you could be tempted to discard the whole thing — including the strong writing. When the exercise is fresh in your mind, the workshop can influence your attitude. You will bend more easily when you are close to this new material.

The workshop's task is to point out the powerful writing in the exercise. This is especially important because the material is new to the author, and the author may feel uneasy about it. Crazy Child writing can be strange and scary. The images might feel raw or embarrassing — or stupid.

---

> . . . *In a carnival seat I'm rushing upward*
> *past ladder rungs at a breathless speed,*
> *holding my brother, a child, in front*
> *of me. He has a long sheet of paper*
> *on which he has written a poem. He is*
> *terrified. I say, "Don't worry, I'm*
> *holding you tight," but the fact is, I'm*
> *having a hard time keeping my hold on him.*
> *I realize he is vomiting on the poem.*
>                CORNELIA VEENENDAAL, *"Dream Journeys"*

---

The syngenetic workshop operates on the premise that all children are creative geniuses. The Crazy Child is no exception. The workshop may recognize the Crazy Child's powerful writing easily. The greater challenge may be to convince the author that you, the workshop members, are correct. You may be working against the author's judgment.

The author may feel like Cornelia Veenendaal's brother in "Dream Journeys." It may be obvious to the listener when an image detail or description of action is powerful. But the author may be looking at vomit, and trying to figure out why you like it. You need to be very clear with your feedback. You may need to repeat your insights a number of times until the author truly understands. You may be struggling against a ton of negative judgment.

When your writing is being workshopped, it is important to believe the feedback. You, too, may be looking at something that seems ugly, and the workshop is telling you it is fine. How can you believe them when your writing looks so bad? The judgment of your Editor might be extreme, and in error. This calls for a major adjustment in your thinking.

When you make that adjustment, you begin to include new material into your writing. You are counteracting the usual editorial bias. You are affirming the wilder and more innovative parts of yourself — your creative unconscious. You are about to discover new power.

## Doors

In your writing, "doors" are places to expand and explore. An image or a phrase or a bit of dialogue can be just like a door. It can open onto another story or another universe. You turn the knob and go through into another world, and a new story, poem, play, or essay begins to unfold.

There is a door in Mary Oliver's poem, on page 69. Aren't you curious to hear what her despair is? In the Christopher Russell poem that follows on pages 81–82, there are two doors: one is the story of the woman screaming in the window at night, and the other is the story of how the man hurts himself. Doors, like hooks, excite the reader's curiosity.

You will easily become proficient at spotting doors. You will feel a signal in your body when you find a door: a twinge, a flare of excitement, a small thrill of mystery, or a sense of something missing. What would the reader see, if the author opens that door?

For this workshop, two things are vital. First, be very clear about the powerful writing in the Crazy Child exercise. Second, point out new possibilities for each author. You may find doors in the missing person piece as well. Wherever you find them, each of you should have doors to enter for the next session — worlds to expand and explore.

## PRACTICE

Did you notice a door in your Crazy Child exercise? Something, an image or a quote, that made you curious? You might open that door, go through it, and write what you see. Include all the things we have talked about: hook, image detail, and slow motion writing. Be sure to include information from your senses. Pull the reader along with you.

Doors may be especially obvious if you wrote a childhood event — it is hard to write about the past and not include parts of several stories. You may have felt these doors as you wrote them. Or perhaps, as you were writing the exercise, another story came along and flirted with you.

### Alternative

An alternative is to make the missing person practice a persona piece. Write a new missing person piece as if you are a different age, gender, or race — or write the same piece as if you are one of the other characters. Another alternative is to do any persona piece. Become any persona your Crazy Child takes a shine to and write a story, poem, essay, or play in that persona.

Does one of these possibilities excite your interest? The best thing is to write something your Crazy Child chooses on its own. For this reason, practices are generally not precisely defined. All these alternatives are meant to help you cast about in the dark, where you might strike some delightful sparks. Your creative unconscious may fan one of these sparks into a bonfire.

## Listen to the Darkness

The Crazy Child is alive and well in the unknown. We find it by listening to the darkness, and in this poem Christopher Russell has a gang of Crazy Children wake up an imaginary poet:

Great Poets

It's tough, being a great poet:
If you are a great poet,
a heterosexual great poet,
the women can't get enough of you
they scream in your window at night,
Great Poets are sex objects:
It holds for Women Great Poets, Men Great Poets
Homosexual Great Poets and Bisexual Great Poets . . .
well, forget it.
You get a Heterosexual Woman Great Poet
with a Heterosexual Male Great Poet —
she'll claw his back, slap his ass, yell obscenities
in his ear and he'll keep it up until he
hurts himself — Why?
Because they're Great Poets. That's why.
It holds for Homosexual Great Poets
and Bisexual Great Poets . . .
Well, the hell with it.

Great Poets don't write.

Archetypical fiends, monsters, angels and combinations
of all three enter the Great Poet's bedroom — if
the Great Poet is fortunate enough to have a bedroom —
late at night and yell,
"Wake up, lamebrain, I'm gonna talk, get the goddamn
tablet and write this down,"
frequently these archetypical types are drunk and
incoherent.
The Great Poet takes dictation.

That is how Great Poetry is written.
Simple as that.

Eventually, however
these archetypes fail to show up.

The Great Poet gets up to read in public
and his/her mouth falls open and nothing comes out.
A crack appears in the forehead, fluid drips down
the Great Poet's shirt and covers the podium,
the Great Poet becomes brittle and suddenly
collapses in a pile of shards,
like a Ming vase dropped on a garage floor.

The janitor comes in with a broom
and a dustpan and sweeps up the Great Poet,
puts the pieces in a special literary trash heap
and the Great Poet lies in state.
Everyone says, "Hey, whatever happened to what's its face,
you know, the Great Poet?"

Listening to the darkness is useful whether you expand the Crazy Child exercise or do a persona piece. Any persona has a way of separating itself from the writer, and as a separate being it may seem to speak to you from a place where there is no light.

## Find a Door

A door opens onto a new universe and I describe doors on pages 79–80. It may take some effort, but you should be able to discover a door on your own. Poke at one of those people in your exercise. Is your brother or sister or friend — or whoever — telling you about something else that happened?

Read your writing with care and use your body as an antenna. Listen for any funny feeling. This may be easier when you read someone else's writing, but you should also get signals from your own work. Twinges of mystery or excitement or anticipation — or of something missing — these are all doors.

You may also get a feeling of dread. You may think, "Do I have to write that stuff?" But do you know what is said about resistance? Where there is great resistance, there is a great story. "Methinks he doth protest too much" is Shakespeare's way of putting it. There are riches behind that door, so dare to go through it — the one that says, "Do I have to?"

Getting through that door may take work. Your Crazy Child might drag its heels, or hook its fingers in the doorjamb. But once you pull yourself through, you have a chance to explore new territory. You are on an adventure.

## Crazy Child and Political Correctness

Your Crazy Child may be politically correct or may not be aware of such things. For the purpose of practicing, it may help to let go of being too careful.

In his poem, Russell pokes fun at rigid correctness. He starts including all gender identifications in his poem, and then he gets lost. "Well, forget it," he says. His poem points out the ridiculousness of being too finicky, yet at the same time he acknowledges the importance of diversity.

We live in sensitive times. You should be wary of publishing something in which you fill in a stereotype or speak for a race or gender not your own. But practice is not publishing, and it is valuable to feel free about practicing any persona.

Choose one as nice as you wish, or as disrespectful, or as vitriolic. *Let the Crazy Child Write!* is about total self expression. The more you get on the page — including ugly, insulting stuff — the more you will learn about writing. You may also learn about nasty feelings.

If you cross the line into insults, you will hear about it. Dumping on others because of sex, race, class, or gender identification will make enemies. But sometimes, if you're clear the insults are coming from a flaw in the persona, you can write with impunity. The persona is being an asshole.

Writing an unlikable persona is a risk, but it may teach you a lot. Some personas teach us about darkness, some about emotional depths, some about how influential our backgrounds are, and some personas teach us about the beauty of diversity.

Most personas teach us about the joy of writing. You are on an adventure, and you will learn the most by giving yourself as much freedom as you dare. Write whatever persona your Crazy Child wishes.

# Chapter 5

## Point of View

*There is, indeed, only one way of understanding a cultural phenomenon which is alien to one's own ideological pattern, and that is to place oneself at its very centre. . . . Before we proceed to judge it we must fully understand it and become imbued, as it were, with its ideology, whatever form it may take. . . .*

MIRCEA ELIADE

Reading is like meeting people: we meet a person in an article, we meet people in stories and plays, and we may get to know a person very well in a novel. In a poem we may experience someone so completely that we feel we are that person — or that person is us. It makes no difference if the person, technically, is the author's persona.

The author uses a "point of view" to lead us toward that person. The reader is guided, in an intimate way, if the author poses as the character. The author may seem to stand and say, simply, "Hello. My name is George, and something very odd happened when I was driving to the market. . . ." This is the "first-person" point of view.

Or the author may stand aside and present someone else. This author refers to another person and may write, "An odd thing happened to Sylvia on her way to the market, when she was thinking about her son. . . . " This author is a ghostly presence, and uses

85

"she" or "he" when describing the main character. This is the "third-person" point of view.

In the omniscient point of view, the author hovers above the scene. "Omniscient" means all-knowing, and this author may write from a godlike position in the sky. "Sylvia was thinking about her son when she pulled up to the stop sign, and she had no idea that George was barreling down the side street, happy as a lark but oblivious, running every stop along the way." This author also uses "she" and "he." But the omniscient narrator presents information that neither character could possibly know.

Point of view can be flexible, and one point of view may blend into another. In fact, when nuances are taken into account, there are many points of view. One study lists thirty-six different variations, with examples of each.

In *Let the Crazy Child Write!* I will explore three fundamental points of view: first person, third person, and omniscient. I will also discuss one common variation, the "shifting third-person" point of view, in which the author slides back and forth between two or more characters.

There is a second-person point of view, though it's not often used. It addresses the reader as "you," and sometimes puts the reader inside the piece — much like the first person does. When I read "you," I may translate it automatically into "I." Mary Oliver's poem, on page 69, is a fine example of this point of view, and so is Thaisa Frank's short story, on pages 217–218.

## Persona and Point of View

Persona is the person you present as you write, and point of view is your angle of presentation. If you pretend to be a cat, the cat is your persona. How you present the cat is your point of view.

If you present the cat as yourself, you may write "I am prowling the backyard, on the lookout for salamanders." This is the first-person point of view.

If you write as if you know the cat intimately, this is the third-person point of view. "Topaz the cat prowls the backyard, sniffing for salamanders."

If you also know what's happening around the cat, this is the omniscient point of view. "Topaz was prowling the backyard for salamanders when a red-tailed hawk swooped down, landed on the telephone pole, and eyed her plump, furry shape."

If you go back and forth between the cat and the hawk, then you are using the shifting third-person point of view.

## Crazy Child and Point of View

Point of view defines and limits your creativity. It is like a playpen: it fences in a territory, but allows unlimited play within that space. One point of view provides your Crazy Child with one kind of play, another with a different kind. Which point of view will work for a piece may not be obvious — probably because there are so many variables. Your creative unconscious, however, is likely to chose one for you.

Your Crazy Child knows very well what you are bringing to your topic. All your knowledge — conscious and unconscious — translates into a kind of pressure. The Crazy Child feels that pressure. The pressure may be a feeling in your body or a whimsical bias or an intuition. It will make some points of view seem too constricting and some too loose, but one will feel exactly right.

---

*I make all my decisions on intuition. I throw a spear into the darkness. That is intuition. Then I must send an army into the darkness to find the spear. That is intellect.*

INGMAR BERGMAN

Your Crazy Child may throw a spear into the darkness, and soon you will be searching out that spear. But before it throws the spear, your creative unconscious can be more or less informed about points of view. In general, you want your Crazy Child to be able to roam freely among the various points of view, and to know what they are about.

The more familiar you are with points of view, the more easily your Crazy Child will make its choice. And the easier it will be to identify that point of view. As you read this chapter and do the writing exercise, the characteristics of these fundamental points of view will become familiar ground.

## First-Person Point of View

We know about first-person point of view naturally. We use this point of view when we talk. We use the first-person "I" in everyday life, and this "I" is the same as the literary first person. It is the "I" of telling a story, the "I" of journal writing, and the "I" of speaking a personal truth in a poem or in an essay.

Whatever you associate with yourself can be written in the first-person point of view. This covers a lot of ground, and we know what that ground is instinctively. That ground is what you think, and what you feel, and what you see. Whatever is in your individual realm is in the realm of the first person.

The limitations of the "I" are automatic also. We are limited to our bodies and minds. Or, technically, we are limited to the body and mind of our persona. If we project ourselves into another body, it becomes our "I." We are then limited by that body and mind — we are limited to what it thinks and feels and sees.

Consider Jane Smiley's novel *A Thousand Acres*. The main character has learned that a neighbor, who is sometimes a friend and sometimes an antagonist, has been blinded in an accident. Her husband thinks she is not being adequately sympathetic:

> "Don't you care? The fucking water tank was empty! You

know what it means as well as I do!"

I said evenly, "It means he's blind."

"Don't you care? This is a friend of ours! What happened to you? I don't know you any more." He headed for the door.

I followed him, my voice rising, "What's wrong? What am I saying that's wrong?" He got in the truck and drove off, his tires squealing on the asphalt.

The fact is, I was too astonished to think anything. The imagination runs first to the physical, doesn't it, so that no matter what, you recoil from the pain, imagine yourself blind, your tissues resonating from the power of what has happened. I actually don't remember how I imagined the accident then, when I hadn't learned any of the details, but it entered my life with a crash and I do remember my hands trembling so violently as I tried to do the dishes that a plate broke against the faucet and I had to stop and sit down. Then I remember almost throwing up sitting there.

The first-person point of view keeps us involved in the main character's thoughts and feelings. She is confused by her husband's reaction, shocked by the accident, and she tries to understand what is happening. The reader makes the same effort. We stay right with the story as her reactions evolve — we think her thoughts and feel her feelings.

Notice how breaking a plate because her hands were "trembling so violently" is an excellent kinetic detail. That, in combination with the image of the faucet and with her thoughts, puts us right at the sink.

Generally, the first-person point of view keeps a piece immediate and dramatic. Whatever happens feels like it is happening to the reader, because we identify with the "I" of the character. This identification is automatic, akin to seeing that three-legged dog. The job of our nervous system, when it reads "I," is to imagine we are that "I."

You may not like the character, however. When a reader says,

"I don't identify with that character," the reader usually means that the identification is not comfortable. The reader is repudiating any similarity between the character and the reader. But the identification does take place. It happens in an eye blink.

## Third-Person Point of View

Kobo Abé wrote *The Woman in the Dunes* in the third-person point of view. He is intimately close to his character, just as Smiley is to hers. He shows us what that character thinks, feels, and sees. And, just as in the first person, he is limited by what that character thinks, feels, and sees.

But Abé uses the word "he" instead of "I." This gives the writing a different quality. His third-person point of view is almost the same as the first person, with the "I's" changed to "he's." This has the effect of making the reader's identification with the character less personal.

In Abé's novel, the main character has been kidnapped. He is forced to live with a woman at the edge of a village — and the village is being encroached upon by sand dunes. The woman's house is constantly invaded by sand. Her job is to scoop the sand out of the house and maintain the village's first line of defense. The villagers hope the man will help the woman, but the man is very angry:

> . . . Yet no matter how he puffed he got only the taste of smoke, an extremely greasy smoke that irritated his tongue; the cigarette was worse than useless. The experience quite spoiled his frame of mind and took away any desire he might have had to speak to the woman.
>
> She attended to the dirty dishes, placing them on the earthen floor and slowly heaping up sand on them. Then she said hesitantly: "I'm going to have to begin right away getting the sand down from the ceiling."
>
> "Getting the sand down? Oh. Well, that's all right with

me." He wondered indifferently why that should have anything to do with him now. It didn't concern him if the beams
rotted and the roof fell in.

"If I'm in your way, do you want me to move somewhere
else?"

"I'm sorry, but would you mind . . . ?"

She needn't pretend! Why didn't she show even a little of
her real feelings? In her heart she probably felt as if she had
bitten into a spoiled onion. But she was expressionless as she
swiftly, with an accustomed movement, wrapped a towel
folded in two around the lower part of her face and tied it
behind her head. She put a whisk broom and a small piece of
wood under her arm, and climbed up on the partition of the
closet, which had only half a door remaining.

Abruptly, he exclaimed: "Frankly, I'm convinced we'd both
feel much better if this house fell to pieces!"

He was surprised himself at his peevish outburst, and the
woman turned and looked at him with an even more startled
look. Well, apparently she had not yet turned quite into an
insect.

We certainly get to know this character. We follow each
thought as it evolves into the next, influenced by what the woman
does. When she looks back, startled, he sneers that she is not yet
"an insect."

But we do not identify as personally with this character as in
the first-person point of view. The reader is not saying "I" as the
story continues; the reader is saying "he." This makes the story
something we watch as an outside observer — like a movie. We
can read it and accept it at face value.

In this sense the third person has more power. There is more
room for curiosity in the reader. There is also less likelihood that
the writing will tangle with the reader's private feelings. The third-
person point of view may elicit a more believing response from the

reader. This accepting response may hold true even if the writer presents a character who is wildly bizarre.

You may also conceal who you are by using the third-person point of view. The reader does not automatically assume that the main character is the writer. On the surface, the author is talking about someone else. When I write, I like to have that anonymity. The third-person point of view provides a sort of cloak the author can hide behind.

The third-person point of view may also be useful for hiding the character's thoughts. This can make for powerful writing of a different, distanced kind. It may be packed with action or tough to the point of being steely. Flannery O'Conner, quoted on page 48, Ernest Hemingway, and William Gibson sometimes write in this manner.

All through Abé's *The Woman in the Dunes* the writer's eye is like a camera mounted on the main character's shoulder. The reader sees only what is directly in front of that character. We can also hear the man's thoughts, as if the camera has a microphone in his head. This "camera-on-the-shoulder" technique is explained on page 100, and you may want to use it when you do the exercise.

## Omniscient Point of View

In the omniscient point of view the author hovers over the scene. The author can present the scene as if the author knows everything about it. Any insight may sound like a true, accurate vision of the world — the author is, after all, the creator of the scene, the characters, and the action. This confers much authority on the writer. The reader responds to that authority automatically.

The omniscient point of view is especially effective for an insight that takes more than one person to demonstrate. Wendell Berry's poem has two crucial participants:

## Creation Myth

This is a story handed down.
It is about the old days when Bill
and Florence and a lot of their kin
lived in the little tin-roofed house
beside the woods, below the hill.
Mornings, they went up the hill
to work, Florence to the house,
the men and boys to the field.
Evenings, they all came home again.
There would be talk then and laughter
and taking of ease around the porch
while the summer night closed.
But one night, McKinley, Bill's young brother,
stayed away late, and it was dark
when he started down the hill.
Not a star shone, not a window.
What he was going down into was
the dark, only his footsteps sounding
to prove he trod the ground. And Bill
who had got up to cool himself,
thinking and smoking, leaning on
the jamb of the open front door,
heard McKinley coming down,
and heard his steps beat faster
as he came, for McKinley felt the pasture's
darkness joined to all the rest
of darkness everywhere. It touched
the depths of woods and sky and grave.
In that huge dark, things that usually
stayed put might get around, as fish
in pond or slue get loose in flood.
Oh, things could be coming close

that never had come close before.
He missed the house and went on down
and crossed the draw and pounded on
where the pasture widened on the other side,
lost then for sure. Propped in the door,
Bill heard him circling, a dark star
in the dark, breathing hard, his feet
blind on the little reality
that was left. Amused, Bill smoked
his smoke, and listened. He knew where
McKinley was, though McKinley didn't.
Bill smiled in the darkness to himself,
and let McKinley run until his steps
approached something really to fear:
the quarry pool. Bill quit his pipe
then, opened the screen, and stepped out,
barefoot, on the warm boards. "McKinley!"
he said, and laid the field out clear
under McKinley's feet, and placed
the map of it in his head.

That shout comes in the nick of time. We see both the man on the porch and the man wandering blindly toward the quarry. The poet is a presence hovering over the entire scene.

The omniscient point of view creates the feeling, for the reader, of participating with an objective mind. This is the unique power of this point of view. We identify not so much with the characters themselves, as with the mind that is describing them. We are watching with the mind of an objective authority — perhaps even with the mind of a god.

There is something comforting about this, or satisfying — or horrifying if we are reading a horror story. In "Creation Myth" the horror was averted at the last moment. A story in the omniscient point of view seems like an ultimate reality. It does not seem like something that happens to just one person. This reality can be pleasant or painful or anything in between — whatever your Crazy Child likes.

## Shifting Third-Person Point of View

Tillie Olsen's story "Tell Me A Riddle" is written in the shifting third-person point of view. She shifts between an aging man and his wife. The man is trying to fix a vacuum machine motor, and he is pleading with his wife to move to the "Haven":

> But while he struggled with the motor, it seethed in him. Why fix it? Why have to bother? And if it can't be fixed, have to wring the mind with how to pay the repair? At the Haven they come in with their own machines to clean your room or your cottage; you fish, or play cards, or make jokes in the sun, not with knotty fingers fight to mend vacuums.
> Over the dishes, coaxingly: "For once in your life, to be free, to have everything done for you, like a queen."
> "I never liked queens."

The lines that switch the reader from person to person are "bridges." The first sentence, "But while he struggled with the motor, it seethed in him" is a bridge from the external world directly to his internal dialogue. His first thought is "Why fix it?" and he continues on, in some anguish.

The woman and her husband take a few acrimonious snipes at each other, back and forth, and the woman finally becomes annoyed and turns off her hearing aid. The man tries some earnest convincing:

> "Look! In their bulletin. A reading circle. Twice a week it meets."
> "Haumm," her answer of not listening.
> "A reading circle. Chekhov they read that you like, and Peretz. Cultured people at the Haven that you would enjoy."
> "Enjoy!" She tasted the word. "Now, when it pleases you,

you find a reading circle for me. And forty years ago when the
children were morsels and there was a Circle, did you stay home
with them once so I could go? Even once? You trained me well.
I do not need others to enjoy. Others!" Her voice trembled.
"Because *you* want to be there with others. Already it makes me
sick to think of you always around others. Clown, grimacer,
floormat, yesman, entertainer, whatever they want of you."

And now it was he who turned on the television loud so
he need not hear.

Old scar tissue ruptured and the wounds festered anew.
Chekhov indeed. She thought without softness of that young
wife, who in the deep night hours while she nursed the current
baby, and perhaps held another in her lap, would try to stay
awake for the only time there was to read. She would feel again
the weather of the outside on his cheek when, coming late
from a meeting, he would find her so, and stimulated and
ardent, sniffing her skin, coax: "I'll put the baby to bed, and you
— put the book away, don't read, don't read."

That had been the most beguiling of all the "don't read,
put your book away" her life had been. Chekhov indeed!

The sentence "Old scar tissue ruptured and the wounds festered anew" bridges to the woman's internal dialogue. The next
phrase is her exact thought: "Chekhov indeed." The author writes
those bridging lines, using — briefly — an omniscient point of
view. We travel across these sentences, like across bridges, to the
other person.

This point of view is difficult to write, but Olsen makes it
seem easy. Her switches are graceful and natural. It helps that she
switches in a rhythm, so we spend about the same amount of time
with each character. It helps more that she has a strong narrative
presence, so we hear her bridges clearly.

It also helps that the positions of the two characters are completely opposed. We do not have to figure out whose thoughts we
are reading — we know instantly. The woman wants to stay home,

and the man wants to move. This poses no problem for the reader.

The great appeal of this point of view is that you can present both sides of an issue. And you can do it intimately. Olsen gives us each character's thoughts in exact, accurate-seeming phrases, like "Why fix it?" and "Chekhov, indeed!" We get the full flavor of the people.

## Point of View in Poems

Point of view works the same in poetry as it does in prose. The first-person point of view, however, is used far more often in poetry: "I" think this, or "I" feel this, or "I" see this. "Come live with me, and be my love . . ." writes Marlowe. "I saw the best minds of my generation . . ." writes Ginsberg. Many, many poems are written in the first person.

The first person is used so much in poems that poets often avoid stating it. The poet may write "I" early in a poem, so we know who is speaking. Then the poet may delete every subsequent "I" — or every one that is not absolutely necessary.

The poets have a point. The reader does not want to be bludgeoned with "I"s. And the poet probably prefers us to be involved with the presentation, instead of with the I-word. It's much better if we are busy absorbing the images and feelings.

Try this with your own poems. Take out all the "I"s, and put back only the ones you cannot do without. You may be surprised how few "I"s you truly need. Does the poem sound different?

## Point of View in Essays

The essay is most often written in the first-person point of view. The author will set up an unspoken contract with the reader, using that first person. That contract goes something like, "This is the truth, to the best of my knowledge." Because of this unspoken contract, we will be disposed, as readers, to giving the material a fair reading.

The "personal essay" is a nonfiction piece, usually about some part of the author's life. It, too, is often written in the first person — naturally. This type of essay less frequently has a point to prove, so much as a story to tell, or some aspect of life the author wants to make clear.

Barbara Robertson's essay, "Looking for Mr. Right Now," hooks us with the first sentences: "Did you see my ad? I'm the 'package deal. Includes intelligent conversation, nice body, kind heart.'" Her thesis comes later: "Opportunity is exactly what the personals are about: opportunity to meet people, to explore possibilities, and to practice being yourself."

In the traditional essay, the author seems to say, "This is what I believe." The reader is open to considering it. In a personal essay, the author seems to say, "This is what part of my life looks like." This is inviting, and the reader opens to the experience. We look forward to it.

## Point of View in Plays

Point of view works differently in drama than in prose or in poetry. The author is not on stage talking in one or another point of view. The characters are on stage, and they are most likely all speaking in the first person.

But the dramatic issue is being presented from an angle, or it is being worked out through one character. Playwrights ask, "Whose play is it?" In Arthur Miller's *Death of a Salesman*, we are more aware of the salesman's plight than of anyone else's. In Shakespeare's *Hamlet*, it is Hamlet's problems that are uppermost. You could say the drama was arranged around Hamlet, or even that it is from Hamlet's point of view.

But the same drama could be seen from another character's point of view. An example of this is Tom Stoppard's *Rosencrantz and Guildenstern Are Dead*, which is *Hamlet* seen through the eyes of the two young men who were sent to England. They do not see much of the drama, and what they do see is remarkably different. The title is a quote from *Hamlet*, in which someone inquires after the two men. What would *Death of a Salesman* look like if the drama were centered on the wife?

As a playwright, it is useful to wonder how your play would change if you focused on a different character. Try imagining the difference. If nothing else, it will help you when you go back to your original position. You may be more certain it is the point of view you want, and you may write it with more assurance and more flair.

Take twenty minutes to rewrite the Abé excerpt, on pages 90–91, from the woman's point of view. Stay in the third-person point of view, as if you are a camera on the woman's shoulder. Use the word "she" for whatever she thinks, feels, and sees. Be sure to check her other senses. At any moment, what is she hearing? Tasting? Touching? Smelling?

You may choose any sort of persona. You can be the woman as nearly as Abé describes her or be as different as your Crazy Child likes. Perhaps the woman is bristling with annoyance, or perhaps she is poised for revenge — for the nasty things the man has said — and she is planning some sort of torture. Or perhaps she wants to jump his bones.

Most of all, show what she, the captor, is thinking. She no doubt thinks very differently from the man. Let your Crazy Child do her thinking. There is no need to be discreet, and no need to be culturally accurate. This exercise is for exploration and discovery. Make her any sort of person you like.

You may use the same lines of dialogue. The woman would hear them, just as the man did — though she will give them different significance. Include the whisk broom, the piece of wood, the half door, the partition, the dishes, the towel, and the sand.

They seem ordinary in the excerpt, but they might be different to the woman. In your writing they could be anything. They could be irritating or sexy — or they could be weapons.

## Camera-on-the-Shoulder

The "camera-on-the-shoulder" point of view is a strict third-person point of view. The writer is fixed on the shoulder of the main character like a camera, with a microphone in the character's mind. You can report what the character thinks and what the character hears, touches, tastes, and smells. But you can report seeing only what is directly in front of the character.

The camera-on-the-shoulder funnels your Crazy Child energy. To get the most from this exercise, let your Crazy Child go wild — and, at the same time, keep it contained in that camera. It can see anything in front of your character, but only in front. If your Crazy Child wants to see something else, you have to turn your character around. Whatever you want to describe will have to face that camera.

Keeping the Crazy Child in that camera-on-the-shoulder keeps the reader on that shoulder, also. It anchors the reader in the character. Once we are firmly on that shoulder, we are ready to believe whatever you present. Your Crazy Child, within the scope of that camera, can say whatever it wants.

## Crazy Child Options

There are many options for this exercise. For one, you do not have to write in Abé's careful, ironic style. Let your Crazy Child choose the style. Your captor might be raging, spewing swearwords like a sailor, or viciously scheming under a polite exterior — or she might be totally serene.

There is no reason, also, to restrain yourself regarding the persona. Why not make the captor a man? Why not a gay man? How about a gay man who is interested in the captive — or is repulsed by him? Take complete freedom regarding the captive, also. The captive could be a woman.

Are there any other alternatives? If there is one you are interested in, go for it — let your Crazy Child write. Write in a contained fashion and wildly at the same time. This is excellent practice in understanding point of view.

## WORKSHOP

You now have a point-of-view exercise to workshop, and also a Crazy Child piece from the persona chapter. By all means read them both. It may be very interesting to hear how other workshop members have handled the point-of-view exercise. You may pick up ideas on how to write your point-of-view practice piece; you may find out how to make yours more exciting or more fun.

The Crazy Child practice, however, may present the same problems the Crazy Child exercise did. Did someone read material in the last session that was difficult to hear? Did you easily discover someone's powerful, raw writing, and the writer could not understand why you liked it? Or did you feel vulnerable about your own writing — did it seem like drivel?

With the Crazy Child practice the problems may be worse. The Editor may have tortured you all week. It may have made you, the author, feel thoroughly rotten. So this workshop should be conducted with compassion, and at the same time with much firmness. It is important that any ugly messages from the Editor are disputed powerfully. You should leave the workshop feeling positive about your writing.

Be sure to follow the kindergarten rules, depicted on pages 16–17. When you are the writer, your job is to believe the feedback. When you are a listener, establish the strengths of the writing first. Make sure the writer understands you — only then can you can give rewriting suggestions. You can comment on image detail, on the hook, on doors, and now on point of view. Remember that one, two, or at most three rewriting suggestions are plenty.

## Apple

Saying "Apple" is a way of indicating an apology. "Apple" applies to any tearful or tragic situation — or to any excuse. The writer declares "Apple" at the beginning of a share, and that is all that need be said. Everyone understands.

It might be that the baby threw up on the manuscript. Perhaps the copy machine reduced the text to 6-point type, and it is unreadable. Maybe the writer crashed into someone who ran a stop sign and both cars were totalled. But the most frequent cause for declaring "Apple" is that the writer feels terrible about the work.

Saying "Apple" is an important convention. It focuses the workshop on the writing and away from disclaimers. A writer's disclaimers are often not valid, anyway — they sidetrack attention from the writing. A discussion of the disclaimers will usually contaminate how the writing is received.

Saying "Apple" also reminds the workshop that the author is vulnerable. You can hardly be more vulnerable than when you share your writing — it is more vulnerable-making than taking off your clothes. You wouldn't be called stupid for your body, would you? But you could be called stupid for your writing. My Editor does that often.

That vulnerable feeling can be intense, especially when you are sharing Crazy Child writing. The Editor may be disgusted with the Crazy Child, and may discount it in extreme terms. The Editor may want to apologize at length. At first!

What you stand to learn from working with the Crazy Child is that it is your strongest voice. The creative unconscious is the foundation of your most powerful and engrossing writing. What you, your Editor, and your Writer stand to learn from the Crazy Child is that you love it — and that your Crazy Child loves to write.

An instructive practice is to write in the camera-on-the-shoulder point of view. If you enjoyed the exercise, simply continue, making up the plot as you go along. If you want to try something different, recast any of the other examples into the camera-on-the-shoulder point of view.

Smiley's pieces could easily be transformed into this point of view. So could Olsen's piece, from either the woman's or the man's perspective. Either main character could be chosen in the Berry poem, also — and the poem could be made into a short story. Extend whatever you do to five pages.

## Point of View and Consistency

An effective point of view is consistent. The reader gets a sense of the point of view in the first sentence, or certainly by the end of the first paragraph. The point of view should be smoothly maintained throughout the entire piece. You are creating a new world for the reader. Writing that world is very much like creating a trance.

When there is a problem with the point of view, the reader's trance will waver. We will sense something is out of kilter and begin to question what is happening. The trance slips a little. The world being created suddenly looks hollow or threadbare. We will see through it, or question it — or simply stop believing.

Remember, as you do the practice piece, to write with consistency. Stay in the camera-on-the-shoulder point of view. This will avoid problems and keep the reader focused. Hold your Crazy Child right there in that camera — even if it wants to jump up and down and scream.

## Alternatives

You could rewrite one of your own pieces, using the camera-on-the-shoulder technique. You could also continue with *The Woman in the Dunes* exercise from a point farther along in the story. In the next chapter, the man ties up the woman. You could show us how the woman gets free — or how she tricks the man into untying her.

Later, you may want to return to this chapter and practice other points of view. You might do the first-person point of view, or the omniscient point of view, or the shifting third person. You can try these out by rewriting the Abé piece as described on pages 99–100, or the examples described on page 103, or on any other piece. Write the point of view of your choice with consistency. Do several pieces and extend each to five pages.

The main thing is to practice, and to have fun while you do. For this first piece, the camera-on-the-shoulder is instructive. Once you feel its limitations and its powers, you will be able to choose other points of view with confidence and savvy. For now, give your Crazy Child the feel of that tightly-focused, camera-on-the-shoulder point of view. And don't forget to have fun.

# Chapter 6
## Dialogue

*The experience of art cleanses the emotions; through it we touch the wildness of life, and its basic intractability. . . .*

AARON COPLAND

Dialogue confers zest and the "wildness of life" to writing. There is dialogue when any character speaks and when that happens, the written word seems to stand up, open its mouth, and start talking. Dialogue shows what is happening at the moment — out loud.

Dialogue displays what is consuming the character. Is the character angry? Bewildered? Happy? That feeling vibrates through the words when we imagine them spoken. The thoughts behind that feeling and the issues engaging the character give the dialogue its flavor. The character seems to come alive.

This aliveness is created by your imagination. As soon as your eye picks up a quote mark, "Did you see both of those?" you imagine the words being spoken. What "both" did I just ask you about? The two quote marks — of course you saw them, and you imagined I was speaking.

That is the human nervous system doing its job. We hear the words in our minds. They seem to be spoken in our presence, or spoken at us. This process is similar to the visual imaging that we do when we see that three-legged dog running. And the aural process repeats itself many times, perhaps hundreds of times, throughout a story, poem, play, or essay. Our imagination makes the speeches sound in our ears as if we were there.

With the help of dialogue, the reader's imagination makes a movie out of words. "Stella! Stella!" yells Marlin Brando in the movie of Tennessee Williams' play *Streetcar Named Desire*, and the words echo through that house in New Orleans. We will convert any written speech into part of a movie. If the speech is embellished with image detail — a gesture, a wave of the arm, a grimace — we seem to be in the film completely.

If there is a reply from someone, so much the better. The reader now witnesses two characters, and they both seem alive. We also sense the dynamic of the exchange. Who will bend at the end of the dialogue? Will the characters become enemies or friends? Will Stella admit that she feels an attraction? Or will she continue to manipulate and scorn her husband?

## Definitions of Dialogue

"Dialogue" is the word used in *Let the Crazy Child Write!* for any speech, whether spoken out loud or muttered under the breath. "Dialogue" is used even when only one character is talking. If the other character is silent — or if there is no other character — the spoken word is still called "dialogue."

Writers also use the word "dialogue" to describe words that are spoken silently — words that are formed only in the character's mind. An example is the chattering or arguing of conflicting thoughts. This is called "internal dialogue." Other terms for this are "interior monologue," "internal monologue," and "interior dialogue," and they are interchangeable.

Spoken dialogue is put in quotes, but internal dialogue usually is not. They both add vibrancy to writing, and they both work in countless ways. I will discuss a few of the ways in this chapter, and then encourage you to experiment freely. By letting your Crazy Child play with dialogue, you will learn how dialogue works. You will get a feel for how exciting and powerful it can be.

## Dialogue and the Crazy Child

Your creative unconscious delights in dialogue. The Crazy Child in you has been grunting and squealing, trying to get itself heard, since you were born. The blank page is quite receptive to whatever it wants to say. What a delight to shout joy or utter delicacies or to rant and rave — and not be shushed.

The Crazy Child is keenly aware of how often it is not heard. Over the years, your creative unconscious has listened to a variety of screwy replies to what it says. It knows how often we, its host, do not hear it at all, or how often we negate what it says. It also has an acute idea of how strange it, the Crazy Child, might sound to the outside world.

Your creative unconscious knows that only once in a rare while are its words received accurately. The Crazy Child has experienced more tension-producing miscommunications and screwups than you can count. It has a finely tuned sense of how skewed our dialogue can be.

Just as finely tuned is the Crazy Child's sense of when communication is truly happening. The delight of connecting — of speaking and being understood — is highly treasured. Your Crazy Child may be able to remember the joy of this happening at an early age. That sense can light up its face like a finger's gentle touch on its tender cheek.

## Dialogue and Communication

Some dialogue is accurate communication. A writer may even make the communication better than it is in life. The characters understand each other so well, they leapfrog ahead and the reader can barely keep up. This creates a super-real communication, and why not? You can have a dream of perfect, total communication come to life on the page.

An example is the ecstatic exchange at the end of Tom Robbins' novel *Still Life with Woodpecker* where Leigh-Cheri and

Bernard rediscover each other. Bernard's hand is shaking, and Leigh-Cheri remembers the color of the camel blanket they wrapped themselves in long ago.

> "With a few stripes of blue."
> "How do you know this?"
> "I had the same dream. It seemed more real than a dream. A hallucination? A ———"
> "At dusk, we made love."
> "You started it by sucking my toes."
> "Your toes are cute. And then the dates took effect."
> The Princess laughed. "You wondered if there was a men's room over at the pyramid."
> "We decided to avoid pyramids. Except as pedestals. We slept by the pool. How do you know this? How do *we* know it? Could we both have had the exact same dream?"

On they go, rediscovering their magical relationship. It must be exciting to put such uncanny dialogue into writing. We deserve to have perfect communication, after all — at least in a story, poem, play, or essay.

## Stairwell Wit

You have the opportunity to exercise your sharpest wit when you write dialogue. It makes no difference whether you are witty in real-life situations or not. "Stairwell wit" is what the French call the reply you think of after the moment has passed. You might say something dumb as you leave your landlord or your ex-lover, but as you walk down the stairs, a snappy reply pops into your head — something superb and cutting.

The moment might have passed in life, but in writing it's never too late. You get to mull over what that landlord or ex-lover said, and two minutes later — or two hours or two weeks later — the perfect reply will come along. You can write it down, and the zinger you wished for is right there in black and white. Timed perfectly.

## Dialogue in Stories

A rule of thumb is that dialogue should deepen the character or advance the action. In the excerpt from Linda Cohen's novel on page 6, each line of dialogue moves the reader forward. We learn more about the characters and the action jumps ahead. Both are done most effectively when the dialogue is given a context, line by line, with description.

> *Dialogue should deepen a character*
> *or advance the action.*

Consider the dialogue in Barbara Kingsolver's novel *Pigs in Heaven*. Turtle, an untalkative child, has seen a man fall into the spillway of a dam and Taylor, her mother, asks the guard to start a search:

"The guy might be banged up," Taylor points out. "Could we speed this up at all?"

Mr. Alvarez has a dark fringe around his bald head, and the eyes of an indifferent hound. He states with no apparent emotion, "There's an eight-foot security fence around the spillway."

"We don't know how he got over the fence," Taylor says, trying to match his tone. The fluorescent lights seem abusive at this hour, and she squints, trying to remember the hillside near the dam. "Maybe he came the other way, down the mountain. Or off the lake."

"We have security personnel watching that area like hawks."

"No offense, but we spent the better part of this night looking for one of your hawks."

"It's a holiday weekend."

"Happy Easter," Taylor says. "Let's go hunt some eggs."

Taylor counters the guard's immovability with wit. Notice how the postures of the two characters are supported with image detail. The guard has the "indifferent eyes" of a hound, and the lights bother Taylor. The guard continues to discount the possibility that Turtle has seen something:

> "Frankly," he says, "I haven't heard her say anything."
>
> "She doesn't talk much. If you leave out all the bullshit in life, there's not that much left to say, is there?"
>
> Alvarez . . . carefully winds his watch. Taylor gets up and walks to the door and back, reining in a real need to kick a chair leg with her cowboy boot. "Do you want me to lie? Do you want me to say I saw it too? If you write that down on your report, then can you call a rescue party?"
>
> "Just tell me what happened. Just the truth."
>
> "Just the truth is: a man fell down the spillway of your wonderful dam, today, right around sunset. My daughter saw him go in, and it would give her a better impression of the human race if you'd act like you give a damn. Because if he dies in there he's going to be just truly dead."

Taylor hits a few bull's-eyes, and at the end she gets her say — her last speech is powerful and to the point. Though the guard may understand her perfectly well, he does not want to act. He has a different agenda.

## Dialogue in Poems

Dialogue works in poems much like it does in prose. It should deepen the issue, if not a character, or move the action forward. A poem can be entirely dialogue, or have internal monologue woven throughout, as in my poem "Feint and Jab":

Feint and Jab

Ray's smile shows square-tipped teeth,
he shouts "Hey, guess what?" and boxer eyes
measure my stance. I tighten my abdomen,

flex hands at sides and double-edged replies
twinge at my tongue. Ray bangs his fist
"I got that promotion!" into my shoulder,

I slide off the punch, raise up arms and
fear of the slam-down widens my nostrils.
"There's talk about me in Modesto," Ray says

and his lips read "You're no good! No good!"
as he dances around the ring. I juke
shoulders side to side, tug up at smile

muscles, quick combination "Nice going,
champ! You must be a good apple-squeezer!"
cross and hook rocks him on his heels.

Feint and two jabs coming back "You jealous?
That's not even half what I'm worth!"
and we are equals, dripping sweat off noses,

bouncing each other off the ropes.
"Sure I'm jealous! Light up Modesto
and someone might see it from here!"

Head-fake and maintain position. Maintain.

The contrast between the jibes and the character's fearful
thoughts — his internal dialogue — keeps this poem interesting.
The boxing match is in the character's mind, and that last
"Maintain" is a command he gives to himself.

We've read other poems that rely on internal dialogue. In
Sharman Murphy's piece, "Three Easy Moves" on pages 30–31,

the events and the internal dialogue are separated in columns. The
Michael McClure poem, on page 32, is a tapestry of observed
detail and internal dialogue, with no spoken lines.

## Dialogue in Plays

Playwrights say that each character has a "goal" in a scene. The
characters' goals are clearly displayed in this excerpt from Sam
Shepard's play *Curse of the Starving Class*. The father has been on
a drinking binge, and, with no memory of the night before, he is
making breakfast. He feels good and thinks everything is fine. His
wife has a different experience:

> *Weston:* (*still cooking*) Where you been anyway?
> *Ella:* Jail.
> *Weston:* Oh, they finally caught ya', huh? *(chuckles)*
> *Ella:* Very humorous.
> *Weston:* You want some breakfast? I was just fixin' something
>     up for Wes, here.
> *Ella:* You're cooking?
> *Weston:* Yeah. What's it look like?
> *Ella:* Who did all this laundry?
> *Weston:* Yours truly.
> *Ella:* Are you having a nervous breakdown or what?
> *Weston:* Can't a man do his own laundry?

Ella is exhausted and suspicious. Her goal is to engage Weston
in the ongoing crisis, and she can't understand why he's so jovial.
She reports she spent the night visiting their daughter, who was
arrested for a series of violations. Weston then acts proud, and calls
the daughter a "fireball":

> *Ella:* Part of the inheritance, right?
> *Weston:* Right. Direct descendant.
> *Ella:* Well, I'm glad you've found a way of turning shame into
>     a source of pride.

*Weston:* What's shameful about it? Takes courage to get charged with all that stuff. It's not everyone her age who can run up a list of credits like that.

*Ella:* That's for sure.

*Weston:* Could you?

*Ella:* Don't be ridiculous! I'm not self-destructive. Doesn't run in my family line.

*Weston:* That's right. I never thought about it like that. You're the only one who doesn't have it. Only us.

Ella is scornful and sarcastic. She's trying to break through Weston's insensible charm. Weston keeps to his agenda, insisting everything's fine. He goes on to accuse Ella's ancestors of being professionals, and Ella becomes enraged:

*Ella:* Are we waxing philosophical over our eggs now? Is that the idea? Sobered up over night, have we? Awoken to a brand-new morning? What is this crap! I've been down there all night trying to pull Emma back together again and I come back to Mr. Hyde! Mr. "Goody Two-Shoes"! Mister Mia Copa himself! Well, you can kiss off with that crap because I'm not buying it.

*Weston:* Would you like some coffee?

*Ella: NO, I DON'T WANT ANY GODDAMN COFFEE! AND GET THAT SON-OF-A-BITCHING SHEEP OUT OF MY KITCHEN!!*

*Weston: (staying cool)* You've picked up on the language okay, but your inflection's off.

*Ella:* There's nothing wrong with my inflection!

*Weston:* Something doesn't ring true about it. Something deep in the voice. At the heart of things.

*Ella:* Oh, you are really something. How can you accuse me of not measuring up to your standards! You're a complete washout!

*Weston:* It's got nothing to do with standards. It's more like fate.

*Ella:* Oh, knock it off, would you? I'm exhausted.

*Weston:* Try the table. Nice and hard. It'll do wonders for you.

The wife succumbs to exhaustion and lies down on the table. She gives up. Her goal changes to getting some rest. She worked hard to engage her husband, but he deflected her anger and glossed everything over. Weston is charming, oblivious, and obnoxious.

The reader's interest lies in the question of who will prevail. We are engrossed as we follow the shifts, back and forth, between the characters. We wonder which one is getting the upper hand, and which one might achieve a goal.

Notice how the two characters are in very different emotional states. They also provoke very different states in each other. Ella becomes furious; Weston stays calm and unprovoked. They may not be communicating with each other at all, but the playwright is communicating something to the audience — about the two characters and their relationship.

## Dialogue and Miscommunication

Strong dialogue, on the surface, is often a sort of miscommunication. The words seem to be missing their targets. If there is some communication, it may be about something different from the topic under discussion.

The Crazy Child's awareness of skewed communication, contrary to what one might think, helps in writing dialogue. A communication screwup points to a deeper truth. Perhaps the characters do not want to hear each other or perhaps they have different agendas. The excerpt from *Curse of the Starving Class*, on the two preceding pages, is an excellent illustration. Those different agendas are the point of the writing.

## Dialogue in Essays

Dialogue works in essays almost the same way that it does in fiction.

The difference is that an essay may have no action and no characters. The rule of thumb that "dialogue should deepen a character or advance the action" will not strictly apply, but dialogue can help illustrate an essay's point.

Some essays profit hugely from a few lines of dialogue. In her essay "Loud Noises" Diane Ackerman lists various ways noise can grab our attention. She quotes one line from Adolf Hitler: "Without the loudspeaker, we would never have conquered Germany." Boom! This one quote conjures Hitler's raspy voice as he foments a mob. She has embellished her point chillingly.

## Framing Dialogue

If a line of dialogue has no image detail or no explanation of how it is spoken, it is a "naked line." A naked line may give no clue for how it is inflected. The characters need to be delineated in advance, and the dialogue needs to be crystal clear. Or, alternatively, the writer can give a context with each line.

The example quoted on page 105, "Did you see both of those?" was meant to be playful. Since *Let the Crazy Child Write!* is written in a good-natured, informative mode, you probably took the question that way. But it could be asked demandingly or angrily or anxiously — or however you like.

Imagine how easily you could set up that sentence in a different manner. "The teacher leaned over, pierced his student with stone cold eyes, and growled, 'Did you see both of those?' " Here the image detail shows the reader that this is an unfriendly context, and we feel a hostile emotion. The teacher is being demanding, and the student might feel unsettled, to say the least.

## Precision in Dialogue

In a short story, poem, play, or essay, every word must contribute to the final effect. If a speech is out of character, or if there are extra words, the reader's trance is broken. But in *Let the Crazy Child*

*Write!* we will write dialogue imprecisely and abundantly.

Our goal in this chapter is to explore. If you begin to get a feeling for how dialogue works, you are doing well. Do not expect your dialogue to be precise, not without a lot of practice. It is fine to be sloppy at first — you are developing your skills.

## EXERCISE

Start with a situation that is rip-roaring with tension. Make up your own or use this one: your protagonist is in a relationship, and has just read a singles ad. The ad is identical to the one your character answered at the beginning of the affair. The lovers are still seeing each other — at least to this point.

What does your main character do? Phone or E-mail the lover right off? Answer the ad pretending to be someone else? Or stew for a while and then break off the relationship? What does the lover do — find some reason to defend the ad? Ask why was the protagonist reading ads in the first place?

> *Innocence of heart and violence of feeling are necessary in any kind of superior achievement: The arts cannot exist without them.*
>
> LOUISE BOGAN

Almost any variation of the exercise will have great potential for "innocence of heart and violence of feeling." Let the intractable wildness of life come through your words — come roaring through the extremity of the situation.

Write whatever variation most appeals to your Crazy Child. Focus on the confrontation, and keep varying the balance of power. When one character gets the upper hand, introduce a flaw so that the balance shifts. One character could be caught in a lie, and maybe the other is arrogant.

Make sure your characters approach each other with extreme feelings — and with different feelings. They may not want to give up those feelings. They may cling to them for a long while, so it's appropriate to stretch the dialogue as far as it will go. Write for a half hour.

Your characters may also have different agendas. One might want to resolve things and the other may not. Or one may be deciding one way, and then another, as the discussion proceeds. One may not hear what the other is saying at all, perhaps because the desire is simply to win and blow the other off.

## Dialects and Accents

Terrence Clarke, in his story collection *The Day Nothing Happened*, wanted to convey the accent of a British officer. He found out how not to write dialect by watching a low-budget British film about Yanks in World War I. The G.I.s were portrayed as stereotypes and every word they spoke was a cliché.

Clarke discovered he needed only to suggest an accent and the reader would get it. His officer says, "The empire has a history on which I can fall back when necessary. Glories for the most part, I should think." That's enough — we hear the accent through reading just the occasional Briticism.

But you might have reason to write a dialect phonetically, as Zora Neale Hurston does. In her novel *Their Eyes Were Watching God*, Phoebe says Janie is taking a chance in romance, and Janie responds, "No mor' than Ah took befo' and no mo' than anybody else takes when dey gits married. It always changes folks, and sometimes it brings out dirt and meanness dat even de person didn't know they had in 'em theyselves. You know dat. . . . " Hurston maintains the sense of a special, separate world with the exact flavor of the dialect.

If you have a purpose for writing speeches phonetically, by all means do so. But if you do not have that purpose, there is no need to be exhaustive — you need only to suggest the accent. A few hints will give the reader a sense of the accent and you can continue.

## Dialogue and Listening

Writing dialogue is mostly listening. Once you have your situation in mind, listen to what the characters might say. Listen to your Crazy Child, and listen also to what each character's Crazy Child might say. Write down the words.

You can do research by listening to how people actually talk. It will not hurt to jot down phrases that you overhear, or that you remember. But the most fruitful listening is a kind of inner listening. Your creative unconscious probably already knows how your characters talk.

Alice Walker used her house almost as a stage set when she was writing her novel *The Color Purple*. She walked around and imagined where her characters would be comfortable, sensing that each one preferred a separate room or alcove. Then, when it was time for one to speak, she went to that character's part of the house. She listened. She wrote down what was said. She even knew, sometimes, when it was someone's turn to speak — because that character started making noise.

An author is deeply involved in a story when the characters start talking on their own. This may not take place immediately, but it is easy to encourage. Just listen. Those words floating at the back of your mind are not to be discounted. They may very well be the words of your character. Your Crazy Child may be wagging its tongue, and you should write the words down.

Get a lot of words on the page. Remember you are not trying to write precise dialogue from the start; just get your characters talking. Your Crazy Child will be making up gems as they chatter away — gems you do not expect.

## WORKSHOP

You now have a dialogue exercise to workshop, and also a point-of-view practice from the last chapter. If you do not have time for both, it is more important to workshop the point-of-view piece. By following up on the ideas from the last chapter, you will have them clearly in mind as you proceed through *Let the Crazy Child Write!*

As before, follow the rules of the syngenetic workshop. Believe the feedback when you are the writer. When you are a listener, establish the strengths of the writing first. Make sure the writer understands these strengths, thoroughly, before you make suggestions. One or two rewrite suggestions are sufficient.

### Listening to Point of View

The workshop should notice whether the practice stays in the camera-on-the-shoulder point of view. It may not be easy to tell, because some sentences can be heard in different ways. The workshop should discuss these sentences — without any help from the writer. You will learn a lot, when you are the writer, if you remain silent.

Often we as writers are not aware when we switch the point of view. You might have shifted to a narrative or explanatory voice, or you might have commented on a character's thinking. This may interrupt the reader's sense of the character. The workshop will be able to identify where the point of view shifts.

For you, the writer, it is useful to see where you have stayed in the camera-on-the-shoulder point of view and where you have not. It is easy to slip — and a slip is easy to correct. What you should learn is how touchy point of view can be. You may need to stay clearly focused to keep it working.

You might also discover that staying in the camera-on-the-shoulder point of view is not necessary. The trance may work even if you do vary the point of view. The third-person point of view can drift into the omniscient point of view, and then drift back. You may be able to shift it quite a bit or you may find that you write most comfortably in a strict camera-on-the-shoulder mode. It all depends on your creative unconscious.

## Listening to Dialogue

If you have time, workshop the dialogue exercise. Point out what exchanges are funny, poignant, or suspenseful. If you find the situation intriguing, say why. Note especially which exchanges can be lengthened. If one character becomes especially interesting, encourage the writer to write more dialogue — and more extreme dialogue — for that character.

Make clunky suggestions, too, if you think of ways the moments of excitement or tension can be extended. When you are the writer, jot down all the suggestions. You do not have to follow them, of course, but one of the suggestions may open doors for you.

## The Weaver and the Weaving

In her classes, Thaisa Frank points out that writing is decisively different from weaving. A weaver can see both the threads going into the weaving and the pattern of the emerging cloth. But a writer cannot. The loom is in the writer's mind. No matter how you twist the manuscript page around, only the threads going into the weaving are visible.

How much red should you put in? That thread might seem like dynamite, and one inch will do. How much green? Perhaps it seems these colors will overwhelm the finished piece, and you could better discern how much to put in if you could walk around and view your words from the outside, objectively. But you cannot.

It is no accident that writers need workshops. It is impossible to tell, on your own, whether your writing is working. You see mostly the color and weight of the threads going into your piece, and not their effect.

During the workshop, believe the praise and be sure to take notes. If your Editor or Writer discounts the feedback, valuable information sinks out of reach — unless you have it down in ink.

## PRACTICE

You have done the exercise, and you have read some intriguing possibilities for dialogue. For the practice you can expand the exercise or you can write a situation of your own imagining.

Before you begin, there is the matter of point of view. Did your exercise automatically have a point of view? Was it the switching third-person point of view? Or the camera-on-the-shoulder? Even if you chose easily, you will benefit from reading the next paragraphs. Point of view can be difficult.

### Point of View and Dialogue

The switching third-person point of view is a natural for dialogue. You can write a speech for one character, give that character's thoughts, then write a speech for your other character, and give that character's thoughts. You are switching from one to the other, in the third person.

Or you might pull back and write from an omniscient point of view. This point of view is best done from a godlike position — from the air above the characters. You involve the reader with your observations and with the dialogue. You can also write what both characters are thinking, and the reader will listen through your mind.

Both of these points of view work fine for dialogue. So does the camera-on-the-shoulder, and so does the first-person point of view. To make a choice, you could listen to your Crazy Child, and let it follow its fancy. You might also pick one simply because you haven't tried it before.

## Choosing a Point of View

You might enjoy practicing points of view by using a new one for your dialogue practice. Every practice in *Let the Crazy Child Write!* requires a point of view. By writing in different ones, you will develop your feel for points of view.

You could also look for one that is perfect for the piece you are about to write — one that suits you, your topic, and your Crazy Child. The ultimate goal, naturally, is to learn how to choose a point of view for every piece you do.

Listen down into your body. The Crazy Child feels the totality of what you are bringing to your subject, and it will send you a clue on which point of view will work. It may have thrown the spear of intuition into the darkness, as we discussed on page 87–88. Finding it will be your job, and your writing will be rewarded.

The Crazy Child's spear may be revealed by a twinge of mental delight or a gritty sense of power in your lower belly. Perhaps a fluid, warm feeling in your neck and head or perhaps — but who can say what the signs are? You may need to do some exploring to find out.

Use your body as an antenna. Do anything physical — run, do some knitting, play basketball, take a nap — and let the question roam in your mind. With any luck, a sentence will come along, a bit of dialogue or a character's thought or a description, and the sentence will seem absolutely right.

That sentence will express a point of view. It will use the first-person "I," or the third-person "he" or "she," or it will use "he" and "she" from an omniscient perspective. Your nervous system has displayed what your Crazy Child has chosen, and you are on your way.

## Write Different Stances

Do what I have suggested: expand the exercise, or make up your own situation. Make up one where people are having trouble communicating, one that is bristling with tension. Usually, the more extreme the situation is, the more interesting the writing. And the more you stand to learn.

Listen to your characters. Let them have very different emotions. Let one character be in one state, and the other in a different state — and then change their states. Remember that most dialogue, on the surface, is miscommunication. Have one character want to say something, and the other not want to hear it.

At some point, you may want to hone your dialogue. You might have written a great many pages for the exercise, and, if so, you are an exception. Now you want every word to be precise. You are ready to take out any flat spots or repetitions, and keep the action moving forward.

You have the option, always, of summarizing dialogue. As, "The teacher asked me if I saw both quote marks, and went on for a half hour about dialogue." You wouldn't want thirteen pages of technical information in an action novel, so you squeeze the discussion into one sentence. Now you are free to get on with the hot stuff.

For most of us, the dialogue practice will be just that: practice. Write a lot of exchanges, four to eight pages would be excellent, and don't worry about how vivid they are. After your pages are done, you will be able to see where your dialogue can be improved and where it is working superbly. For now, do as we have throughout *Let the Crazy Child Write!* Practice, have fun — and get those characters talking.

# Chapter 7
## Plot

*In the writing process, the more a story cooks, the better.
The brain works for you even when you are at rest.*

DORIS LESSING

"Plot" is what happens. Plot is the first thing that happens, followed by the second thing, leading to the third thing, and so on, all the way to the end. Broadly, plot is this pattern.

Plot is what holds the reader's attention. If the piece is built on action, as a thriller or a play, plot is that *sequence* of events. If the piece is built mostly on emotion, as a story or a poem, plot is the *progression* of feeling. If the piece is built on an idea, as an essay, plot is the *chain* of logic.

Since plot usually contains a combination of all three — action, feeling, and ideas — it can get complicated. If an undercurrent is dominant or tension slacks off here and there so it can increase later — then plot becomes downright intricate.

But even the most intricate plot is built on a simple foundation. An overview will reveal basic elements in that foundation — the "structural" elements of plot. They are all you need to know.

### Hook, Issue, Resolution

The three structural elements of plot are hook, issue, and resolution. I discussed the hook in chapter Three. The second element is the issue, and it is the focus of this chapter. The third element, resolution, is the topic of the final chapter in this book.

Every plot has these three elements. The other components — action, feeling, and ideas — are the "content" of the writing. The content, whatever its proportions, is always fashioned into a plot. We will find a hook, an issue, and a resolution in every piece of creative writing.

These elements are displayed when we follow an example of a hook to its logical conclusion. Remember that tiger on page 47? A saber-toothed tiger was prowling near a village, and a scout saw it. The scout had to alert the villagers without attracting the tiger. He needed a clever hook.

The issue and the resolution follow the hook. The issue is how to avoid that hungry tiger — obviously. Staying away from that tiger was the life-and-death issue for the villagers. The resolution is whether or not the villagers escaped the tiger — and whether or not anyone got eaten.

In the same way, every few hours in the life of a toddler has a plot. The child will use a hook — hooting, crying, or banging a pot — to attract its caretaker's attention. The issue is the child's hunger. The resolution becomes whether it gets fed, and how. At root, plot is very simple.

Hook, issue, and resolution are parts of a whole. The hook draws us into the issue and the issue works itself out until we come to a resolution. All three make up the plot. But the issue is the central element — it is pivotal. The other aspects of plot revolve around the issue.

## Plot and the Crazy Child

Your Crazy Child knows all about plot. This should be no surprise, since every topic in this book is familiar ground for the Crazy Child. *Let the Crazy Child Write!* is mostly a journey of rediscovery. I am not the first to propose this as a way of learning, however.

Socrates argued, in a dialogue with Meno in 500 B.C., that learning is remembering.

The Crazy Child is well versed at getting attention, as we discussed on pages 46–47. The Crazy Child also knows how to keep attention, in much the same way. Keeping attention is what plot is about. An effective plot holds our attention to the last page.

Plot is in our ancestral background, and that saber-toothed tiger will show you how. The tiger was prowling near a village, and a scout saw it. Let's say the scout deduced that the tiger was heading toward a kill under a nearby tree. The scout desperately needed to get the attention of the villagers. The scout also needed to keep their attention long enough to convey the problem.

A shout of "Tiger!" would not do. That shout would also attract the tiger. Pointing and whispering "Tiger" might start people running in various directions. Someone would likely end up near the tree where the tiger was headed. Wouldn't the tiger like that? Two meals on the same spot — one of them fresh.

The scout needed to devise a purposeful hook. Perhaps the scout could have pointed toward the tree and said (in Neanderthalese, of course), "Don't run now, I'm not saying saber-toothed tiger. But there is a recent kill by that tree, and a saber-toothed tiger coming from this other direction." With the first sentence, the scout grabbed the villagers' attention. This is the hook.

With the second sentence, the villagers became engaged in the issue. How would the villagers escape the tiger? The scout, by pointing first toward the tree and then toward the tiger, had indicated what areas to avoid. The villagers had a chance. The villagers would now be involved in the problem of escaping.

You can bet the villagers' attention was riveted. It would stay riveted until the problem was solved. Their lives were at stake. The outcome would be the resolution. Our attention, as readers of the story, is seriously aroused also and will stay aroused until the villagers are safe — or eaten. We imagine, automatically, that we are the villagers.

A one-sentence summary of the plot, so far, might be, "How the scout warns the villagers about a saber-toothed tiger, without also giving the tiger a meal." As the story unfolds, our sentence might become, "How the villagers avoid (or do not avoid) a saber-toothed tiger, through the cleverness (or mistakes) of their scout." Of course, we do not know what the best sentence would be. The story has not been written.

Now, you are not that scout, and you probably never tried escaping a saber-toothed tiger. But the tiger and situations like it were a daily occurrence in Neanderthal times. The instinct to survive is in your body. In fact, since our species has survived, that instinctive knowledge is in everyone's genes.

Much closer to home are our childhoods. When you were a hungry babe, you needed to attract and hold the attention of those who fed you. To an infant, that issue is just as life-and-death important as avoiding a prowling saber-toothed tiger. You needed to involve your caretaker's attention long enough to have your hunger satisfied.

Your Crazy Child became practiced at holding attention. You probably use this ability in your daily life — since that tiger, in transformed, modern versions, is all around us today. Or your ability may seem buried. But even if you are a quiet person, your creative unconscious knows all about eliciting attention.

You may feel this knowledge as a twinge in your stomach. That twinge has great power because it is a survival mechanism. The Crazy Child, alive in our bellies or chests, definitely knows how to survive. Your creative unconscious knows what makes an effective plot.

## Plot as Obstacles

When we read about an obstacle, we imagine trying to overcome it. The process is as automatic as seeing that three-legged dog. We become almost instinctively involved in how the obstacles are overcome — or not overcome.

The characters in John Tinloy's story face quite a few obstacles. Notice how the obstacles hold your interest. They might remind your Crazy Child of difficulties it had before finally getting fed — or before escaping that tiger:

## Malady in Madrid

Libby got really sick the first night in Madrid. She figured it was the paella we shared for dinner, but I was all right. The white-and-red tiled bathroom in our hotel room was sparkling clean, and Libby embraced the shiny toilet for several hours. Her face was pale green.

We had that three-star room for one night only. In the morning Libby could barely drag her backpack to the lobby. I got busy phoning around for another room while Libby drank some agua mineral con gas to settle her wooziness. Breakfast was out of the question.

I made a reservation and the bellhop flagged a taxi. Other drivers honked and dodged as our cab swerved curbside. We stuffed our packs in the back seat and piled in. We traversed from the bustle of wide boulevards into narrow passages of winding streets through ancient, dark buildings.

The door to the hostel was flush with the street. Libby marshalled her last energy to push and pull her pack up two flights of stairs to the desk. But we had no room. The woman who had vacated had missed her plane to Morocco and had already come back to reclaim the room.

All Libby wanted was to lie down and rest. She was groaning softly while the clerk made a few calls. He found a vacancy at the Hostel Santa Maria. He said it was near a mesón called "Museo de Jamón." Libby moaned at the word for ham. She looked like she was going to puke.

We found the Museo de Jamón after an hour's trek. There

were hundreds of huge, red, smoked hams hung around the ceiling. Patrons leaned around the island bar drinking beer, eating thinly sliced ham sandwiches and socializing. Deli paper and used paper napkins covered the floor. The cacophony of downtown traffic and the smell of car exhaust washed through the airspace. Construction workers were yelling and hammering all over the scaffolding on the building next door.

Libby looked green again. "Let's get out of here," she said.

The Hostel Santa Maria was on a side street around the corner from the Museo de Jamón. We climbed up a long flight of stairs and checked in. Then we walked to the end of a hallway to our room.

Libby dropped her pack and plopped herself on the bed. She was seconds away from retching. She sank into the worn, flaccid mattress and the bedsprings squeaked and creaked. It was hot and she asked me to open the window.

The glass was opaque yellow, the kind that distorts light so you can only see fuzzy images. The open window exposed the airspace between four exterior building walls. From a clothes line, about three feet across from our window, hung a half dozen huge chorizo sausages. Libby's eyes opened wide in horror. We smelled jamón. Our room was directly above the Museo de Jamón. Libby was out the door and down the hall for the bathroom.

Libby resigned herself to the fetal position and tried to sleep. That night she clung to the bed as the room spun around and around. The smell of smoked ham wafted into the room from below. The workers next door hammered without pause or rhythm. Tubes of drying meat dangled in the air. The revelry from the mesón got louder.

Libby's mattress turned into quicksand. Only her green head stuck out of the bed. She thought she was being punished for skipping Hebrew school years ago and for sneaking out and enjoying BLTs.

Each new, annoying obstacle keeps our interest piqued. We want to know what happens — and everything seems to conspire against these two people. When Libby finally does find a comfortable room, it makes her more ill.

In "Malady in Madrid" the obstacles are external. They could as well be internal or some combination of the two. One of your characters might have a flaw that keeps that character from attaining a goal, and your character could be conscious of the defect. The plot would then involve the character's struggle with the defect as well as with the goal.

Libby, for instance, could have been pregnant, or she could have been brooding about her relationship. That brooding might have caused her to make poor choices — and her situation could become worse. Or, from the beginning, Libby could have been sure those BLTs were her damnation. That could give the story a hilarious twist. There are probably as many other possibilities as there are people.

## What Is the Issue?

The issue is often obvious, as in "Malady in Madrid." We can put it in one sentence: "Will Libby find a comfortable room where she can get some rest, or will circumstances — and that fragrant Spanish ham, jamón — defeat her?"

The issue is more subtle in David Shaddock's short prose piece:

### My Childhood

People came in, dropped off rage, and left. My father entered and snored to *Gunsmoke*. On weekends there was roast beef and we could really get down to fighting. *Tante* Bessie would knit and grow increasingly catatonic. The house sucked up dogs and cats and postmen who were never seen again. A Hell's Angel chased my mother with a sprinkler turner-oner.

James Arness lived across the street. It was a high-toned neighborhood and we were terribly out of place. My mother would chase my father into the street with a kitchen knife. He would jump in the Pontiac and drive around and around the block honking the horn to taunt her. All the kids shook me down for my lunch money.

At night, after bedtime, I would watch the westerns through the slats in my louvered doors and dream of the infinite peace I could find in a real gunfight.

This piece makes me laugh, but I also get very anxious. I wonder how anyone can survive in this wacky household. When I had that thought, I realized it was the issue.

We could put it in one sentence: "How is the character going to stay even partly sane in that bizarre home?" All those nutsy things that happen are obstacles. They are rather intimidating obstacles, in fact — obstacles to any sort of peace of mind. They are not as terrifying as that saber-toothed tiger, but they create plenty of anxiety.

Obstacles are at the root of other terms commonly used for the issue, too. The issue may be called the "tension" or the "problem" or the "conflict." These terms are nearly interchangeable, for they all point toward the central issue. And each one implies an obstacle.

In "My Childhood," the character releases the *tension* of the household by dreaming of a real gunfight. In "Malady in Madrid," Libby solves her *problem,* as best she can, by giving in and curling up like a fetus. In the saber-toothed tiger story, a *conflict* brews between the tiger and the villagers.

When we ask what the issue is, we are asking what keeps our attention. We are asking what pulls the reader through the piece. Answering this question may bring into focus responses that tweak your nervous system. It's best to state the issue as succinctly as you can.

## Plot in One Sentence

I have made a number of one-sentence summaries already. If you take everything that happens and boil it down to one sentence, you have the essence of a plot. This sentence is usually a statement of the issue.

For Margaret Atwood's novel *Surfacing*, that sentence could be, "How a woman attained her personal power as she explored memories of her father." For Ernest Hemingway's *The Old Man and the Sea*, it could be, "How an old man asserts his dignity in a battle with a huge marlin."

Your missing person piece, from pages 59–60, has a plot. Its summary might be, "How Henry found and came to love his aunt after he discovered she was missing." Or it could be, "How Joyce decided to join her ex and become a bank robber, and then decided not to since she remembered what a creep he is, all while standing in line at the post office."

Most authors, however, will not write this sentence for us. We will feel its effect as we read, but it won't be spelled out. We have to figure it out as we read. This takes practice. We will probably refine our sentence, adding some words and whittling away others, as we think about it.

The best one-sentence summary conveys the plot accurately and concisely. It will state exactly what holds our attention. When you read, it's good practice to compose that sentence. You will be able to apply this skill to your own writing. Knowing exactly what the issue is will help you revise your pieces.

What about poems and stories in which nothing happens? The piece might be a pattern of emotions, a juxtaposition of memories, or a weaving of irony or intellectual tension. But one of these patterns will work just as well as a chain of events. It will draw the reader through the piece. And that pattern, too, can be summarized in one sentence.

## Plot in Poems

Gail Ford's poem has a pattern of events and insights that keeps
our interest. The poem has a hook, too, the same as a story does:

### Two-Sided Coin

I sit very still and focus.
The dime-sized piece of air
between my forefinger and thumb

glistens, then thickens,
opens like an eye's iris

letting in light from my world
and me
head-first after

to the other side

to the place where the cats go
when I know they are somewhere here
but can't find them

where the rules of the world
are written in the clouds

where good humor and mal-intent
are clearly lit for all to see,
no confusion, no obscurity.

When I am here, I remember.

When I go back, I forget.

The world blurs and thins.

I reappear in my original chair
with a dime-sized piece of air

between my fingertips.

Curious, I toss the coin.
It flips up and over
flashes high, then falls
to land in my open hand.

The coin clears, then disappears
leaving only the lines
on my palm
to be read.

The hook is that dime-sized slice of air. When it starts transforming, the reader's attention is aroused. We wonder what magical thing will happen next.

The coin becomes a door into another world, where "good humor and mal-intent" are obvious. The poet glimpses that other world — which could be this world, seen accurately. You might have a sense of déjà vu as you read the poem. I think people often have a feeling like the one described.

When the poet flips the coin again, she finds — instead of the other world — the lines on her own palm. They seem mysterious. The inference is that human nature, or the poet's destiny, makes for a world that is difficult to understand. Perhaps her palm, in some way, does contain those clear rules — if only she, and we, could read them.

I will try stating the plot in one sentence: "The poet glimpses a truer world, by flipping a magic coin and going into trance, and then comes back to face her own nature more clearly." This sentence doesn't cover all the inferences. You may be able to do better than I have.

## Plot in Plays

Theater has no easy way to give the audience a build up. From the moment the curtain rises, live characters are on stage. That makes the plot quite visible to the audience. It also means the author needs to be instantly clear about plot.

Consider these lines from Tennessee Williams' play *Orpheus Descending:*

> *Lady:* Well, what in God's name are you lookin' for around here?
>
> *Val:* — Work.
>
> *Lady:* Boys like you don't work.
>
> *Val:* What d'you mean by boys like me?
>
> *Lady:* Ones that play th' guitar and go around talkin' about how warm they are. . . .
>
> *Val:* That happens t' be the truth. My temperature's always a couple degrees above normal the same as a dog's, it's normal for me the same as it is for a dog, that's the truth. . . .
>
> *Lady:* — Huh!
>
> *Val:* You don't believe me?
>
> *Lady:* I have no reason to doubt you, but what about it?

Val has a plainly stated goal. He wants a job, and that means giving up his free-floating ways. Lady is resisting him, and she states her resistance plainly: "Boys like you don't work." She becomes an obstacle to Val, since she has her own idea of what Val is after. As the play continues, she changes her mind — and that, too, becomes part of the interest.

Give your main character a goal, and have other characters resist, or develop goals of their own. Goals are like engines that drive the characters. When goals conflict, those conflicts drive the plot — the goals become obstacles to each other. Strong goals and plenty of obstacles are the ingredients for gripping drama.

## Plot in Essays

The discussion of the saber-toothed tiger in "Plot and the Crazy Child," on pages 126–128, is a short essay. It has its own plot. As you read it, you become involved in how the hook and the issue work in the tiger story. And how that dynamic is similar to the experience of a hungry infant.

These ideas are the hook, issue and resolution of that section. A one-sentence summary could be, "How a story involves the reader in the same ways that our ancestors needed to involve their peers, and also in the same way a hungry infant involves its caretaker."

In an essay, important obstacles are outside the writing. They are in the reader's mind. The obstacles may be simply a lack of knowledge, or they may be public misconceptions that the writer wants to correct. Any objections the reader might have would be obstacles, too, and the essayist could try to answer them in advance. You will want to guide your reader's thinking so that your conclusion is inescapable.

In *Let the Crazy Child Write!* the plot involves blending examples with the step-by-step expansion of one basic idea. Careful thinking went into the order of those steps, as it should in any essay. This book takes the most simple, most demonstrable examples — image detail and the three-legged dog — and builds from there.

The one basic idea is that our creative unconscious or Crazy Child is the primary source of strong writing. The main obstacles are the common myths that writing is discouragingly difficult and intellectual. And that it requires a rare talent.

## Plot as Magnet

Plot is like the sweep of a powerful magnet. It pulls the reader through every page. It attracts us at the hook and sweeps us through the issue all the way to the resolution. "Magnet" combines the structural elements of a plot into one image.

The Crazy Child's sense of plot is also represented well by the image of a magnet. The Crazy Child magnet is the feeling the writer follows as a plot develops. Most plots are not thought out, in detail, in advance. Many plots are not thought out at all. The author simply follows a feeling, like following the pull of a magnet.

> *The laws you can lay down are only so many props to be cast aside when the hour of creation arrives.*
>
> RAOUL DUFY

A first draft may be a glorious unfolding of plot. You are the first audience for what your Crazy Child writes. And you may have no idea what is going to happen. You find out as you move your pen or type the words. You are being pulled along by a magnet.

All the intricacies of plot fit into this image. You may not have to plan at all as you write. You may experience a tightness in your belly, or a sweaty feeling, or a flush of excitement. The Crazy Child is tugging at you — like that magnet. "Come this way," it is saying. "Write this!"

## EXERCISE

### Plot Germs

This exercise has two parts. First we imagine goals for characters, and then we make up obstacles to those goals. This is very like the germ exercise on page 55. The results will be sentences or short paragraphs that could be seeds for full-blown plots.

Take fifteen minutes to write goals. Write the name of a character and write what that character needs or wants. Write each goal in one sentence. Any kind of goal is fine — any kind whatever. The more outrageous the goal, the better.

By making up outrageous goals, you will glimpse the huge territory where the Crazy Child romps. Your creative unconscious has endless possibilities. There's no point in having your Editor or Writer limit its horizons. You might have more fun being outrageous, too. Be as wild as your Crazy Child likes.

If you already have a plot in mind, you have an alternative. You could make up goals for your main character. You could state the character's single, essential goal. You might learn more, however, by writing absurd or irrelevant-seeming goals — at least at first. The purpose of the exercise is to explore. If you write a lot of wacky goals, you might discover new things about your story.

Here are a few examples:

> Paul needs to find his father and discover what Paul really feels about him.
>
> Phyllis needs to survive the winter in Alaska.
>
> James wants to find a magical gift so his lover will ask him out.
>
> Ron wants to know why punks are showing up at his baseball team meeting with guns.
>
> Jori needs to control her angry thoughts before she loses it and slugs her boss.

It is best to listen down into your body as you write. See if you can engage your Crazy Child's interest. You will know the Crazy Child's ears are perked when you have a fluttery feeling or a vulnerable feeling or — whatever. By now you know what signs indicate your creative unconscious is engaged.

Do not worry if your sentences seem to lack intelligence. The exercise will work just as well if your sentences aren't sharp. In fact, if your sentences seem off, you may be doing the exercise in the most useful way possible.

Your Editor or Writer may think that any new material is dumb — when it is not. Go ahead and allow your Crazy Child to sound silly. That may mean your material is poignant and vital — or shocking. You will find out when you share it with a friend or when you look at it with fresh eyes in a day or in a week.

Take another fifteen minutes for the second part of this exercise. In this part, put obstacles before your characters. They can be internal obstacles or external obstacles or both. Write several sentences for each character, if you like. And let your Crazy Child make up the list. Write in the same free manner as you did when making up the goals.

Here are examples:

> Paul has no idea which of three trails — up the canyon, across the creek, or into the brush — his father could have taken.
>
> Phyllis's wood stove has a leak in it, and it is snowing so hard she can't find the woodpile. Or it is difficult to cut the wood, and her ax was borrowed by her ex-FBI sister who lives down the road. Her mind is getting numb, so that she can't remember where she put her matches! And her gloves have a hole in them, which is letting in the cold air. She keeps thinking of the sun in Phoenix.

This list for Phyllis is certainly not logical. I wrote it fast, and I wrote it with a playful attitude. The list gives hints of possibilities for other stories.

Writing rapidly may work well for this exercise. Write a lot of different obstacles. If you have an extravagant impulse, write that. If you want to be ordinary or vanishingly subtle, do these things, too. The more variety the better. Your Crazy Child will show you what it finds interesting as you go along.

## WORKSHOP

Read the plot exercise to your group or to your writing partner. Read all of your plot germs, even ones you think are stupid. And when the workshop gives you feedback, be sure to mark down what is said. Pay special attention to positive feedback.

## Listening to Plot Germs

Positive feedback is crucial for this exercise. When you are the listener, say which germs you find intriguing. You are reflecting back to the writer which ones are working well. And the writer may not have a clue. Be firm and very clear about what you like.

The most useful feedback comes from your uneducated nervous system — not from what your Editor or Writer may think is correct. Your natural responses are the valuable ones. Your body may be intrigued by something you would not mention otherwise. Another way to put this is: Listen with your heart.

By definition, plot germs are doors. They make us curious. And plot germs, like doors, are places for the writer to go through and expand and explore. When your germs are being discussed, note which ones your listeners find most exciting.

Train your Editor and your Writer to accept what the workshop says. They may resist, so it is very important to write down the positive feedback. You are discovering what your Crazy Child knows about plot. And your germs may be excellent plots for stories or for your next practice.

## Listening to Dialogue Again

You have a dialogue practice from the last chapter. Bring copies for everyone in your workshop. If you have started a play, it may be useful to hear other people read the parts. You might learn how well the lines are working. Having someone else read your prose can be informative, too.

When you are listening, give positive feedback first, as in every syngenetic workshop. You will know, of course, when a speech is humorous. Listen also for places where you stay involved — for whatever reason. It takes concentration to notice these spots. When the writing is strong, we automatically flow with the words, and slide into a kind of trance. You must step out of the trance to recognize that you were involved.

The author may have written a lot of dialogue. As you listen, it is only important to point out where you are attentive to every word or where you are on the edge of your chair. It is the writer's job, later, to cut what is uninteresting. Your job is to notice the sections that are working, even the short ones. Pointing out a vibrant two lines might be very valuable to the author.

## What Does It Need?

After giving its appreciations, the workshop will think about what the piece needs. There are two or three common things to notice. One is the overuse of "she said" and "he said." A first draft often uses too many of these indicators. The workshop will pick this up right away.

You can substitute an image detail for "he said" or "she said." Pick a detail that identifies the person, and shows what they are thinking or feeling, as Linda Cohen does on pages 6–8. A gesture or a stance or a quirky expression will work nicely. The image detail then does double duty: it identifies the speaker and it adds something to the character or to the action.

The workshop should also notice if the naked lines are working. The author may give a vocal inflection that is not in the words. When you are listening, the author's inflection may be convincing. Notice this, and at the same time notice whether the words indicate the inflection — on their own. This is tricky, but with a little practice it comes easily. The flaw is also easy for the author to fix. Add an image detail that shows the character's mood.

## Mini-Beats

When a character's speech changes, that marks the beginning of a new "beat." This is a third thing the workshop can notice. The change can be a change in the goal — or in the feeling or the thought — of the character. I call the moment of the shift a "mini-beat."

"Beat" is an acting and playwrighting term. If you are writing a play, you are not required to indicate each new beat. It is the actor's job to search them out — although you can have a character speak in a changed manner or give a stage direction or write "Pause." Poets and prose writers do not have these techniques, so they must use image detail.

Image detail can easily indicate where there is a mini-beat. If the tone of a speech shifts, there should be a detail that points to that shift. An effective detail will show a change in the character's thoughts or emotions.

In this example from my story "Saturday," a lady describes a modeling party, and then her attitude changes. She begins to recruit her young friend:

> "Of course models should be paid! But we're a small operation, we can't afford professional models. We rely on friends, and on beginners who want to practice." The lady put her chin on her hands and stared at the young woman intently. "You would be good at it, I can tell by how you hold yourself. Have you ever tried modeling?"

With the sentence describing the physical detail — the lady putting her chin on her hands — we focus on the mini-beat. We could understand the speech without that line, of course. But the change is important, and deserves to be highlighted.

A line of interior monologue would work equally well to show the mini-beat. The lady could think something about how the young woman looks. Or, if the story were in the young woman's point of view, she could observe some detail about the lady.

## Check with the Author

By the end of the discussion, the workshop may lose sight of the strengths of a piece. Check with the author and ask how the session went. If the author does not mention the positive feedback, repeat that feedback. Summarize it clearly.

You should leave each workshop with positive and accurate feelings about the strengths of your writing. Your Editor may already be obsessing on what needs to be fixed. That is the Editor's job, but it should not overwhelm your sense of your real strengths. Keep in mind what you and your Crazy Child do well.

## PRACTICE

Did one of your plot germs seem exciting? Expand that one. Work it up into a story, poem, play, or essay. And make the situation fraught with tension — as soon as your character solves part of the problem, present another difficulty. Keep the tension going. If you're writing an essay, keep knocking down obstacles in the reader's mind.

### Missing Valuables

Here's an alternative. Say your character's first meeting with some-one is ending and the character cannot find something valuable. A purse or wallet is missing, or something that has personal meaning — a notebook or a photograph.

The other person might be seeing your character to a cab or to the subway, or offering a ride in an automobile. The two might be saying good night in the living room. And the missing thing may have nothing to do with the other person. What has happened to that precious item?

Begin your piece "one heartbeat after the action has begun," as you practiced on pages 60–61. This will give your writing a dynamic hook. The hook will pull the reader directly into the action and directly into the issue.

If you are writing about a missing valuable, your first sentence could show your character putting a hand where the valuable was. On the mantle, where a bust of the Pope rests — or a sports tro-phy or a piece of contraband. Or the other person could ask, "Where is your notebook?"

These beginnings are one heartbeat after the action has started. Your plot germ has several ways to begin one beat after the action has started, too. Your Crazy Child can imagine many ways to do this.

Go on from that second heartbeat. Any necessary information can be conveyed in the sweep of the action. The magnet is starting to pull you into the issue.

## Image Detail, Slow Motion, Persona, Point of View, Dialogue

This practice is fertile ground for your writing skills. You could make your plot germ a persona piece. Why not? Your characters can be any age, race, or gender — and so can you, the narrator. Follow whatever twinge your Crazy Child might have.

Keep the point of view consistent. You might try one of the points of view you have not yet used, especially if it's intriguing. Have you written as the omniscient author yet? Or you could experiment with the camera-on-the-shoulder point of view.

Put in some lively dialogue, and a slow motion section might be fun, too. Use plenty of image detail. Remember how small, odd, and dissonant details have considerable impact.

## Follow the Magnet

Whether you do a plot germ or a missing valuable, keep putting obstacles before your protagonist. Don't make it too easy to solve the problem — you create tension by making the solution difficult. A happy ending will be vivid if, for a while, the difficulties seem insurmountable.

Let your Crazy Child pick the obstacles. Try using some internal and some external obstacles, or some that are illogical or bizarre. The sweep of action as you overcome obstacles is the pull of that Crazy Child magnet.

> *In effect [writing a plot] is like driving in the fog. The headlights show only the next short space, and you see farther ahead only as you move forward.*
>
> SUE GRAFTON

It may be a good idea, as you write, to have a sense of what will happen next. But it is not necessary to map out the plot in advance. A feeling is enough. Sue Grafton confesses she has not a clue what her detective is going to do from minute to minute.

When Grafton says plotting is like driving in the fog, she affirms how unconscious most writing is. She does not work out her plots before she begins. She gets out of the way and lets her Crazy Child do the plotting.

You can do the same. Write four or five pages — more if you like. Be alert for that feeling of intrigue. If, as you finish one scene, you have an inkling what the next scene is, you have discovered a feel for the plot. That's all it takes.

You are following a Crazy Child magnet. Whatever seems intriguing to have happen next, whatever might be exciting, write it down — even if it seems wild or whimsical. Your Crazy Child is making up the plot.

# Chapter 8

## Narrative Presence

*You have not grown old, and it is not too late*
*to dive into your increasing depths*
*where life calmly gives out its own secret.*

RAINER MARIA RILKE

"Narrative presence" means simply that the storyteller is present in a memorable way. The person telling the story — the "narrator" — becomes known to the reader as the piece unfolds. If the reader receives a vivid impression of that storyteller, we say the writing has "narrative presence."

We can become quite involved with the narrator. Many stories, poems, plays, and essays revolve around the narrator. The main point might be, in fact, how the narrator interprets the action. We can become more involved with the storyteller than we are with anything else.

At one extreme, the narrator might be highly animated. Opinions and ideas could splash out of the storyteller's mouth like an auctioneer. We could identify with this narrator, or we might be curious how extreme this narrator can get. We certainly know a narrator is present: a loud narrator cannot be avoided.

At the other extreme, the narrator may hover quietly in the background. This storyteller might report the action with a calm, seemingly unbiased eye — like a newspaper reporter. The narrator might pretend to be completely objective. We may not notice, at first, that there even is a narrator.

A discrete narrator can have as strong a presence as a forthright one. The quieter narrator can convey, little by little, an uncanny sense of being there. The difference may be only that this narrator does not draw immediate attention to itself. This narrator does not dress in loud colors. But those quiet tones can invade the writing completely.

Just as with dialogue, the reader automatically imagines the narrator speaking — even though the narrator's words do not have quotes around them. We respond as if the narrator is in our vicinity. The writing conveys a sense of the storyteller's personality: the narrator may be clever, interested, oblique, or full of attitude.

## Persona, Point of View, Narrative Presence

*Persona* is the kind of person the narrator pretends to be — what race, age, sex, class, and temperament. *Point of view* indicates how the author presents that persona: as the same as the author and thus identified as "I," or as someone the author knows very well and denoted as "she" or "he," or as a godlike person watching from above. *Narrative presence* describes how conspicuous that persona is and whether it penetrates all aspects of the writing.

Any persona can have strong narrative presence. The persona's race, age, sex, class, and temperament do not matter. Neither does the place or the time of the persona's supposed birth. You may choose a persona that is loud or quiet, abrasive or demure, sweet or nasty — all these can have strong presence.

A strong narrative presence can work through any point of view, too. The first-person "I" can have strong presence through an entire story. So can the third-person "she" or "he." So can the omniscient narrator. For whatever narrator you choose, a strong presence is created by making that narrator's mind pervasive.

## Attitude

Narrative presence is obvious if the author has an attitude. A strong attitude naturally provokes a strong reaction in the reader. Lots of attitude can be appealing. But narrative presence works just as well if the author pretends to have no attitude. That, in itself, is a kind of attitude.

Remember the piece by Lillian Almeida on pages 66–67? It overflows with personality. "And then — geezus! — he really did what he's been sayin' on the phone! Spattered red truck comin' out of nowhere up that muddy drive again. We'd just been blowin' spun sugar up Ma Bell's dress all these weeks, is what I'd figured."

Almeida's narrator comes across with a truckload of exclamations, reflections, and emotions. Her responses are an important part of the message. Our interest is captured as much by her personality as by what is happening.

In contrast, Mark Peterson's piece on page 51 displays no feeling. "A teenage boy crosses a street. He walks ten yards and stops in front of a video game store; he expected his best friend would be here by now. Beginning to pace, he rotates on his heel and discovers a policeman rolling his motorcycle onto the sidewalk."

Peterson's narrator uses words that have so little feeling they are transparent. The action is conveyed without any attitude. He views it as if through a camera lens, taking the posture of an objective observer.

On a scale of 0 to 10, measuring attitude, Almeida's narrative presence rates close to a 10 — say 9.5. She has tons of attitude. Peterson would rate a 1 or 0.5. Both authors, in their own ways, have considerable narrative presence.

## Steeped in the Narrator's Mind

The essence of narrative presence is consistency. First, a writer comes to a frame of mind and adopts it. Then the writer picks every detail and every thought with precisely that frame of mind. Every single detail — down to the smallest and the most mundane — reflects this mental state. The writing is "steeped in the narrator's mind."

If the narrator is freaked out, then every sentence will show that freakiness. A doorknob might look like an eyeball. If the narrator is calmly observing, then every detail will reflect that calm. A doorknob might be worn brass. If the narrator is sexually excited, then every detail will display that excitement. A doorknob might feel like smooth flesh.

That is how narrative presence gives writing strength. In this excerpt from the novel *Paradise* by Connie Spencer, the details unerringly reflect the narrator's mind. The mother has been looking at an advertisement and decides on a present for her daughter's husband, R.T.:

> . . . "I am going to make a *ornament!* For Christmas! For R.T. Ain't it beautiful?"
>
> It took a minute, so splendidly tacky was the item pictured and so plain and straightforward was my husband, to put the two together mentally. The ad showed a kit — and I use the term loosely — for the assemblage of a beaded, sequined sphere, whose unabashed gaudiness was actually quite grand, in its own way. It looked to me like some sort of Adoration; I supposed I was looking at the Renaissance right there, or such dregs of it as had washed up on this far, far shore. It hung, it spun, it certainly glittered, all this to be achieved by fastening things to a styrofoam ball. And all for only twelve ninety-five.
>
> "Mama — "
>
> I was going to mention highway robbery, but thought better of it, impressed, though not for the first time, by the fortunes to be made off bad taste. What the hell; homage is as homage does; if this was how she felt about R.T., I could only honor the expression.
>
> " — I think it's lovely."

"You do? I was *hoping* you would! See this part here," she said, "I am goin' to do this part in purple," and as her knobby finger moved over the page, I imagined I was rich, not in material things, but in love. I imagined I was rich in love.

The narrator is simultaneously dismayed by her mother's taste and pleased that she cares. The writer does not let the reader off the hook — we are honored by the love, or made squeamish by the taste, in every sentence.

The ornament is described by a narrator who is both attracted and repelled. Internal dialogue takes this uneasiness further: " . . . such dregs of it as had washed up on this far, far shore." Spencer's narrator has a colorful presence, and it is strong because the state of mind is pervasive.

## Crazy Child and Narrative Presence

The Crazy Child finds narrative presence appealing because of its pervasiveness. The Crazy Child's primary motivation is to express itself, and a strong narrator expresses itself through all aspects of a story. For the creative unconscious, to be present on the page is fine. To be present in every detail, large and small, is glorious.

We have already read several examples of narrative presence. One writer's Crazy Child spews out feelings and opinions at every turn. Another's Crazy Child is delighted with presenting a story like an unbiased camera. Between these extremes are as many variations as there are people.

Your creative unconscious may need some coaxing to come out and play with narrative presence fully. It takes confidence to put a narrator's mind into every twist of every sentence. If you choose a wild narrator, it takes confidence to the point of brashness — but it certainly can be fun.

How extreme can your Crazy Child become? What kind of silliness — or seriousness or objectivity — will work for you? Can your creative unconscious be that wacky or that super-steady narrator that you dare to imagine? In every detail?

Yes, of course. The more extreme the better, and definitely be extreme in every detail. Read how extreme J. Maynard is, in the ending paragraphs of the story "Gorgeous":

> . . . I made lots of money by letting them photograph me. They sat me down on a soft velvet couch with lots of pillows. They'd give me lots of great food and plenty to drink. They even gave me all the pot I wanted. Man, if the "cool" girls could see it! Smoking pot in a circle with a bunch of sophisticated artsy types! Just the sort of thing they'd all die for, but it was just thrown on my lap without my even asking.
>
> When I started college, one of the photographers told me he was my man. I told him that generally most men were mine, anyway. He said not like Sean or Scott, but a man who did manly things, lived a manly life. He bought me all sorts of exotic clothes and gave me all sorts of wild drugs and did things to my body that I didn't know could be done. It was great. It was wild!
>
> We've been together for months now. He gave me this crazy apartment with shag carpeting, a zebra-skin rug, chandeliers, artwork on the walls and the walls themselves — one wall is cherrywood, another velvet and gold leaf, another simply white marble and mirrors. He likes variety. He told me it was all mine. It's crazy! It's wild!
>
> We've had tons of parties with lots of different men and women, women like me who are women, beautiful, not preppie but beautiful, not feminists or dykes — beautiful — not cute, not cheerleaders, but goddesses — like me. We've got this whole big scene full of gods and goddesses, and everybody lies down with each other and tells each other how beautiful they all are, and then touches each other and groans with pleasure. My boyfriend says it's better than Rome, so, gosh, I guess I'll never have to go there.
>
> So if there's a moral to this story, you find it. I'm just too gorgeous to have to bother.

"Too gorgeous to have to bother"? This narrator is a 100 percent material girl, and she's oblivious. Maynard plays this stance to the hilt.

Maynard is likely very smart, but this narrator is brainless. The author does not justify the narrator, nor minimize her, nor apologize for her. Maynard simply records every thought and every detail directly from brainlessness. Steeped in this state of mind, the narrator displays it over and over. This must have been a riot to compose.

Narrative presence is a playground for the Crazy Child. Your Crazy Child can be as smart or as cool or as sophisticated as it likes — or as dumb. The creative unconscious can take a state of mind into each small detail, into each turn of phrase, and into each expression. Your Crazy Child can choose any stance whatever, and then amp it.

## Distancing

The writing technique that conceals an author's true feelings is called "distancing." If you choose a "distanced" narrator, you can write about something tragic and your tears will not show. You can write about a subject that curls your guts and no one will know — not immediately. You might even make jokes about it.

Distancing works in literature like a coping strategy works in life. Faced with something fearful, we might want to conceal what is going on inside. We might act tough, noncommittal, irreverent, mean, intellectual — or we might poke fun.

In this story, set in the past when a corpse was burned rather crudely, Pat Bentson chooses to poke fun:

### Mom Was Cremated

Mom was cremated. What remained was returned in a box ten inches by seven inches by two inches. When examined, it was found that the remains were not ashes like one finds in a fireplace or in an ashtray. They resembled kibble. Chunks of charred bone. A staple was found that (presumably) had held the tubes in Mom's throat after the tracheotomy was performed. Dad then went over Mom's kibble with a metal detector. The charred bone was in interesting shapes. One piece looked like a face. Daughter kept it, thinking perhaps of making an earring, a conversation piece. "What's that you're wearing?" "It's my mom. . . . " Family decided to spread the ashes in the backyard (an illegal act in this state) but the kibble was not the consistency for encouraging garden growth. So Dad put all of Mom's remains into the meat grinder. For three hours Dad ground, weeping all the while, to get Mom to the correct consistency. One moonlit night, Dad and daughter shared a glass of wine and fertilized the hydrangeas.

She wants to make earrings of her mother's bones? This writing establishes its presence with irony and bittersweet jokes.

You might laugh as you read "Mom Was Cremated," but you are probably not fooled. Tragedy lurks behind the zany lines. The sentence about weeping and grinding the ashes — "for three hours" — is a poignant clue.

We feel the grieving without being told directly. For this narrator, in fact, an explicit emotion would be out of character. Bentson draws the reader in by using ironical humor at every turn, giving this sad event a flippant, playful surface.

## Distancing and the Surface

By presenting the situation as if you have no feelings — or feelings different from your true ones — you create a "surface" for the reader to land on. That surface can be softer or funnier or cooler or blander than the event itself — or less upsetting than the event.

This makes distancing a supremely effective way of "showing." We land on that surface, and look at the event from a safe distance. We are not put off by the author's feelings. Neither do our own feelings put us off. We are tricked into taking in a difficult or

heartrending situation easily, as if it were bizarre or entertaining —
or of no import. Our true response comes up later.

Bentson's narrator is playfully sarcastic. We may read "Mom
Was Cremated" for its surface humor, but we take in the scene
nonetheless. In the following piece, David Shaddock's narrator is
deadpan — like a bored weather reporter:

### K.'s Childhood

He was born with three feet and a harelip. They cut off his
extra foot a centimeter at a time. This took five years, once a
week. Then they wanted to start on his lip but his mother was
sick of driving him to the hospital. She decided she could do it
just as good at home with the stapler. K.'s dad was always doing
yoga or making money. He never heard K. screaming, but com-
plained mildly when he found his stapler empty. K.'s mother got
crazier. As the years went on her only worry was that someone
would touch something. She forgot K.'s name and their only
contact was when she screamed at him for touching something.
K.'s father's wealth increased sevenfold. K. joined the circus and
became a dog. Still disguised as a dog he joined a family of itin-
erants who taught him to sing the blues.

There's not a whisper of personal feeling in this piece. The
narrator is indifferent throughout — as if reporting the weather on
another planet.

The reader is not invited to respond. We bring a response to the
story on our own. This response might be much stronger than anything an emotional narrator could elicit, and that is the beauty of
this style. Our response may be however much feeling we can afford
or however much we can tolerate. It could be our true response.

## Narrative Presence in Poems

Narrative presence works the same in poetry as it does in prose.
We receive a sense of the author's mind — not necessarily of a

storyteller, since the poem may not tell a story. But we feel a mind working out the poem's issues, or untangling its feelings, or displaying its images.

Walt Whitman seems entranced with the ideas in these seminal lines from "Song of Myself":

> A child said What is the grass? fetching it to me with
>                                                 full hands;
> How could I answer the child? I do not know what it is
>                                               any more than he.
>
> I guess it must be the flag of my disposition, out of
>                                     hopeful green stuff woven.
>
> Or I guess it is the handkerchief of the Lord,
> A scented gift and remembrancer designedly dropt,
> Bearing the owner's name someway in the corners,
>               that we may see and remark, and say Whose?
>
> Or I guess the grass is itself a child, the produced babe
>                                         of the vegetation.
>
> Or I guess it is a uniform hieroglyphic, And it means,
> Sprouting alike in broad zones and narrow zones,
> Growing among black folks as among white,
> Kanuck, Tuckahoe, Congressman, Cuff, I give them the
>               same, I receive them the same.
>
> And now it seems to me the beautiful uncut hair of
>                                         graves.

We feel the breadth of the poet's mind — and his sense of wonder — in this passage. Whitman continues for nearly two dozen lines linking death to the grass. He ends by saying, "To die is different from what any one supposed, and luckier."

You do not need the authority of Whitman, or of anyone else, to write a poem with narrative presence. You need only the authority of your creative unconscious. You can be witty or sour, petty or objective, elusive or full of attitude — or whatever. You can do anything your Crazy Child likes.

Just as in prose, you create narrative presence by bringing a pervasive mind into the writing. Every detail, every image, every observation, and every expression should display that state of mind.

## Narrative Presence in Plays

While a narrator is rarely used in drama, each character does tell a story. Each speech tells the story of what is going on with that character at the moment. We learn what the character thinks, and what the character dislikes, what the character loves, and what the character wants. We learn the character's "goal."

The character's goal is the personal issue of the moment. Each character is steeped in a personal issue, and "presence" is absolutely essential. Actors talk about stage presence, but here I mean a presence in the words — narrative presence.

In the excerpt from Sam Shepard's play *Curse of the Starving Class* on pages 112–114, Weston's speeches stay with his goal. He will see good everywhere — no matter what — and he also insists on being the authority on everything. When Ella swears at him, he replies, "You've picked up on the language okay, but your inflection's off."

Ella changes her goals. In the beginning she's accusative and ironic: "Are you having a nervous breakdown or what?" and "Well, I'm glad you've found a way of turning shame into a source of pride." All her speeches display this state of mind — at first.

Then Ella gets angry, and every word is caustic: "What is this crap! I've been down there all night trying to pull Emma back together again and I come back to Mr. Hyde! Mr. 'Goody Two-Shoes'! Mister Mia Copa himself! Well, you can kiss off with that crap because I'm not buying it."

In the excerpt from Tennessee Williams' play *Orpheus*

*Descending* on page 136, Val's speeches have presence in a less obvious way. "That happens t' be the truth. My temperature's always a couple degrees above normal the same as a dog's, it's normal for me the same as it is for a dog, that's the truth. . . . " These words are quietly insistent, and they stay on target. Val's speeches are imbued with his issue.

An effective speech needs to fulfill the requirements of strong prose. It requires that every word reverberate with the character's goal. Each written word should display the state of mind, or the personal issue, of the speaker.

## Narrative Presence in Essays

Narrative presence works in the essay just as it does in stories, poems, and speeches. In *Bird by Bird*, Anne Lamott deals with the negative voices in a writer's mind — the Editor and the Writer when they're in a thoroughly bad mood:

> . . . First there's the vinegar-lipped Reader Lady, who says primly, "Well, *that's* not very interesting, is it?" And there's the emaciated German male who writes these Orwellian memos detailing your thought crimes. And there are your parents, agonizing over your lack of loyalty and discretion; and there's William Burroughs, dozing off or shooting up because he finds you as bold and articulate as a houseplant. . . .
>
> Close your eyes and get quiet for a minute, until the chatter starts up. Then isolate one of the voices and imagine the person speaking as a mouse. Pick it up by the tail and drop it into a mason jar. Then isolate another voice, pick it up by the tail, drop it in the jar. And so on. Drop in any high-maintenance parental units, drop in any contractors, lawyers, colleagues, children, anyone who is whining in your head. Then put the lid on, and watch all these mouse people clawing at the glass, jabbering away, trying to make you feel like shit because you won't do what they want — won't give them more money, won't be more

successful, won't see them more often. Then imagine that there is a volume-control button on the bottle. Turn it all the way up for a minute, and listen to the stream of angry, neglected, guilt-mongering voices. Then turn it all the way down and watch the frantic mice lunge at the glass, trying to get to you. . . .

A writer friend of mine suggests opening the jar and shooting them all in the head. But I think he's a little angry, and I'm sure nothing like this would ever occur to you.

When she gets to the end, of course it seems natural to shoot those mice. Why not? Her narrator stays right on target — with heavy sarcasm.

In an essay, there is no room for apologizing for your thesis. Anne Lamott takes a stance of utter confidence, and you can do the same. Let every sentence resound with conviction. If you become querulous or snarling or arrogant or completely monstrous — no matter. Take no prisoners.

## Voice and Stride

When an author matures, we say the author has found a "voice." We recognize voice easily and enjoy it as readers. The details of voice can be mysterious or subtle, but, broadly, voice is the essence of your Crazy Child. It is something you already have, and you probably only need practice to let it out.

Voice emerges from the mixture of everything a writer does — voice is in the words. It comes out of narrative presence, action, internal and external dialogue, point of view, persona, image detail — everything. All aspects of the writing contribute to voice.

As a teacher, I often see writers hit their stride, and that is when voice starts emerging. The writer has discovered how to keep sentences moving. Components of the writing are working together, paragraphs flow, transitions are seamless — the trance is unbroken.

Narrative presence is a major part of voice. Practicing different sorts of presence is an effective way to help your voice come out.

Perhaps your creative unconscious can automatically breathe its voice into your words. Some writers are lucky, and their Editors and Writers do not interfere. They let the Crazy Child voice come out loud and clear.

More likely, you are exploring. Perhaps you are working to give your creative unconscious more confidence. It's not difficult to find some chutzpa and let your Crazy Child speak however it wants. The exercise and the practice are designed to help you gain that confidence. The arena they present for your Crazy Child is large and forgiving.

## EXERCISE

Write two pieces, taking fifteen minutes for each. Make the pieces very different. Choose one narrator for the first piece and a different narrator for the second. Blast away in one piece. Then change your narrative stance and blast away — or dance or complain or poke fun or whatever — in the second one.

You might want to do one piece with attitude and another with no attitude. This can be interesting. In the attitude piece, be sneering or exultant or flip — anything — but put in lots of it. In the other, put in none. Be the clear eye of a camera or be that deadpan weather reporter.

Be courageous. Don't worry about what people think. A stance that you think is unpopular, might actually be one you do very well — and one that readers like. An angry narrator, for instance, can be very appealing. You never know. Follow whatever twinge your Crazy Child presents, and play it to the hilt.

Don't bother about other techniques, either. Don't worry about image detail or about forming good sentences. Make your narrator's mind pervasive, and the narrator will shape your writing. That Crazy Child narrator will select image detail, choose dialogue, create action, and compose sentences.

## Twelve-Sentence Childhoods

As a variation, write a childhood in twelve sentences. Do your own childhood or the childhood of someone you know — or make one up. Cover the entire childhood in twelve sentences. Then write another childhood, using a different narrator.

David Shaddock's pieces can be useful models. "K.'s Childhood," on page 155, was written deadpan, and "My Childhood," on pages 131–132, was written with humor and a ladle-full of chagrin. These stances work fine — as will almost any attitude.

## Hidden Connotation

For part one of another variation, pick something that you like or love dearly. It can be a person, a place, an object, an animal — you name it. Write about it for fifteen minutes like a heartless scientist. Use words with no feeling whatsoever.

Words with no emotions — direct or implied — have no "connotation" or no "connotative meaning." They are descriptions: colors, shapes, textures, sounds, smells, tastes, or actions. The description of the teenager in Mark Peterson's piece on page 51 is an example, as is his description of the motorcycle police officer.

For part two, pick a topic that riles you — one that gets you upset in every imaginable way. Write for fifteen minutes like a scientist, the same as in the first piece. Use words with no hint of that upset. Your narrator will naturally become distanced, and the result can be very powerful.

These exercises are designed to stimulate very distinct forays into narrative presence. Use any of the variations — attitude pieces, childhoods, or pieces with no connotations. Let your Crazy Child choose two different narrators and be those narrators in all aspects of the writing.

## WORKSHOP

Listen to the exercise pieces and follow the kindergarten rules —
as in every workshop. Say what particular images or sentences
work for you. Mention phrases that capture your attention, and
watch especially for those that display a powerful narrator.

Listen for phrases that are full of attitude. These are easy to
spot, but it is not so easy to appreciate attitudes you disagree with.
Effective listeners will say when the lines are powerful, even if they
don't agree with the attitude. A well-expressed attitude of any kind
will snag our attention. Ears will ripple.

Listen carefully, also, for sentences written as if by an objective
observer. These require some alertness to hear well. Those deadpan
phrases might seem flat at first — but they contain a unique and
steadfast power.

As you give feedback, you might be giving the author support
for going out on a limb. This not a bad thing. Out on limbs is
where we find styles that sizzle. The phrases you hear may have
lower voltage, but if they have some current, mention them. You
are pointing out strengths for the author to develop. This is the
goal of the syngenetic workshop.

When you are the author, the feedback may seem strange to
you. It will probably not be strange, however, to your Crazy Child.
Your creative unconscious is showing your Writer and Editor what
it does well. Your writing may be making sparks where you least
expect — or where your Writer or Editor least expect. This is especially likely if you use an unusual narrator.

Write down everything the workshop appreciates, just as you
have before. If the workshop likes a line, your job is to write it
down — or to underline it, or to mark it with exclamation points,
or to put stars around it.

## Listening to Plot Again

Everyone will benefit if you read the plot practice pieces from the last chapter. Listen carefully to how each piece begins. Does it sweep into the action or do you wait while the background is painted in? Exactly where do you get hooked?

When a piece starts taking off, tension rises. A sensitive listener will notice where this happens. It might be better to start the piece at that point and splice the information from the first few paragraphs into the flow of the action. Often very little explanation or setup is necessary.

If your piece starts slowly, do not be discouraged. It is commonplace to warm up, or to get the feel of your characters, and then get into your piece. You may not know you were only warming up, but this is not a loss. After the first draft, it's easy to begin a paragraph or two — or even a page or two — further into your piece.

## What Is the Piece About?

This question generally provokes a useful discussion. When the workshop members asks themselves, "What is it about?" it is asking for each listener's summary of the plot. The discussion will reveal how the plot is working. If everyone agrees, including the author, then you know the plot is working well.

The workshop will often come up with several possibilities. Perhaps the author, in the first draft, was not yet settled on the issue. This is not unusual. Perhaps the story, poem, play, or essay heads in one direction, and then turns somewhere else. There may be more than one plot trying to direct the writing.

Suppose a woman's sports trophy is the missing valuable in your plot practice piece, from page 148. Suppose some paragraphs are given to the father, who was her mentor and coach. Suppose, also, that there is mention of the father's second marriage. Both of these people need to have a role in the plot if the piece is to be tight and effective.

The workshop will try to understand how the father and his second wife contribute. There might be some way that they further the suspense or highlight the daughter's character. Perhaps the father is responsible for the flaw that allowed the daughter to lose the trophy. Or perhaps the father is background that is not needed. The discussion should indicate to the author whether the father is necessary.

If you, as a listener, disagree with what others are saying, be sure to state what you think. Point to the paragraphs that support your thinking — but do not argue about them. It's useful to the author to hear what the different positions are. The author will already be mulling over various options for a revision.

## Presenting Options

"Presenting options" is different from giving clunky suggestions. Clunky suggestions point out how a small thing, like confusing image detail or conflicting dialogue, can be mended. Presenting options, in contrast, shows ways to improve the overall structure of the piece.

Here are some examples. If the father in the missing valuables piece does not seem to fit, the workshop could suggest taking the father out. That's one option. If he might work as a contrast to the daughter, spreading small mentions of him throughout is another option. If he could be more dynamic, someone might suggest how he could discover the trophy — or he could have stolen it. That makes a third and a fourth option.

## Let the Author Speak

When the workshop discussion ends, the author may have a desire to speak. If you are the author, you may be surprised — even shocked — at how your work is interpreted. The workshop may have a very different take from yours.

The disparity is probably in the writing. Perhaps you meant for the father to be a major force in your piece. Speak up, and say what you intended. Then give the workshop a chance to respond. They may say, "Oh! If that is what you want. . . . " and present you with new options for augmenting the father's role.

Perhaps you thought the father's effect was clear. The workshop should give you a couple of new ways to make him stronger. You now have options that will further your own — original and important — point, and you can come away from the workshop encouraged. You have several ways to change your piece for the better.

## PRACTICE

In each of your exercise and practice pieces you will have done at least one thing well. Every person's Crazy Child has a native talent. Perhaps yours is vivid image detail, or perhaps it is snappy and entrancing dialogue. Perhaps it is something else, like the flow of your sentences or your honesty. Every piece you write will display this natural ability.

Other techniques you have to learn. You have been picking them up as you go through this book, but we have been moving rapidly. Now is the time to focus. With a rewrite, you can develop and consolidate your ability in another technique. You can add to your natural skills.

### First Rewrite

A rewrite is almost always necessary. A story, poem, play, or essay rarely comes out perfect in the first draft. Four or five rewrites are often necessary to get on track. More revisions may be needed for a piece to attain its most powerful form. One of my plays has been revised twenty times, and is finally ready for production. This is not unusual.

> *Writing is rewriting.*
>
>                            reported by DOROTHY BRYANT

Which piece should you rewrite? You probably have several you would like to improve. Pick the story, poem, play, or essay you are most excited about. Rewriting takes a lot of energy. You will want to be thoroughly engaged throughout the process.

How should you rewrite your piece? Focus on one basic aspect of your piece, and strengthen that. Often a piece has too little image detail, or too much internal dialogue, or too little action. You can correct one of these in a single sweep through your piece. As you do so, you may instinctively solve other problems.

Taking out extra setup or background makes for an easy rewrite. So does taking out extra dialogue or description. More difficult problems are weak crucial scenes or a wavering point of view. For any of these problems, you will want to look at every sentence.

If the narrative presence seems inconsistent, make that what you improve. Have the narrator's exact attitude ooze through all the sentences, just as we have discussed. Get thoroughly steeped in the narrator's mind. This means, again, looking at every sentence and changing most of them — possibly all of them — a little.

If the dialogue seems weak, you might look at each speech, along with its supporting description. Remember the rule of thumb about dialogue? Each line should move the action ahead or tell us something new about the character. Look at each speech you have written and ask if it is doing its job.

Rewriting is "revisioning," according to the poet Adrienne Rich. This is a valuable insight. You can sometimes fix things here and there, like replacing parts on a car. But those weak spots often are symptoms of a deeper problem. You may need to think more about what you want to say.

Dream your piece again. Start by getting thoroughly into the frame of mind you were in when you first wrote it. This takes some thinking — or meditating or daydreaming. Your Crazy Child will eventually oblige, and you'll come up with a new vision of the piece. You'll sharpen or alter that frame of mind. With your changed frame of mind, review every sentence.

My preferred time to mull over a piece is late at night, so I can dream about it before going to sleep. By morning my creative unconscious may have shifted and I'll know exactly what to do. Or I may wake with only a vague feeling of warmth and hope. But that's enough. Feeling that the next step is easy is a signal that I'm ready to begin.

These are rules of thumb for a first rewrite. You are beginning a process that is crucial to writing. You may do many passes before your piece is finished. As you change one thing, you could expose another problem, and this will need work on the next pass.

Rewriting can be an aggravation. It helps if you take it one step at a time and do not try for a perfect rewrite. You are improving your piece, not finishing it — you are making your piece one notch stronger. If you stay in touch with some Crazy Child enthusiasm, so much the better. A little zing from the joy of creating certainly helps.

# Chapter 9
## Good Clichés

*The intensity with which a subject is grasped . . . is what makes for beauty in art.*

PAULA MODERSOHN-BECKER

A cliché is an overused phrase, like "You'll understand when you're older." It has lost its meaning, especially if you are young, because you have heard it too many times. It no longer packs its original power.

We recognize a cliché automatically and discount it. We laugh and judge the speaker on the spot or we get bored and think about something else. It is often said that a cliché is a tired phrase.

More precisely, it is our ears that are worn out. The cliché is only words, after all: it cannot be tired. But our nervous system develops a callous — or a bruised or a tired or a bored spot — where the phrase hits.

Have you come to a place in your life where you notice that a cliché has turned out to be true? The meaning of "You'll understand when you're older" could change over time from insulting to false to boring to fact. As you get older, you may find yourself saying the same words you used to dread — because they are true.

Most clichés are true, in appropriate situations. "It's an ill wind that blows no good" works for many circumstances, so it has stayed in the language a long time. "We're in this together" and "Eyes like deep pools" are two more of thousands of clichés. They seem to make communication easy.

But writing a cliché is dangerous. You may write the phrase with its pristine intensity in mind, and your reader takes a nap. Two or three clichés can give your reader an overdose. It takes only a few clichés to poison the reception of an entire poem, story, play, or essay.

Authors are generally afraid of clichés. Our Editors and Writers learn right away that a cliché is bad — very bad. Some authors avoid writing clichés to such an extent that, at times, they cannot write at all. Many authors despise clichés their entire lives.

This chapter, in contrast, will show that the impulse to write a cliché is fine. You will not want your finished piece to sound like a cliché, but that is a matter of revision, not of creation. In the act of writing, to be bold enough and free enough to write clichés gives you transcendent power.

## Clichés and the Crazy Child

Your Crazy Child may know nothing about clichés. Your creative unconscious may live in a universe of images and stories that has nothing to do with worn-out phrases. Your Crazy Child may not even recognize what a cliché is.

At the other extreme, your creative unconscious may live entirely in clichés. Your Crazy Child may relish them and roll in clichés like a puppy in a field of daisies. Between these extremes is an infinity of worlds, and not one of them is bad.

Sometimes my Crazy Child is a ball of energy, picking up images and stories like mad, sometimes it sits and plays quietly with cards or guns or dolls. It has its reasons for doing whatever. Behind any phrase the Crazy Child chooses is a ton of power — whether or not that phrase is a cliché.

The great, mysterious wisdom of the Crazy Child has no rules we can recognize. Any phrase from your creative unconscious contains that wisdom, or some part of it. If your Crazy Child lives in a steamboat trunk full of silly clichés, no matter. Its words contain power and wisdom.

The Crazy Child is what psychologists call the "excluded self." This self becomes excluded because we make judgments against it and shut it in a closet. In *Let the Crazy Child Write!* we counter those judgments. We are training the Writer and the Editor to accept the creative unconscious as it is.

The author's job is to translate Crazy Child intensity into fresh language. We begin by honoring whatever words the creative unconscious gives us. If you define Crazy Child clichés as good, you are able to include them as raw material. You can then tap the immense energy behind clichés.

## Going into Clichés

There are several possible clichés in the following passage from the novel *Jane Eyre* by Charlotte Brontë. The narrator, a young girl, has been caught hiding behind a curtain by her brother:

> John . . . bullied and punished me; not two or three times in the week, nor once or twice in the day, but continually: every nerve I had feared him, and every morsel of flesh on my bones shrank when he came near. There were moments when I was bewildered by the terror he inspired, because I had no appeal whatever against either his menaces or his inflictions. . . .
>
> . . . I came up to his chair: he spent some three minutes in thrusting out his tongue at me as far as he could without damaging the roots: I knew he would soon strike, and while dreading the blow, I mused on the disgusting and ugly appearance of him who would presently deal it.

I would bet you stay involved when you read " . . . every nerve I had feared him, and every morsel of flesh on my bones shrank when he came near." You might be less interested if Brontë wrote, "my heart trembled" or "I trembled to the core of my being." The meaning of these phrases is similar to what she did write, but they are overused. Your response might be a yawn.

Brontë taps the energy behind the possible cliché by delving into it. She feels the situation clearly and describes it in exact detail. She does the same with the boy's tongue: he was thrusting his tongue out as far as he could "without damaging the roots."

Did you notice that Brontë's writing has strong narrative presence? She is steeped in caring for the young girl. This narrative presence helps her to be startlingly clear about the girl's circumstances. It also helps her go far into the possible clichés and make them vivid.

## Twisting Clichés

Another way of returning power to clichés is to twist them. First, let a cliché come up freely. Next, twist the phrase a little as it blossoms. Change the order of the words, or extend the phrase, for instance, by inserting a slice of real-life description.

This strategy works well for Marge Piercy in her collection of poems *The Twelve-Spoked Wheel Flashing*, as the beginning of "What is permitted" shows:

> How beautiful to be let
> to stare into your eyes
> from inches away, eyes of a shallow
> sea with rock on the bottom
> volcanic and jagged, rocks that slide
> from the pass of scarlet poppies.

"I love staring into your eyes" is a cliché, but Marge Piercy writes "To be let to stare into your eyes." This small change runs counter to the reader's expectations.

Staring into someone's eyes is an invasion, unless permission is granted. Piercy's "to be let to stare . . ." acknowledges this reality. She invites the reader to think alertly, which wouldn't happen if she used the cliché.

Her next words " . . . from inches away" bring the reader in close. She does not write "Your eyes are like deep pools," but, instead, she twists this cliché adroitly. Her words "eyes of a shallow sea" keep the reader wide awake.

You could suspect her partner is shallow, since the next lines display objects — "volcanic," "jagged" rocks — that could not be seen in deep pools. But she is saying that some of her partner's depths are visible. This affirms a multilevel relationship, as does her previous image.

Piercy transforms possible clichés into windows of vision. What we see through the windows are images of a caring intimacy. "What is permitted" is one of the more remarkable poems of our time.

## Gushing Clichés

Writing clichés one after the other, without changing them, can be surprisingly effective. As the clichés roll along, they accumulate power like a snowball rolling downhill gathers snow. Perhaps they gather intensity because of their rhythms. Perhaps, by bouncing off each other, they set up fresh meanings.

Many authors write like this. Tom Wolfe's prose in "The Red Tide," from *The Electric Kool-Aid Acid Test,* seems to crawl with clichés:

> Stranded in an up-tight town; no roads leading north and no roads leading south; nine or ten hours of hell by bus to Guadalajara the only way to git back to the rest of the world; can't git out in the daytime and do anything because of the heat; can't git out at night because of the mosquitoes; the jungle beyond the Rat Shack filthy with cocoa palms and all sortsa jungle shit; itching crawling alive like a chigger-ridden groin; all manner exotic vermin; sting inflame chigger-blister mosquito heaven, with scorpions for good measure coming up outta the dung dust like lobsters as the crab louse is to the crab.

We learn loads about this author's persona, along with particulars of the story, as the words cascade. Wolfe's style allows both to
happen. He rolls out near clichés with enthusiasm and verve.

Most of these images are not quite clichés. Each phrase adds a
kernel of information important to the scene, and something
unexpected keeps happening. The reader stays alert. If Wolfe were
afraid of clichés, he could not have achieved such liveliness.

Piercy, similarly, displays no fear of clichés. Her powerful
poem "The window of the woman burning," from *Circles on
the Water*, is built with gushing images, if not clichés. The lead-in
phrase, "Woman you are not..." sets up a string of negative
pictures:

> Woman
> you are not the madonna impaled
> whose sacrifice of self leaves her
> empty and mad as wind. . . .

The next lead-in, "Woman you are . . . " is followed with positive images:

> Woman
> you are the demon of a fountain of energy
> rushing up from the coal hard
> memories in the ancient spine. . . .

These free-wheeling lines seem to come from deep inside, as if
Piercy is listening intently into her body. Forged together with the
images is historical and psychological wisdom. The combination
gives the poem immense impact.

---

*The dream of every cliché is to enter a great poem.*

CHARLES SIMIC

## Clichés and "Like"

The word "like" has tainted many pieces with clichés. It is an invitation for facile comparisons. In *Let the Crazy Child Write!* we will take up the dare: why not compare a feeling or a thought to anything the Crazy Child might want?

If Shelly Nielsen were afraid of the word "like," she could not have written the poem "I Know." The repeated "like" gives her room to explore a common and universal topic:

I Know
Today someone asked me
what I know.
"What do you really know?"
I am unaware of what I know.
Completely oblivious.
I know nothing.

Not true.
I know what morning smells like,
sweet and hopeful,
like baby powder,
newborn every time.
I know what the moon looks like
in the middle of the day,
a chalky promise of a beautiful night.
I know what the air tastes like,
clean, clear, cold water.
I know what the wind looks like,
a woman's long gauzy skirt.
I know what music feels like,
lots of fingers and toes.
I know what the sunlight does to my hair,
the hidden red of my spirit.
I know what I look like on the inside,
you.

Nielsen uses "like" as an invitation to see precisely. She does not limit herself because the words might seem like clichés. Her crystal-clear perceptions give rise to fresh and entrancing images — and to that stunning ending.

It takes daring to write so transparently. The poem is captivating, whether or not you agree with it intellectually. Our hearts may not, after all, be so very sophisticated. My nervous system takes in these images and finds them true.

## Clichés in Plays

Tennessee Williams' character Val gives a speech, quoted on page 136, that is nearly a cliché. "My temperature's always a couple degrees above normal the same as a dog's, it's normal for me the same as it is for a dog, that's the truth. . . . "

Val implies that he is hot-blooded. If he had used that phrase, "hot-blooded," and nothing more, his speech would be a cliché. The audience would miss the ambiguity that makes Val's character riveting.

But Val comes up with an odd image. His "temperature . . . the same as a dog's" sets up resonances in the audience's mind, and adds a funky aspect to hot-blooded. We wonder if Val is calling himself a dog.

The playwright avoids the cliché by going into it, just as Brontë does in her prose. Val's insistence pushes his speech beyond cliché. That same insistence, as I noted on page 158, gives Val's speech narrative presence.

Characters on stage, however, can speak in clichés. This is a luxury of the theater. Your character might say a cliché archly or mockingly or bitingly — twisting it with attitude. Since the attitude is live, the audience will relish the cliché.

The stage also allows the playwright to challenge clichés in a lively manner. For instance, if Lady were more contentious in Williams' play, she could insist that her temperature is higher than

Val's. She might want to have fun with Val, or to compete. The situation could get inflamed — quickly.

## Clichés in Essays

An essay should be tightly reasoned. Your Editor and Writer know this, and they might restrict the freedom of your first draft. The Editor may think a Crazy Child perception is clichéd — but it could be the engine that drives the essay.

Would an argument about capital punishment be advanced by a mud puddle? Or by a stray dog? Both seem ridiculous if you consider them in advance. Read how they function in this excerpt from George Orwell's essay "A Hanging," from *Shooting an Elephant,* as a prisoner is led to the gallows:

> A warder, detached from the escort, charged clumsily after the dog, but it danced and gamboled just out of his reach, taking everything as part of the game. A young Eurasian jailer picked up a handful of gravel and tried to stone the dog away, but it dodged the stones and came after us again. Its yaps echoed from the jail walls. The prisoner, in the grasp of the two warders, looked on incuriously, as though this was another formality of the hanging. It was several minutes before someone managed to catch the dog. Then we put my handkerchief through its collar and moved off once more, with the dog still straining and whimpering.
>
> It was about forty yards to the gallows. I watched the bare brown back of the prisoner marching in front of me. He walked clumsily with his bound arms, but quite steadily, with that bobbing gait of the Indian who never straightens his knees. At each step his muscles slid neatly into place, the lock of hair on his scalp danced up and down, his feet printed themselves on the wet gravel. And once, in spite of the men who gripped him by each shoulder, he stepped slightly aside to avoid a puddle on the path.

It is curious, but till that moment I had never realized what it means to destroy a healthy, conscious man. When I saw the prisoner step aside to avoid the puddle I saw the mystery, the unspeakable wrongness, of cutting a life short when it is in full tide. This man was not dying, he was alive just as we are alive.

That troublesome dog is simply expressing its nature. When the prisoner does the same thing, by avoiding the puddle, he becomes especially vivid. We have an image of the dog's liveliness in mind already. As the prisoner takes that sideways step, he becomes equally lively — and human, besides.

Orwell presents the puddle and the dog as crucial parts of his argument. He did not worry, evidently, whether they might seem like clichés. He sees the situation clearly and goes far into it, just as Brontë and Williams do.

## Have No Fear

Perhaps the sum of what I am saying is to have no fear. Clichés are to be used, and to be transformed, without hesitation. Consider this poem by Marc Hofstadter:

Poetry

My cat
begs me five times,
with plaintive cries,
to pet him.
I am too busy
trying to write.
At the sixth meow
I put my pen down
and stroke his gray,
smooth fur.
He purrs.
I say to myself

this grateful flesh
is where the poetry is.
I pet him until
he settles down by my side,
happy.

Do you suppose Hofstadter was surprised at what came out?
The poem may simply have flowed out of his pen, as Keats desired,
as "naturally as a tree grows leaves" — and with no fear.

## Clichés and the Editor and the Writer

This chapter gives the Editor and the Writer a fresh education. I
am proposing to the Editor and the Writer that clichés are all right
in our first drafts — more than all right. The impulse behind a
cliché is the source of strikingly powerful writing.

The cliché will express at least part of that impulse, and it
should be set down in ink every time. It will remind you what the
impulse is. It will face you with a feeling or thought that is crucial
to your Crazy Child, and this will point you directly to the core of
your piece.

To follow that pointer, you must get the cliché on paper. If
your Editor and Writer cannot approve of clichés, they should at
least accept them in a first draft. And they have the option of turning their heads away. They should definitely learn to get out of the
way, somehow, and let your Crazy Child express itself.

EXERCISE

Pick anything you feel strongly about, a person, a place, an object,
an idea, whatever. Be sure your topic arouses plenty of emotion —
strong emotion. It can be something you know well or something
brand new to you.

Write for half an hour. Use Piercy's "The window of the

woman burning" as a model. Substitute your topic for "Woman."
Address the topic as "you," as Piercy does, and follow with a string
of images. Write "(Your topic), you are . . ." and go on at length.
When you are done with the positive, begin again, this time with
"(Your topic), you are not . . . ."

Or you could simply describe your topic. Write "(Your topic)
is . . ." and follow that with images — objective, flamboyant, sarcastic, or loving images. The negative lead-in phrase would be
"(Your topic) is not . . ." Follow that with images.

Roll out the words one after the other, clichés or whatever, in
all their glory. Be as wild as you like — the wilder the better. Write
in a positive mode for the half hour, or entirely in the negative. Or
switch back and forth whenever the impulse strikes you.

Write either prose or poetry. If you find yourself composing a
story or an essay, go right ahead; if you find yourself writing dialogue, that is fine, too. If you start running out of energy, come
back to one of the lead-in phrases. Come back whenever you need
to fire up your Crazy Child.

## Crazy Child, Writer, Editor

The Crazy Child, Writer, and Editor are busy every time you
write. A group I led in 1982 demonstrated this vividly.
Miniaturized typewriters had appeared on the market and writers
were excited. For the first time you could fit one comfortably on
your lap, and you could work on an airplane or while riding in a car.

A woman brought one to class. Her Crazy Child became the
typewriter and it snicked along, bopping and humming and spewing out images. Then the typewriter went haywire: a chip card fell
out of the case, smoking, and the words went screwy. Everyone
laughed. I asked, "How did it feel to write that?"

She said it felt awful, and I was surprised. "Why? Wasn't your
Crazy Child having a great time?" She said yes, it was having fun,
but the whole while her Editor was shaking its head and snorting,

"Neh-neh-neh-neh-Neh-neh." She felt like an animal trainer in a cage with a lion.

Her Editor was a lion, and her Crazy Child was playing with the typewriter. Her Writer took up a whip and a stool. The Editor would come over and stick a claw into the keyboard and the Writer would crack her whip and push at the lion-like Editor with the stool, forcing it back. Then the Writer would murmur and coo to the Crazy Child, and get it playing again.

The Writer needed to keep the Editor from damaging the Crazy Child. The Writer needed to provide encouragement, too, so the creative unconscious could write freely. Managing the whole process is the Writer's job. You do not want the Editor to eat your Crazy Child for lunch.

## Write the Next Word

As you do the exercise, simply write the next word. William Stafford does exactly that in this workshop version of his poem "Not Very Loud *(What?)*." He puts his Editor's thoughts in parentheses:

Not Very Loud *(What?)*

*Now is the time of the moths that come (How, when, where?)*

*in the evening. (Ok, I guess) They are around, just being (What?)*

*there, (Oh) at windows and doors. They crowd (Who, what, where?)*

*the lights, (That's better) planing in from dark fields*

*and liking it in town. They accept each other (Why, how, when?)*

*as they fly or crawl. (Well, it's an answer) How do they know (What?)*

*what (What???) is coming? Their furred flight (What now?)*

*softer (Unh) than down, announces a quiet (What?)*

*approach under whatever is loud. (Where's this going?)*

*What (What! What?) good are moths for? Maybe they offer (Who?)*

*something (Pretty vague) we need, a fluttering (Why, when, where?)*

*near the edge of our sight, and they may carry (What now?)*

*whatever (???) is needed for us to watch (When, where?)*

*all through those long nights in our still, (What???)*

*vacant houses, (Now what?) if there is another war. (Ouch!)*

It is hilarious when his Crazy Child writes "what" and the Editor howls back, *"What???"* This Editor is working pretty hard, even when he is sniping or bored. I like the lukewarm *"Ok, I guess,"* the sarcastic *"Well, it's an answer,"* and especially that final *"Ouch!"*

"Not Very Loud *(What?)*" is an example of the Editor, Writer, and Crazy Child working together. The Writer sets up the situation and makes the request, "Write the next word." The Editor helps shape the piece by prodding the Crazy Child. "What, where, when, how?" are questions for the creative unconscious to answer.

The questions do not interfere with the process. Words are flowing from the Crazy Child, and even though the Editor has no idea what will come next, he seems to respect that flow. The Editor squawks, but he does not try to stop the Crazy Child.

The Crazy Child senses this. Its images keep right on coming, almost as if the Crazy Child is oblivious — but I think it is not. I think the Crazy Child does hear the Editor's questions, and lets itself be guided. The three voices have created something that is entirely the poet's and — as Georgia O'Keeffe suggests — it is exciting.

> *Paint what's in your head, what you are acquainted with. Even if you think it doesn't count . . . doing something that is entirely your own may be pretty exciting.*
>
> GEORGIA O'KEEFFE

## Gushing Clichés and Twisting Clichés

If you feel daring as you do the exercise, twist any clichés as they come up. This gives your Editor a job. While the Crazy Child is busy pushing up words, your Editor can be bending and twisting them. Clichés are like dried herbs and the Editor can help bring out their vital, pungent scent.

But, mostly, you should keep the words coming. Do not let the Editor stop the flow. The safe course is to let the clichés gush out however they want. There is no overriding need to twist them in the exercise — this can be done later. Keep your pen moving on the page.

A single nasty remark from the Editor can halt the writing. This is not good. Write down the Editor's remark, as if you are paying attention. Mine often says, "Clive, that's the same old drivel." I put those exact words in parentheses, just as I suggested on page 73, (Clive, that's the same old drivel) and go on. The Editor has had its say, and now my Crazy Child can continue.

Write the Editor's criticism in parentheses, and continue with the Crazy Child's words.

## Trail of Clichés

Each word and the next — even if it is a cliché — form a trail. The words are attached one to the other, like the animals in a story told by poet Robert Bly. A man suspects something is wrong, and he questions his partner. The story becomes "The little old lady who swallowed a fly" in reverse.

The woman protests, no, no, there is nothing wrong. "Are you sure there isn't one small thing," he asks, "that you need to tell me?" No, there is not. Nothing. He continues to ask and she continues to protest. The man goes so far as to plead, "Isn't there one, teensy-weensy thing on your mind?"

Yes, she admits finally, there is one small thing. A little furry tail seems to be tickling the back of her throat. She pulls at the tail and out comes a mouse. The mouse is attached to a cat, the cat to a dog, the dog to a hyena, and so on through all the animals of Noah's Ark. Soon there is a rhinoceros in the living room.

Continue just as the woman did in Bly's story. Pull out phrases and clichés by their tails; they may be animals that get larger and larger. On pages 14–15 we followed a trail of details as they linked one to another. Here we follow a trail of images and clichés.

The purpose of this exercise is twofold. First, by gushing out clichés or possible clichés, you encourage the Crazy Child to put its feeling into words — any words. You are releasing yourself from restrictions. Your creative unconscious can now write exactly what it wants.

Second, you encourage your Editor and Writer to accept clichés in first drafts. Your Editor and Writer need to get used to plenty of clichés, whether or not they try changing them. The clichés are footprints of the wisdom of your creative unconscious. Be as clichéd as your Crazy Child likes.

## WORKSHOP

You have the cliché exercise and your rewrite practice from the last chapter to work on. Start with the gushing clichés exercise. When you are a listener, you have something valuable to offer the author.

Ordinarily, the author's Editor and Writer will be struggling mightily with clichés. To see clichés in a positive light may be almost impossible for these judgmental characters. They might be having a sort of fit.

If you listen attentively, you will notice what phrases are working. When you hear a cliché that is uniquely phrased, or powerful, or marvelously twisted, point it out. It does not matter if there are stale clichés nearby. They were probably a warm up for the good cliché — the one straight from the Crazy Child's mouth.

Be forceful, and be certain the author writes down your comments. The author needs to hear you through the noisy chatter of the Editor and the Writer. You will need to do the same, as a listener — you must hear the piece through the flak from your own Editor and Writer. Does this give you an inkling of how well you must listen?

When you are the author, follow the kindergarten rules. Listen well, say nothing, and write down the positive comments. You are taking in information that will counteract your Editor's and your Writer's prejudice against clichés. You are opening doors for your Crazy Child.

## Workshopping the Rewrite

As a listener, you will be hearing a piece for the second time. This requires new discipline. Listen with fresh ears, as if you have not heard the piece before. This is quite a trick — ultimately, of course, it is impossible. But the more nearly you do this, the more useful your feedback will be.

"Virgin ears" are people who are truly hearing a piece for the first time. Perhaps they missed the last session or perhaps they are guests at your workshop. In my classes we listen to those virgin ears first, before the rest of us speak up.

The workshop may interpret a rewrite piece the way it was intended because they know the author's intention from the previous session. Virgin ears, however, know nothing about this. They won't know whether the piece expresses the author's intention, and they can report only what the words say. Theirs is the more valuable feedback.

With a rewrite, follow the syngenetic rules as usual. Listen carefully. Repeat what snags your attention word for word, even if you mentioned the same words when you first heard the piece. You might be surprised how some parts seem changed that are in fact not changed. You are naturally reading the piece with a slightly different mind.

The workshop should ask again what the piece is about. The discussion that follows will be different from the previous discussion because the author has changed the piece. There is most likely more work to be done, and the workshop should ask themselves what the next step is. Remember, one or two rewrite suggestions are plenty — three at most.

## Baby Steps

When you bring your rewrite to the workshop, you will probably be hoping the piece is finished. You are in for a surprise. Your workshop will usually find as much to say about the second draft as it did about the first.

You may feel that you are taking baby steps. Do not be discouraged. This is precisely how rewriting often goes: one baby step at a time. You are zeroing in, little by little, on the most powerful version of your piece.

---

*Start wherever you can, fixing up a little thing first, perhaps, to give you courage to tackle a big one. Then fix up whatever you disturbed by fixing, because rewriting leads to more rewriting.*

DOROTHY BRYANT

Dorothy Bryant's admonition is true for poems, stories, plays, and essays as well as for novels. When you rewrite one thing, you jostle the rest of the work. Its parts are interconnected. Take a character out of a story, or add a character, and something else goes out of whack.

Maybe your workshop will tell you that a different character needs to be bolstered, now. Or if you have changed an image in one stanza of a poem, the workshop may say another stanza is weak. It's impossible to tell in advance where a misalignment will occur.

Go ahead and record the new feedback. You may not know at first how to alter your piece, so be wise and sleep on it. You will know later what to do with it, either in the middle of the night or the next morning — or in a week or two.

## PRACTICE

For the practice, you have three options. The first is to continue the gushing clichés exercise, the second is to write a new piece, and the third is to do a rewrite. You could do another rewrite of the piece you just revised, or you could rewrite a different piece.

If the cliché exercise got your Crazy Child going, by all means continue. This is the first option. By now you know how to expand an exercise into a larger piece. Get that story, poem, play, or essay down from beginning to end. Quickly and roughly. Do this with the confidence that you are doing one thing well — at least one thing.

It can be useful to ask yourself what the piece is about. This is your target. To hit that target, you may need a harsh conflict, or you may need piles of image detail, or sharp dialogue, or a strong narrator. Aim at that target and write wildly — in the spirit of the exercise. Gush out those images and possible clichés.

The cliché exercise might also have pointed to something new. This is your second option. You were following a trail of clichés and you might have brushed up against something in the dark. It could be a big, furry animal — a wild beast straight from your Crazy Child. Chase that critter.

Your third option is to do a rewrite. If you're tempted to do another rewrite of your revised piece, it's wise to sleep on it first. After a little time has passed, your mind will clear. You'll be working on a new set of problems and you'll have fresh eyes.

You could rewrite a different piece. The gushing clichés exercise has a way of exposing raw feeling — feeling we may not realize we have. You may be ready to bring startling emotion to an old piece. Perhaps you realize you love that erring relative in the missing person practice, on pages 59–60, though at first you cast the relative in a bad light.

Or perhaps you will want to redo the missing valuables practice, on pages 144–145. You might have discovered that your protagonist is more angry than you first imagined. Your narrator should be sizzling with anger. The piece could use a rewrite — one that gives off smoke.

## Anger and the Crazy Child

The topic of the gushing clichés exercise could have made you angry, too. Honor this. Anger is an engine for powerful writing — especially the anger of the just. Anger chooses smoldering details. Anger ignites your sentences with fire. Anger can pull the reader right into its bloodshot world.

The Crazy Child stores anger we are not aware of, and this anger can bend clichés automatically — without our realizing it. It does not matter if you begin with dozens of clichés. Spew them out. Anger has a way of forging them into carbon steel.

## Amping the Attitude and Pushing the Envelope

"Amping the attitude" and "pushing the envelope" might both be clichés — and they might work for you. You are enlarging the area where your Crazy Child is free to be itself. Amp the attitude in your practice piece. Push that envelope.

It will be difficult to tell on your own whether your clichés have recovered their power. It is better simply not to make a judgment. Keep the Editor and Writer in abeyance — off to the side. You are teaching them to accept the Crazy Child's flow of words. After a few days have passed, you may be able to assess which words are powerful.

For now, simply write. Whether you expand the exercise, write a new piece, or do another rewrite, let your Crazy Child gush out those clichés.

# Chapter 10

## Character

*I always try to write on the principle of the iceberg. There is
seven-eighths of it under water for every part that shows.*

ERNEST HEMINGWAY

"Character" is the complex of traits that makes up a person. These
traits distinguish each person from all others. In life we recognize
the person in front of us, moving or talking or quietly thinking, by
that person's traits.

Height, weight, eye color, and hair color are obvious physical
traits. Character includes a plethora of subtle traits, too. Manicured
hands, an alert expression in the eyes, a slight limp as that person
pulls a chair up to a restaurant table — all these show character.

The list of character traits goes on: dress, tastes, habits, man-
ners, emotions, everything right down to intangibles. Little habits
are part of character. Style is part of character. How a person eats
a soft-boiled egg in a cup for breakfast or cereal with raspberries;
how that person holds a coffee cup or a cup of herbal tea.

Traits that drive the character are in each person's history.
Religious, cultural, and racial factors exert pressure at every
moment, and so does a character's upbringing. How the character
speaks to the waiter, how the character responds to what the waiter
says — all this is rooted in childhood.

The complex of traits is vast. If we list all of one character's attributes, our writing would go on forever. But the reader does not need to know everything. Authors learn to display character succinctly, without using lists.

## A Few Traits Convey Character

Character is best conveyed by a few traits. Two or three salient details, thoughts, or actions will bring a character into focus. A few more scattered through the writing and the character becomes full-blown.

These few details seem to set up a triangulation. One detail from history, plus one physical trait, plus one thought, and the character gains an outline. If the character pushes against someone else's action, or pushes against the world, the shape of that character becomes clear. Write that interaction, include a quirky speech or another detail, and suddenly you have created a lifelike character.

These guidelines are simple. But exactly how you choose those details from the infinite number at hand is a mystery. The Crazy Child has some insight that is sure, decisive, and inexplicable.

> The chief use of the 'meaning' of a poem . . . may be . . . to satisfy one habit of the reader, to keep his mind diverted and quiet, while the poem does its work upon him: much as the imaginary burglar is always provided with a bit of nice meat for the house-dog.
>
> T.S. ELIOT

I will explore, more thoroughly, several ways that character is conveyed. These suggestions will be like the meat in the T.S. Eliot quote — they serve as morsels for your conscious mind to chew on while your creative unconscious does the real work. The Crazy Child knows something we do not.

## Character and Belief

Characters in creative writing are fictional — in the final analysis. But writers want us to forget about fiction and to believe the characters. Readers agree. We want characters to be so lifelike they seem to stand in front of us.

You might, as a writer, want a swimming pool attendant to be flirty and snobbish, or a gold digger to be truly sexy and raise goose bumps on the reader's thighs. A car thief might seem respectable and yet display a streak of larceny, even when he is eating lunch. He reaches and takes butter from another table, without anyone noticing.

You could write the opposite of these types. A lifeguard could be a physical nerd, but has a freckly magnetism. Maybe a gold digger is plain, and yet there is something in her eyes that promises heaven to her victims — and no one else can see it. A car thief could have an awkward walk and seem unable to put together a shirt and a clothes hanger, let alone two hot wires.

Any well-written character seems real to the reader. Our nervous system automatically creates the character from those few vivid traits. We feel the emotions, think the thoughts, see what the character sees — no matter what sort of character.

## Character, Point of View, Narrative Presence, Persona

The character I am discussing could be the main player in a story, poem, play, or essay. It could be your narrator, in whatever point of view. It could be a first-person narrator, a third-person narrator, an omniscient narrator, or any other person in the piece.

In the chapter on persona we saw how a writer can be many different people. In this chapter we investigate how any character becomes vivid. This includes your persona as well as your other characters.

Your main character is the most important, of course. It is vital that the reader believe this character. Others may be minor. They might be constructions the main character bounces off of or gets bruised by. They can be made of cardboard.

## Character and the Crazy Child

Your Crazy Child knows character, and why this is true is not a mystery. We deal with different people every day — in the world and in our minds. We make thousands of decisions and the sum total is us, but at any moment several decisions might be more typical of other people.

All these decisions amount to proposals of character. Your creative unconscious remembers them — and remembers the decisions we consider but do not make. When we wonder whether to ask someone out, we propose one character to ourselves. When we are paranoid about someone we propose another character to ourselves — or several nervous characters.

My creative unconscious can zoom into character through a single detail — as if that detail is the external sign of a decision, or of a series of decisions. I think of the tuck in someone's blouse when I need a character, or the knot on a bootlace, or the angle of a tilted jaw. Or I find a photograph and study it until a detail catches my eye.

My Crazy Child expands that detail easily. I need see only the tuck of that blouse and I dream who did the tucking, why the tucking was done, the shape of the hand that did the tucking, the disease that shook the hand, the smell of the room — and how the character made the blouse smell pungent.

An old photo of my father shows him on a runway, as a young man, standing beside one of the first planes that ever flew. He is listening to an engineer. The soft curve of his shoulder seems to echo an adoring look in his eyes. I've conceived a number of characters from this photo.

Near relatives are a fine source of characters. Our distant history contains an astonishing variety of people, too. Go back a century and you have some sixty-two blood relatives, go back five centuries and you have sixty-seven million. This crowd is in your genes. There are a few robbers, princes, and gold diggers in a group that large.

The Crazy Child seems to tap into this knowledge. The creative unconscious does know everything about any character — about any character whatsoever. World literature supports this. Authors, through their imaginations, know all about the most unlikely characters.

This knowledge is in your psyche, and it is yours through a sort of dreaming or remembering — just as with plot. You will find your own particular way of retrieving it. The process is easy. When you imagine a character, it's like remembering someone your Crazy Child knows well.

## Character and Action

Character is expressed through action. How people act reveals their character. How people react to a friend — or an enemy — displays a ton about character, and how imaginary people react in a story, poem, play, or essay is crucial.

Your character may confront danger quietly, or your character may wish for a weapon and reach into a coat pocket. If a gun is there, does your character use it? Or is that simple gesture — reaching into a pocket — barter for escaping from a dark alley?

"Action" does not mean violence, necessarily. It simply means that something is happening. Action can be confronting a strange situation, or holding to an ideal, or taking a risk — generally moving through life. No blows are struck in this excerpt from P.A. Combs' short story "Ulysses," but there's plenty of action:

> . . . Just as I was tilting the carton of milk up for a deep
> cold swallow I heard the snore. I froze. As far as I knew no one
> should be snoring in my apartment, no one but me anyway. I
> wasn't asleep, wouldn't have made any difference anyway, even

though as many an ex-girlfriend had told me I snored to wake the dead, I never heard myself doing so. I was always asleep when I did. So, who was snoring? Putting the quart of milk down I grabbed an old squash racquet from the top of the fridge and, crouching down, duckwalked behind the chipped Formica counter to where I could see over the pass-through into the living room. Hanging over the end of the couch was a huge, sun-bronzed foot clad in, of all things, a gilded sandal. Lifting the racquet in a sweaty hand I crept closer to the back of the couch. The snoring had stopped. I crept closer. I raised the hand gripping the racquet and peeked over the couch to see who had come to visit. From beneath a mass of auburn curls any one of my ex's would have killed for, one brown eye transfixed me.

"Is this how you greet a guest?" a musical voice issued from the slumberous lips.

"Who the hell are you?"

Glancing up at the squash racquet quivering in my hand he answered, "I am one whom hundreds learned to their sorrow that it was folly to have turned their hand against me. All. Every one I sent down to the cold darkness of Hades." His voice rose to a rumbling crescendo on the last word. I looked from the raised racquet in my hand, back to him, and then lowered it.

We feel this character's feistiness, and his foolishness, when he picks up the squash racquet. Someone else might scream or sneak out of the house or yell or phone 911 — or find a real weapon. How this man picks up the racquet and how he duckwalks toward the stranger shows his character.

Combs adds internal dialogue to the action. The man thinks about snoring and about his ex-girlfriends in a rambling, offhand way. This odd, self-deprecating chatter adds more to his character.

## Character and Internal Dialogue

Internal dialogue gives the reader a fresh take on character. Linking thoughts to action or to dialogue can make a character more vivid, because we get to know those thoughts in context.

In the preceding excerpt, we see how Combs weds thoughts to action. Gayle Staehle weds thoughts to external dialogue in this adaptation from her novel *Virtually Alien*. In it Sheila listens to Kesh explain how he entered a nightmare memory while testing a computer game:

> . . . I buried my head in my hands, acutely aware that the migraine was growing worse.
>
> I heard Kesh say, "All right, Sheila, a damaged CM on the visor might account for the phantom orange. But that can't explain the memory."
>
> "What exactly do you mean by memory?" I asked, propping up my elbow to press a hand against my forehead.
>
> "I'm not talking about computer storage," Kesh snapped.
>
> I knew I deserved it. It was another rotten day, one more bead to add to a string of misfortune. One more day that said I didn't belong at Virtually Real Technologies. I never even desired to live in California.
>
> Kesh looked down at his feet, shaking his head. "I'm telling you, the images were too precise to be either a dream or a hallucination."
>
> "Well, that leaves only one other hypothesis," I said, bewildered by the implications. "We've just invented a time machine."
>
> "I'm not making this up!" he fumed, jutting his jaw.
>
> Perplexed, still reluctant to believe what had happened, I shook my head. "Sounds like a wolf cry to me," I answered.
>
> "Get off my skin!" Kesh exploded. He picked up Ian's mug, the object closest to him, and threw it against the nearest wall. A loud clank sounded as it bounced off.

I stared at the ceramic pieces on the floor. That made three accidents in one day. I decided to take a break, calm down, and let the meds work against the migraine. I made one last attempt at a flicker of dignity. "Well, that's mature," I said over my shoulder to Kesh and Ian. "I'm going for coffee, while you two cyborgs grow human brains."

Sheila's thoughts are a world apart from her caustic remarks. She struggles with the computer problem, she struggles with her migraine, she tries to maintain dignity. Her character has these vulnerable aspects, even as she calls Kesh and Ian "cyborgs."

## Character and Image Detail

Character is revealed through the small — small actions, small thoughts, small details. Small, odd, and dissonant traits are most vivid, the same as with image detail. Odd traits are especially memorable, because they display the wrinkles that identify an individual.

Perhaps your character asks for a rare-medium-rare burger or for a veggie burger. Does she squeeze or knife her mustard on the patty or on the roll? When these small details are written precisely, they compel the reader to place the burger up close, in imagination, so those distinctions can be made.

These are superficial details, but every deep current has a suite of superficial — and obvious — details. Those details reveal inner traits. Something like an iceberg, which shows a tenth above the water, these surface details are keys to a character's depths.

Remember the excerpt from Jane Smiley's novel *A Thousand Acres* on pages 88–89? The narrator brings terrible news to her sister. Rose listens, but she seems more interested in adjusting her ponytail:

> I got up and hurried down to Rose's place. I burst in with the news. . . . I said, "My God, can you believe this?" I stepped over the pattern pinned to the fabric on the floor and fell into

an armchair. Rose knelt down and resumed setting the facing pieces on the fabric. "Rose?"

"What?" She sounded annoyed.

I didn't dare say anything else. I guess what I thought was that I'd offended her somehow. I always do feel a little guilty when I break bad news to someone, because that energy, of knowing something others don't know, sort of puffs you up. She picked pins out of her tomato pincushion and poked them into the oniony tissue paper, then sat back on her heels and cocked her head, surveying the fabric. She was wearing a ponytail. She lifted her arms and idly pulled her liquid dark hair out of the elastic, then made the ponytail again, more tightly. . . . She said, "Well?"

Sudden blindness in a relative should be shocking, but Rose fiddles with pins and adjusts her ponytail until her sister stops talking. These odd, superficial details display her mood. She is distant and unresponsive — if not hostile.

This mood, especially at such an emotion-laden moment, is part of her character. A deep current has surfaced. She seems to be angry, or in denial, or possibly she has a private agenda. We must read on to find out which.

## Character and Quirks

A "quirk" is a particularly odd trait. It is a peculiar part of a character, and everyone has one, or a few. They might be off-putting, hilarious, bizarre, or just plain silly.

Quirks mark an individual, and give the reader a unique angle into character. In Linda Cohen's novel, a quirk of Sal's character is shown on page 7 when he "took a spoonful of cereal and watched it move toward his mouth." A quirk of Rose's character appears on page 6, when she went to the bathroom, "put down the toilet seat and sat on top of it."

In the excerpt from Lillian Almeida's short story on pages

66–67, the protagonist is full of quirky expressions: "Overgrown half-dressed babes fresh from our first fuck," "another piece of ecstasy pie come and gone," "blowin' spun sugar up Ma Bell's dress." In Christopher Russell's poem on page 84, fiendish muses are quirky, too, when they rouse the writer: "Wake up, lamebrain, I'm gonna talk. . . ."

Less obvious are psychological quirks, as displayed by the narrator and his date in Larry Beresford's poem:

Mister Funky's Date

Margaret arrives at my door
with an enormous smile:
literally disarming.
I feel weaponless, naked,

witless, tongue-tied,
wondering how to impress her,
wishing I could bottle
some of her liveliness.

"Are you hungry?"
she asks eagerly.
I shrug and she replies,
"Good. I'm starving!"

That enormous smile displays Margaret's overly buoyant — and oblivious — character. The narrator, in his self-negating thoughts, shows a quirkiness of his own. He feels helpless before Margaret's enthusiasm.

Quirks make both these characters memorable. Any aspect of character can be quirky, such as dress, speech, thought, a habit, or a mannerism. The reader may think a quirk is only odd at first, but — like Margaret's enormous smile — it may point to the character's essence.

## Character in Plays

On stage, character is expressed through dialogue — naturally. A playwright puts the characters' quirks and depths in their speeches, and this should be done efficiently. You do not want the audience to nap while the characters describe themselves.

The main character in Susan Griffin's one-act play, *Thicket*, which was written for performance artist Ruth Zaporah, grieves the loss of a close friend. In this excerpt she walks around the stage describing the friend's room, where they had often visited:

> . . . the whole space was different then. I mean the walls and the floors are the same. Exactly the same. Except maybe the paint's a little worn. But it was her furniture that made the place what it was then. Her things. She had them in such a way that. . . . The table was in front of the sink, see. It was oak. An oak table in front of the sink. Not round. It wasn't round, it was oblong. Small. Antique. *[Pause]*
>
> And the stove was over here. The stove was on my right. Because I always sat in this chair. This chair facing the sink. So she could sit in the other. They were little folding chairs. So she could sit in the chair right in front of the sink, next to the stove, across from me. And the table was about a quarter, no maybe about a sixth, no maybe about, about somewhere between a quarter and a sixth into the room. And not quite centered. Just a bit off center. Just a bit off center. You see, to know it was meant to be off center. Just a bit to the side. To the left. And the chairs were . . . they were just centered. But the table was small. Not so small as a café table. But small. And I would sit facing her and she be sitting. . . . *[Pause]*
>
> And then she would get up for the teapot and pour all in one motion never stopping our conversation. . . .

Her obsession with the arrangement of the room is striking.

The table is "Just a bit off center," and she repeats this. She even figures precisely how far the table projected into the room. These small-scale, particular observations reveal the depth of her loss.

This character is also attentive to her friend's mind. We get a sense of the friend's character as an added benefit. How exacting she was in the arrangement of the room, and her final, graceful sweep of motion as she poured the tea.

## Character in Poems and Essays

Character works the same in poems and essays as it does in stories and plays. The narrator, however, may be the only character, and the author wants the person making the argument to seem authentic. The reader needs to believe the character, just as in a story or a play.

In the excerpt from George Orwell's essay "A Hanging" on pages 177–178, we noted the careful, observant character of the narrator. He watched from a receptive frame of mind, and he did not do this coldly. He was alert to the ridiculousness of the dog and the puddle — and to their impact. He was keenly aware throughout the piece.

The narrator should be consistent and believable as well in a poem. In her poem "Two-Sided Coin" on pages 134–135, Gail Ford is curious, playful, willing to accept, and able follow the images of her imagination. She makes poignant associations as she enters a surreal vision "where the rules of the world are written in the clouds."

When the poet returns to the ordinary world, her character is intact: she is still curious. She flips the coin again to see what will happen, and she invites the reader to be curious with her. Then the coin disappears. In the last stanza, both the reader and the poet are looking at the lines on her palm.

Wendell Berry, in his poem "Creation Myth" on pages 93–94, shows a similar consistency. He sounds like a country person spinning a yarn when he writes " . . . about the old days when Bill

/ and Florence and a lot of their kin / lived in the little tin-roofed house. . . ."

He keeps that mentality intact throughout the poem. Leisurely, exacting, amused at the foibles of his fellows, and, at the end, good-hearted. He seems very like the person in the tale. Bill finally lays out the map in his friend's mind by calling to him, after his friend gets lost — but before he hurts himself.

## Steeped in Character

When your Crazy Child is steeped in a character, whatever you write will show that character. You will find yourself writing the character automatically. You will write details that the character perceives, from the mindset of that character and seemingly in that character's mood. You will write that character's unique thoughts, speeches, and actions.

Your Writer and Editor can think about techniques for making character vivid, but your Crazy Child does the important work. When it is thoroughly steeped, your creative unconscious is the authority. Your Crazy Child will pick details that fit the character — no matter what your Writer or Editor think.

> *The training of a poet consists in learning how to tap that secret part of yourself which connects with the communal unconscious.*
>
> ERICA JONG

You are steeped in character when your characters start acting of their own accord. This is a benchmark. You, the writer, will simply report what the characters think, say, and do. You are writing the characters that your creative unconscious presents. Your Crazy Child is doing the creating.

## EXERCISE

Write two character portraits. Do one portrait of a person who is at the beginning of some sort of action and do another portrait of this same person at the end of the action. Take fifteen minutes for each portrait.

The action could be meeting someone new, or getting involved in a car wreck, or going alpine backpacking alone, or discovering that a relative has fallen ill — anything dramatic. The action could be the plot of a new piece. The first portrait could become the first part of a story, poem, play, or essay, and the second portrait could be its end.

Pick a character you have some interest in. Using a character that is already part of an exercise or practice is fine, and so is using a new character. Make it someone you are curious about or piqued by or love — a character that has some spark for you. This marks a character that your Crazy Child likes.

Write several aspects of the character in both portraits. Describe the person in small, physical details — both before and after the action. Show the character's personal habits before and after. Give examples of the character's dialogue and some of the character's thoughts. Be sure to include the person's more quirky traits.

All the traits will be different in the two portraits — at least a little different. Focus on the differences as you write. You are creating the character before and after a change, and these two poles will help you dream into the character deeply.

### Character Before and After

This exercise is called "character before and after." The missing valuables practice on page 144 can provide a useful before-and-after contrast. If you have an urge to rewrite this piece, use this character for your exercise.

At first, the character has an area of ignorance. The character either finds the valuable in the end, knows where it is, or at least knows where it isn't. That ignorance could be due to a flaw in the character, or due to an accident, or due to someone's connivance. Things could be very complicated.

Maybe the valuable becomes irretrievable in your story. Maybe the character gets confused and the world becomes a dangerous place, or possibly the character realizes the acquaintance is a malicious enemy. The reverse could as easily be true. The acquaintance — known only slightly at the beginning — could become a true and loyal friend.

In any case, the "before" and "after" portraits will be different. This difference displays the evolution of the plot. Your Crazy Child is probably interested in the growth, or in the decay, of this character. Your character might even get engaged to be married at the end of the piece. Or your character might die.

## Get Wild

As you write, the character may take over your mind. If so, stop the exercise and write the fullblown story, poem, play, or essay. Sometimes a student will skip my writing class when the Crazy Child starts percolating: "I'm not coming because I'm writing." This is a legitimate excuse. Jump into the piece that's cooking.

When you begin the exercise, be as extravagant or as mundane as you like. Make that "before" character vastly different from that "after" character — or only slightly different. Check in with what your Crazy Child wants. The differences will be crucial in either case, whether they are flaming or subtle.

Write as much as you can in the two fifteen-minute sessions. Write tiny details as well as wild quirks. Write the small, the peculiar, the dissonant — even things you suspect are not important.

Write down everything. It's difficult to tell which details are revealing while you're writing them. You may know an hour later.

Or you may gain perspective after several days have passed — or a week or a month.

## WORKSHOP

When you workshop the exercise, listen especially for how vivid or full a character seems. This is new. The author may think the details about character are trivial, but you can inform the author when those details show character. You are helping train the author's Editor and Writer to respect the creative unconscious.

You also have the rewrite or the practice from the last chapter to workshop. You can now include observations about character. Do this in the manner of every syngenetic workshop: follow the kindergarten rules. Your comments should further the intent of the writing.

## Unpleasant Characters

If you dislike a character, that's a sign the writing is effective. You do not have to be warmly disposed toward a character for that character to be vivid. Reading is a physical process. If you have a powerful negative reaction, the writing is penetrating to your gut. The writing is strong.

You might have uncomfortable reactions to small things, too. We bring a plethora of personal reactions to what we read. These reactions indicate what is on our minds — but not necessarily what is in the writing. I often dislike characters that do not meet my expectations. But the story goes on its powerful or vivid way, regardless.

In order to hear what the words express on their own, you must listen attentively. Your sense of a character may be deepened by small details — even ones that seem bland. Let them sink in before you react. Listen to what is happening inside you: the sense of a character may be mild, subtle, and deep.

Your role as listener is much more obvious, of course, when

your reactions are dramatic. If you like a character, everything is copesetic, and you know what to say. You can pick out the vivid lines easily, and quote them verbatim to the author.

If you dislike a character strongly, this is equally informative. A feeling of intense dislike is a signal to repeat those vivid phrases back to the author, and you know why. "I like this writing, and I know I do, because I hate that character. I want to kill him."

## The Complete Crazy Child Exercise

The complete Crazy Child exercise has three parts. Each part defines the role of one voice: Editor, Writer, or Crazy Child. You are familiar with the first part, from pages 72–78. You banish the Editor and Writer, and let the Crazy Child write whatever it wants. You know when part one is done, because the writing stops. Your Crazy Child takes a nap.

The workshop has been doing parts two and three. Part two starts when you invite the Writer back into the room. The Writer's job is to sort the strong writing from the not-so-strong writing. The workshop does this, as a group, when they point out memorable words and phrases.

Say your Crazy Child has written four paragraphs about a piano player in the "character before and after" exercise. Each paragraph has several vivid details except for the second, which has a dozen. The Writer types out all the vivid details, and the Writer is done. The workshop does the same, in effect, when they say, "These details are striking."

In part three, the Editor comes in and shapes the work, treating it like someone else's. The workshop has been doing this, as a group, when they give rewriting suggestions.

Say all the details in the second and fourth paragraphs are about the character's fingers. But the second paragraph has so many details about so many things that the piece is out of balance. The Editor decides which ones to trim. The workshop performs this role when someone asks, "Are all these details necessary?" A discussion indicates which ones work best.

But the Editor and the workshop do not throw away the extra details. They put them back in the Crazy Child's play box. Your workshop should emphasize this by telling you to save your phrases. That play box is a valuable resource. A description or a quote or a sentence or a character can be born in one piece, and find its home in another. This happens frequently.

The Editor does not have the right to nix a whole piece. That is not its job. It could decide, however, to ask the Crazy Child to replace an image. If the relationship between these inner voices is smooth, the request will be honored. The Crazy Child could even like the Writer and the Editor — and the workshop — strange as this might seem.

## Give More

Workshops often exhort an author to "Give us more." Sometimes the author is skating over the surface of a gripping story, poem, essay, or play, and does not go far enough in. This is a shortcoming beginning writers often have, and it is easy to remedy.

You are doing something well, but you do not quite believe it, so you pull up short. You stop before you have given enough detail, or enough dialogue, or enough internal dialogue, or enough action. You have not opened the door wide enough for the reader to step into the piece.

This is a signal for your Writer and Editor to encourage your Crazy Child. Giving more might seem extreme at first because the scene might provoke feelings you don't want to face. But you should believe the workshop. You may need the Editor and the Writer to help your Crazy Child push the envelope.

Knowing when to ask for more is a challenge for the listener, also. You may not be sure that anything is lacking. At first it's useful to review what parts of the writing are working well. When the entire workshop reports what they like about the piece, you will probably understand its stronger currents. One of them could be truncated — and expanding it might be exactly what is needed.

## PRACTICE

Write a new character. Make this character different from any you have done, and the more different the better. Try basing the character on a wild person you have heard about, or on one of your more bizarre relatives, or on someone very ordinary. Your Crazy Child could make up someone out of the blue, too. Anyone.

Place this character in the center of a new story, poem, play, or essay. You could, as an option, create a new piece by taking a minor character from a previous piece and making it a major one. Your new main character could be the other person in the missing valuables practice, or the criminal in the missing person practice.

When you make a minor character into a major one, you learn about your Crazy Child. This character is not one you chose automatically. You will probably find, nevertheless, that your creative unconscious can imagine it just as well. Your Crazy Child can be anyone.

### Dreaming into Character

Writers deepen characters by dreaming into them. "Dreaming into" a character means imagining what the character is like. You simply pretend you are this other person. You pretend you have this person's mind, body, feelings, impulses, background — everything.

Allow yourself to dream a lot. This will seem more like daydreaming than working, but it is fruitful Crazy Child activity. The Crazy Child loves it. It can be an attractive sort of voyeurism, and it certainly is a way of becoming another person — and enlivening, or escaping, our own lives.

We dream we are in the character's shoes. We wonder, what does this character do next? Think next? Feel next? Accept whatever wild, crazy, improbable — even stupid — thing that comes to mind. Write it down, and write down that next thing, too. Follow this character wherever it goes.

You might adorn your computer with flowers and dream your character is in Puerto Rico. Or sit out on a boat deck with a cigarette dangling from your lips, or imagine your lawn chair or couch is a yacht.

You may dream for an hour and the time is not wasted. The next five minutes may find you thinking this new character's thoughts or later as you fall asleep that night, you may suddenly know your character well. That hour was your research. Your Crazy Child is busy doing research when you daydream.

## Character and Personal Issues

Writing a character too much like yourself can be problematical. Your character may be floored by issues that you are grappling with in life. You might have to both write the piece and solve your personal issues at the same time.

If you're committed to writing about yourself, try fooling your Crazy Child with a disguise. Make some part of yourself, some obvious part, very different. Make your hair red, if it is not red naturally, or be a tall person if you are short, or short if you are tall. Make your own disability vanish, or give yourself a gimpy arm or leg.

Whenever you call your character to mind, you see someone who is physically different from yourself. Your character is different in a way that is unavoidable. You have fooled your Crazy Child, and now your Crazy Child can have fun. The story is free to go wherever your creative unconscious wants.

## Mix and Match

You might want to describe one or more people you know, but you don't want to embarrass them. You don't want to blow their cover. If you write something unsavory, you don't want them to be angry, either, and you don't want to end up in court.

The same technique for avoiding personal issues will work here. Give your characters superficial and starkly different traits, like curly black hair or a mean streak or a limp — or make each a composite of several people. Give one character the red hair that belongs to someone else, and give that second person the first person's limp. You are doing "mix and match" — just like a puzzle.

This frees the story, poem, play, or essay to go its own way. You are releasing your Crazy Child from the constraints of reality. You are taking off from real-life characters, not copying them, and your characters can do what they want.

You might be surprised how many stories and novels are taken from life. Most novels are inspired by things that actually happen, and the characters are composites of various people the author knows. Those people may not recognize themselves, however. They have a different life in print.

For the practice, you are writing a new character. You are letting your Crazy Child develop that character in different and mysterious ways. You can mix and match, you can write quirky details, you can do a take off of a relative, you can put a bizarre person into action. One or more of these should appeal to your creative unconscious.

You can daydream. You are doing creative writing, and the wisdom of your native impulses is coming into play. Dream into this new character. Writing is an adventure.

# Chapter 11

## Surrealism

*All good writing is swimming under water and holding your breath.*

F. SCOTT FITZGERALD

"Surreal" writing contains a significant portion of dreamlike material. "Dreamlike material" is anything with the shifty, unpredictable feeling of nighttime dreams. That shifty feeling is a hallmark of surrealism.

Dreams push so vigorously at reality that it becomes distorted, and we never know what to expect. In a dream I had last night an adult said he was four years old, in another dream I leapt thirty feet straight up. Any part of reality that is bent or warped qualifies as dreamlike — and thereby as surreal.

Things that move faster than usual are surreal. Things that move slower than usual are surreal. Sunlight that is brighter than life is surreal, so is grass that is greener than green and super-flat roads and trees with apples that change color and grow while you watch.

Material may be dreamlike because of its images, because of its pacing, or because of its logic. Those famous clocks that flow like putty, painted by Salvador Dali, are dreamlike in themselves. So are fun-house mirror reflections. So are X-ray photos that can walk.

Connect two objects not ordinarily found together and you have dreamlike material. A frog riding on an alligator is a surreal juxtaposition. Eyeballs that roam around out of their sockets are surreal. Ant-sized people skating on bald heads, a baby crawling on the ceiling, city streets with rivers and yachts — these are all surreal.

A fifteen-second TV ad might use dreamlike pacing — hopping from bedroom to morgue to gun barrel to pool to ballroom. These segues are so quick that they condense time. They can make the viewer feel our lives are fulfilled in a minute, in forward or in reverse time. This is definitely surreal.

Whatever twirls our waking, objective mind is surreal. The tone doesn't matter. We will read stories by Nancy Peterson and Jeff Karon where the logic is dreamlike, and the pieces have very different tones. Surrealism can be contradictory, harsh, soft, violent, warm, jumbled, shadowy, sexy — you name it.

When I see something surreal, my eyes widen. I feel I am peeking into a special universe. Whimsy might be real in this new place, or my barely conscious desires might be real. I may glimpse the secret of the ordinary universe. I am about to be honored and gratified in ways I can hardly imagine.

Surrealism has power because it hooks these unconscious wishes. It seems to say our dreams are real. Surrealism also appeals to the certain knowledge that our everyday world is only a thin surface. The universe runs by a deep magic we cannot understand — and surrealism might show us that magic.

Hard-core surrealism maintains its intense, dreamlike feeling throughout. The distortions, or the pacing, or the logic is pervasive. Other writing gains power with touches of surrealism. A poem or a story can include surreal lines that zing straight to the unconscious.

In this chapter we will read a variety of surreal pieces. We will read prose that is surreal through-and-through; poems with soft, surreal images; and lines that are like surreal lightning bolts.

## Surrealism and the Crazy Child

Any surreal universe is interesting in itself — it engages a wider range of ourselves than ordinary reality. This makes surrealism satisfying to read and to write. The appeal of creative writing is that it "lets you in," as Patricia Hampel says in her book *A Romantic Education,* and the operative word here is "you" — meaning all of you.

Surrealism lets in the creative unconscious. It's a free-for-all for that wild part of your mind — it's a neon sign that says, "For the Crazy Child Only." Surrealism is where your creative unconscious can do whatever it wants, however it wants. We know this is Crazy Child territory because the name says so: "dreamlike."

> *When I walked down the corridor and saw that fire hose there, you know the kind of mind I have, I wondered what it would be like if that hose were a snake, and started moving after you, you know, with that brass snout.*
>
> STEPHEN KING

*Let the Crazy Child Write!* shows how the engine for creative writing is the creative unconscious. This engine is not always acknowledged, but in surrealism it is. Surreal writing is obviously, unmistakably dreamlike; it is labeled as coming from the unconscious.

Surrealism is where your Crazy Child can play without restraints — without any restraints at all. There are no rules, because the rules of the ordinary universe have been abandoned. The Crazy Child makes up its own rules, or breaks them — even ones it just made up. In surreal writing the Crazy Child gets to romp.

## Surrealism and Imagining

A simple act of imagining can bend your writing into surrealism. When we imagine something is different from usual, we have entered a dream — if a small one. It could be a large dream, too, as large as fire-breathing monsters, or flying saucers, or as large as that snake in Stephen King's imagination.

Surreal worlds are not far away. Imagine a rose bush swarming with virulent, life-threatening insects. You're dreaming a surreal world. That swarm of bugs, though not a threat to humans, could be there in actuality. They might even be more numerous than you imagine, and a lot smaller.

Take one more leap of imagination, and those bugs are as large as dogs. They could be monsters, or they could be friendly — that's up to your Crazy Child. Another leap and their bite is psychoactive, or the person bitten can hear what the bugs are thinking. Or what plants are thinking.

Maybe a house finch knows what you are thinking. You could imagine its song directed at you. It might be in fact, since ornithologists report that some birds proclaim, "This is my territory." Imagine its next phrase: "Pay a toll if you approach"? Or "Come to dinner"?

When your imagination stretches the ordinary world, you come up with surreal images. Bugs and birds are commonplace — before the creative unconscious starts to play. The surreal is just around the corner, inches beyond what you usually notice. What will you see, as you walk out to pick up the morning paper?

In the following poem, George Staehle takes one small and startling step into the surreal:

An Outside View

They meet week after week
in each poet's house
crafting brand new windows
to see our side.

With straight rules they write
that we are dying fast.
Our seasons peer back worried
through engineered glass.

When they think they've polished
perfect eulogies
our brittle leaves scrape past
their panes to say,

Not dead.
Not so fast.

We glimpse a dream in this poem, or some special magic of the universe — those leaves can talk. They have power as truth sayers and as symbols of the natural world.

The leaves are effective image detail, also. They combine brittleness with the kinetic detail of scraping. Those two images pull the reader sharply into the poem.

## Surrealism and a Different Universe

One flash of imagining can start a world unfolding. The author can lead us into a new universe, step by step. We might view each layer with surprise, or pleasure — or chagrin.

Thaisa Frank's very short story starts in an ordinary way. But as we recognize a man long dead, the world becomes bizarre:

A Brush with Kafka

As you stand in the terminal of Chicago's O'Hare Airport, you happen to see Franz Kafka, hurrying past with a steaming hot-dog in his hand. Yes, you're waiting in line, also for a hot-dog, and there's Kafka, in a grey suit, grey felt hat, rushing to a counter where people are positioned like pillars. With a bitter expression on his face, Kafka unwraps the hot-dog and prepares to eat. His grey-fringed scarf falls into a pot of mustard and he raises the food to his mouth. Then his jaw-bone travels to his ear, and he begins to chew, consuming half the hot-dog in a few bites. As you watch him eat, you happen to notice that his hot-dog is covered with a brackish, dark green sauce, not available at the counter. You think that asking where he got it might be a good way to start a conversation, but just as you're going to approach, a dog runs by: You turn to look. Kafka *also* turns to look. And your eyes meet, cancelling all sense of urgency.

Suddenly the reader is back in an ordinary world, standing in the airport. Kafka and the observer are isolated from each other again. The "you" is unable to talk to the fabulous visitor, and we are left with a sense of loss.

This understandable predicament makes the scene convincing. So do the odd details — the gray clothes, the brackish sauce, the scarf getting dirtied in the mustard. I feel certain I have glimpsed a parallel universe.

You might have noticed this piece addresses the reader as "you." The author says you are in the airport, and you imagine you are. She tells you what you see, what impulses you have, and what you feel. This is the second-person point of view, and it's done well.

Jeff Karon's story also starts off in an ordinary reality. When this reality starts distorting, the distortions increase and then go exponential:

## Mother Love

I squeeze myself behind the living room couch, pressed against its cool springs. The carpet is thick like an unshaved sheep and my mom comes in vacuuming. The vacuum cleaner is a dinosaur. With a throaty growl it chews and swallows a penny. The fire eyes singe the carpet tips as my mom rides it through the room. I stay still as a rabbit.

"Are you still hungry?" my mom asks as she and the dinosaur disappear down the hall. Is she talking to me or it?

Yes, I am hungry. I run out from the couch. "I am hungry. Very very hungry. See!" I tilt my head back and open my mouth — a hungry bird waiting for Mom to spit up down my throat.

But there's no one around. There is no growling rumble, no throaty whistle. I am alone.

"Mom, Mom!" I run down the hall and into the bedroom. The sheets on the bed are damp and twisted, smells of oil and perfume mix in the air. Like her and the dinosaur have just been sleeping there. I could see them leave if only I could whip my head around fast enough.

Above the bed the curtain swells as a cold wind blows in. And I am colder than the wind and hotter than the center of the earth. The center of the earth is hot coal and fire. So hot — hot like hell it could burn a person and turn freezing rain into ashes.

"Mom — Mom!" I run through the house. Just ahead of me smells of motor oil and perfume like orange juice mix into my chest and start a fire.

I cannot live with this burning. "Mom!" I run back into the bedroom and from my singed stomach past my burning throat I throw up hot dust, carpet lint and scarred pennies.

Boundaries dissolve and we are engulfed in childlike fantasy and terror. The child becomes the vacuum cleaner — or worse, the vacuum cleaner bag.

This surreal piece conveys exactly what the child feels. It could be argued that no other writing is capable of doing that. Objective reporting would describe the scene from the outside, but could not give the reader the complete feeling.

## Bold Surrealism

Surrealism can be bold. In Gabriel García Marqués' book *One Hundred Years of Solitude*, the characters laugh, cry, make love, give birth, maim and murder each other in a bizarre world that echoes this one — with many twists. Baroque, wild, and impossible things happen.

Marqués' characters fit a dream of the strangest sort. In Nancy Peterson's story the protagonist lives in a dream that is fully as weird:

### Mud Pie

I'm making a pie. A mud pie full of delicious wet earth with a rainbow of grays and streaks of black in every sticky handful. I pile the mud until it's thick, let it warm in the sun, and before it hardens I smash it into my face, my mouth wide open. It has the stench of stagnant pond water, it scratches my teeth, plugs up my nose with silt, cakes my eyelids so I can't open them. I eat the whole pie and lick the clay from my lips when I'm done.

I'm enjoying my mud pie because in a split second disaster will strike. An arrow will go through my head; the earth will crack beneath me; a lightning bolt will charge me to a crisp; my heart will attack from the inside, swallowing my lungs and liver and spleen; a spaceship will flatten me; molten lava will spill over my head; acid rain will eat holes in my skin; pythons will squeeze me; vipers will strike me; and God will send me to Hell. Thank heavens I have time to eat a mud pie.

Eating a mud pie makes sense in the world Peterson creates. The protagonist might ingest whatever is at hand. She believes she should enjoy anything that is not yet destroyed — even if it's mud.

All the small details relating to the body pull the reader in. We cannot read this piece without tasting that disgusting — and pleasurable — mud. "Mud Pie" also provokes a fresh look at our lives. Am I eating mud pie, without knowing it?

## Surrealism and Emotion

Not much in everyday life allows for emotions at full strength. Even when an emotion finds a home, it usually can't live in all its power and complexity. Mown grass or asphalt streets or newspapers are not often accurate correlatives.

Why should they be? Emotions range from the minute and subtle to the huge and earth-shattering. They call for something from the imagination, something surreal — they call for full expression. The surreal is large enough for emotion: it can expand as far as any emotion's farthest boundary.

Many poems have images so jam-packed with emotion that they bend into surrealism:

"fingers hooked / inside each other's bodies, faces / red as steak"

SHARON OLDS

"sleeves intersect my wrists as though they would cut off my
    hands"
"your lips wrapped around / a block-long siren"

JAN RICHMAN

"a root, bare / and silvery, groping upward through air"

PHILIP LEVINE

"washcloths are / being wrung out inside my ears"
"the sky drifts into salmon and remains at just that moment"

BRUCE HAWKINS

"thin rainbow-colored nets / like cobwebs all over my skin"
"I am pregnant with murder"

ROBIN MORGAN

"the sidewalk is crumbling into diamonds"

DIANE DiPRIMA

"Your heart beating wildly at the tips / of your fingers like a blue
    ticket"

STEVE KOWIT

"Refugees sit up / studying old photographs they enter / like
    water"
"women are standing / at their windows, like lit candles"

KIM ADDONIZIO

"in the voice / of my friend, there was a thin wire of grief"

ROBERT HASS

Some of these lines stand in poems that are otherwise quiet or
meditative. They are like lightning strikes, bringing the poem's
emotion starkly into the foreground.

## Surrealism in Essays

Virginia Woolf uses a dreamlike image in her book *A Room of
One's Own*. She is sitting at the river's edge on a beautiful evening,
thinking about writing:

> Thought — to call it by a prouder name than it deserved
> — had let its line down into the stream. It swayed, minute after
> minute, hither and thither among the reflections and the
> weeds, letting the water lift it and sink it, until — you know
> the little tug — the sudden conglomeration of an idea at the
> end of one's line; and then the cautious hauling of it in, and the
> careful laying of it out? Alas, laid on the grass how small, how
> insignificant this thought of mine looked; the sort of fish that
> a good fisherman puts back into the water so that it may grow
> fatter and be one day worth cooking and eating. . . .
>
> But however small it was, it had, nevertheless, the myste-
> rious property of its kind — put back into the mind, it became
> at once very exciting, and important, and as it darted and sank,
> and flashed hither and thither, set up such a wash and tumult
> of ideas that it was impossible to sit still.

That fish is a touch of surrealism. By using it to represent an
idea, Woolf gives the idea vitality. The reader sees its liveliness in

the liveliness of the fish, as we watch the fish tease and tug and then stimulate a powerful "wash and tumult. . . . "

You could read this passage as a guide for dealing with clichés. They accumulate meaning the way a fish grows flesh. Putting one back in the water could mean leaving it in our writing, or letting it dwell in our subconscious. When it surfaces, it might be sleek and lovely.

## Surrealism in Plays

Surrealism in plays can be exciting. In the "mythopoetic" tradition, characters represent some mythological aspect of life, or even a classical myth itself.

An angel drops onto the stage in Tony Kushner's *Angels in America* and offers a magical escape. Actors live in garbage cans in Samuel Beckett's *Endgame*. In a Dorothy Anton play, one character is presented by two actors — one actor speaks the dialogue, another speaks the person's thoughts out loud.

In another contemporary play-in-progress, one character represents toxic thoughts, and speaks lines that live in our minds — lines we can barely tolerate. A dead father, in another play, walks around with a growing child who embodies the father's flaws and strengths, and the audience hears the father's reactions. All these are surreal strategies. They make for intense drama.

The surrealism is in the setup. The actors are given surreal roles from the start, and the roles are obvious. Since the actors are live, they can give the dreamlike material more reality than we could in our imaginations. Drama, in this way, can be stunningly more powerful than prose.

If you are tempted, by all means try a surreal setup. Make one character the symbol of all homeless people, or another the police, or another a fantasy of love — or what have you. Your characters can represent something of any size, as small as a human quirk or as large as a force in society.

The challenge is to keep your surreal characters interesting. Once the audience grasps what the characters represent, the characters need to change or influence the other actors or clash with the issue — in novel ways. You do not want them to be predictable. Keep them active. Have those surreal characters push the action at every moment.

## Locating the Surreal

Once you see it, you will notice surrealism almost everywhere. Fantasy, horror, and science fiction are mostly surreal, and so are many paintings and movies. It is ubiquitous in advertising.

Look up at the sky and an intuition may spawn a surreal dream. So might eating an ice cream cone, or sitting on the bus, or swooping around a corner on in-line skates. You may start with a casual detail and find it's the first step on an intricate, surreal trail.

Annie Dillard was picking up something off the floor of her bathroom when a spider web caught her attention. A train of thought came, and she began an essay. Another writer began an essay while rummaging around his desk. These subjects were stumbled upon by serendipity, but they are not meaningless. They were chosen by the Crazy Child.

> *When we are dreaming, we are fully conscious and aware of ourselves; we are oriented in time, place, and person. The dream world is a real place with real people in it. We experience a dream as real because it is real.*
>
> WILLIAM DEMENT, M.D.

You are mostly in your head when you write surrealism, and your brain is working harder when it is not looking at the external world. It needs to supply externals with its own energy — instead of simply noticing them. This gives surrealism a power the ordinary world does not possess.

You probably are doing some surreal writing naturally. You may have written lines like the examples in this chapter, and you can locate the surreal simply by noticing what you do. You could expand some dreamlike aspect of your style however you like.

When your Crazy Child wants to convey an idea, it might use a dreamlike image, as Woolf did. When it has a feeling, your Crazy Child might distort reality, as many poets do. Your Crazy Child might write a character emblematic of a trait or dive into a dream sequence in which the character says exactly what it wants, or what it hates, or more. Much more.

Your Crazy Child can create its own world — with a logic that bends or breaks or confuses or dazzles. When you dive into surrealism, you dive into your creative unconscious. Your Crazy Child may jump up and surprise you.

## EXERCISE

Recall a vivid dream and write the last scene. You will need to dwell in that scene. See it as clearly as you can and write plenty of image detail. Capturing a dream's feeling involves looking at it closely.

Then continue the dream, writing for a half hour in all. Continue it any way you like, using dream logic. Keep the same characters and flow of action or introduce new characters and new action — whatever strikes your Crazy Child's fancy. Your continuation does not have to make sense. You are starting out in dream logic, and the exercise continues that logic — or illogic.

Image detail is vital. The reader will not have ordinary reality to help locate where you are, so you need to draw us in by painting a picture of the scene. Include small and peculiar details, especially those peculiar ones — everything may be peculiar.

*Write with the internal logic of the dream.*

## Dream Logic

Organized by the "internal logic of the dream" is one definition of surrealism given by art critic André Breton, who offered many definitions for this twentieth-century art form. The virtue of this definition is that we can use it as a guide.

In dreams, one thing follows another according to a kind of logic. Dream logic is unhinged logic — logic not attached to ordinary reality. It is different from the minute-to-minute and hour-to-hour sequencing we experience every day. There are no other rules for this logic.

The moon truly can be green cheese in surrealism, or the grass can turn into an army, or a weed can be a handkerchief from the Goddess, or guns can shoot love bullets. There are as many versions of dream logic as there are dreams. It is whatever your Crazy Child likes.

## An Object Becomes Surreal

For an alternative exercise, begin by looking at an object — a real one or one you imagine. Assume it represents a blood relative and describe the object in detail. Be a scientist, using only descriptive, nonconnotative words. In part two of the exercise, become the object and describe what it feels like to be the object. In part three, change the object.

Choose anything — a wrench, a lemon, a piece of wood, a feather, a television set. Sometimes in my classes I fill a basket with random items and dump the contents onto a table for my students to rummage through. Who knows what will work? Nothing can predict what inspires the Crazy Child — that's a mystery.

When you begin part three and change the object, you are entering a surreal world. Go for it — change it wildly, fantastically, bizarrely. Change it using dream logic, and let your Crazy Child do the writing.

## Crazy Child as Big

The Crazy Child may not be a child, or little. "Crazy Child" is simply another name for the creative unconscious. Your Crazy Child can be as big or as old as it wants, or as subtle or as wise or as silly or as peculiar.

> *The idea of [inner] child is a means to express a psychic fact that cannot be formulated more exactly. . . . It is a system functioning to compensate a one-sidedness of conscious mind.*
>
> CARL JUNG

My Crazy Child can be a tiny kid wandering around in my bloodstream. It is able to shrink that small, and this is a kind of power — the power of the very small and the very mobile. More often I feel my Crazy Child is just a quarter of an inch under my skin. Or it can be bigger than I am.

My Crazy Child can break down buildings, climb walls like Spiderman, and do powerful things. It can transform the moon into goat cheese or turn my enemy into a sneering bull's-eye. Maybe your Crazy Child can sneeze and cause a butterfly to be born or a concrete wall to become whipped cream. Maybe your Crazy Child can clap its hands and be on Mars.

For either of these exercises, ordinary rules are on holiday.

They are upside down, or playing Crazy Child themselves. If your Crazy Child wants to be humongous, be humongous. Write with the internal logic of the dream.

## WORKSHOP

It may be difficult to give feedback for a surreal piece. The exercise may have very little you can grasp with your conscious mind. You may not be able to find a hook, or an issue — or even a character.

Listening to surrealism requires that you listen well. Clear your mind and let the piece tell you what it's about. It is best to listen with your gut, too, or with another part of your body — your spleen or your heart or your funny bone.

Do a syngenetic workshop, as usual. Listen to the piece, and pick out things you like — simply because they grab your attention. You may have nothing more to offer, and this is fine. You are identifying the impulse of the writing.

The piece may give you a distinct feeling. You can monitor that feeling, pointing out its ebb and flow, and this can help the author see when the Crazy Child clicks in. That may happen in the third scene of the dream, or when the object is transformed. Suddenly the Crazy Child comes along, cool or sizzling, and gives the writing fresh power.

### Apple Again

When you are the author, feel free to say "Apple" — or "Apple sauce," or "Bushel," or "Apple-" whatever. We have been using "Apple" to represent an apology, as I mentioned on page 102, and it could also mean you have no idea what you wrote. This might be true for the surrealism exercise.

When you say "Apple," you are clearing the atmosphere for feedback. You are telling your Editor and your Writer not to get involved in the intricacies of doubt, and you are telling yourself to get ready for the next step. Read out loud, listen to the feedback, write it all down — and take it lightly.

## Real Time

When you workshop the character practice, notice how the author gives you details. In life, you receive a complete picture of someone the instant you meet — but the picture is mostly unconscious. Only three or four things are likely to strike you at first.

As you get to know the person, you notice other details. Some details change — some add meaning and some lose meaning. When you write details in the same sequence as they are discovered in life, you are writing in "real time."

In the character practice, notice how the author interlaces details with action. As the character changes, the author will notice different details, and present these new ones to the reader. To keep the piece moving, the details should be woven in as the action proceeds. It's trickier to give descriptive details in a block, since that can interrupt the flow.

Writing details in real time gives the reader a sense of being there. Linda Cohen describes the scar on Sal's face several times in her novel, and we see it twice on pages 6–7. Each time it appears, it looks different — and it takes on a different meaning. We keep seeing Sal anew, just as we would in life.

## Bracketing

Revising a written piece can work the same way "bracketing" works for photographers. They "bracket" when, while taking pictures, they adjust their cameras for a range of light to dark exposures. They are looking for the setting, between extremes of light and dark, that will produce an ideal picture.

"Bracketing" describes written revisions that go beyond what you want. Perhaps your workshop asked for more detail, and you did write more, but you wrote so much that you shot past the ideal. Bracketing is a signal for your Editor, Writer, and Crazy Child to make a small adjustment.

If the workshop asks for more and then says you have done too much, breathe a sigh of relief. You might think, I cannot do anything to please this workshop. They say "more, more, more" and then they say "too much." But you know now what is too little and what is too much. Back off just a touch. You will be on target.

## PRACTICE

Go to a place that has a buzz of activity, and write with no agenda. Bring a laptop computer or a notebook and pen, but have nothing on your mind — no goal except the goal of not having a goal. Your Writer and Editor will help by being attentive and, otherwise, by staying out of the way.

Write whatever occurs. Describe bits of the landscape as they snag your attention, a passing thought, or a memory as it comes up — whatever occurs next, either in your mind or outside. Don't try to make sense of anything. Do this for an hour.

The place you choose is crucial. The buzz of activity should be loud enough that it keeps commanding attention, but it should not be so loud that you cannot hear yourself think. The kitchen in the home of an active family is a fine place for this practice. So is a cafe, or a delicatessen, or a locker room, or a stoop, or a bus station — or the bus itself.

At a cafe, you could write each of these as they happen: a snatch of a song from a radio as someone walks by, a memory the song provokes, a twinge in your shoulder, a newspaper headline you notice on the next table, a thought that hops into your mind, and so on. For example:

Light curves off the steel table edge. "I'd rather die, than give you control." Money eating away at the soul. Roar of a bus. Grandpa burning the charcoal he was going to sell until it was ashes. Light curves under my lids, into the knot under my shoulder. Bend my back. "Gulf Policy Unclear." Two teenagers, one with purple, one with green hair. Oil on the gulf, on the President's mind. Oil on the woman's lips, bending light into a helix. "Grumble, gurgle, gulp." A gulf between the stroller and the mother, two feet away at the round table. Lamp unlit, twisted blue crepe around its edge. Roar of the bus. Somebody's party the night before. How much money lost. Down the tubes for the last nightmare. My father fighting his father by not saying anything. Strands of barbed wire choking the words.

This example is hopping with possibilities. It could develop into a piece about the father, or one about money, or one about politics. If you go on for an hour, you may have fine raw material for a story, poem, play, or essay.

You can report what happens with a clear eye or you can report with a twisted mentality. If your Crazy Child wants to bend reality, go ahead. Why not see everything through the bottom of a soda glass? Stay clear, though, of organizing the piece. Write without caring whether there are any connections.

## Synchronicity

This practice is called "synchronicity" writing. The only immediate connection between events is that they happen at the same time. Synchronicity is observation in the moment, with no judgments or boundaries: everything that comes to your attention is equal.

Some poems of the New York School, which began with Frank O'Hara in the 1960s, are written like this. They will include the buzz of a refrigerator, simply because it snapped on while the author was listening. With such attention to the moment, you may write unexpected and startling things.

Synchronicity allows your Crazy Child to select material in broad daylight. When you truly write with no conscious agenda, the agenda of your creative unconscious takes over. That agenda may come up in chunks throughout the writing.

You will be writing the evidence that the world is presenting — evidence of your creative unconscious. However, the piece may seem to have little cohesion. It might seem scattered or whimsical or gritty or randomly surreal or pure chaos. Or, to your Editor's surprise, your Crazy Child could create a well-organized piece.

John Oliver Simon's poem could have been taken from a synchronicity practice. The world seems to jump up and support what he is talking about — as he is writing:

### Habitual

Jack and I drive into the glass and steel
center of the city
talking about addiction,
his sugar and cream, my smoke
not even to mention coffee
and the women, my God
the women we keep around
not to leave a vacancy,
a hollowness. Jack says he sees
the people he saw at Overeaters Anonymous
walking around the neighborhood
and they're still fat.
I put a little mark in my calendar
every day I don't smoke dope.
The city draws us in for our own reasons.
As we add up the years past 40
it's harder to stay clean.
At the red light I glance
across the blonde profile
of the woman bobbing to the music

in the red Toyota wondering vacantly
would she soothe who I am
or who I'm not. Out there
on the corner a guy
is not doing so well,
his pants in rags
his perception in tatters
we're both glad we're not him.
We visualize an easy time
when we run hard,
eat all we want, stay stoned
come home to someone who listens
and murmurs and laughs.
Sure we do.
Past downtown Skid Row steams in smoke.

The woman in the Toyota and the guy standing beside the road support the poem's thesis. They would probably not have been noticed if the poet weren't having that conversation. The poet sees evidence for whatever is on his mind, and nothing could be more natural.

Simon could have made up the details after the drive or distilled the poem from pages of notes. But this poem has the feel of being written in the moment — he most likely reported what he saw as it caught his eye.

## Editor, Writer, Crazy Child

The synchronicity practice is a call for the three voices to work together. Your Editor, Writer, and Crazy Child need to agree on how to do this. It is best for the Editor not to quarrel and best for the Writer not to strain to keep the peace.

Generally, the Writer oversees the project and gets the Crazy Child writing. The Editor can be quality control, keeping the phrasing crisp. If the Editor insists on making a critical comment, write it down ("Clive, you've said this before, on page 73!") in parentheses, as if it's part of the landscape. And then continue with your practice.

If your Crazy Child starts wandering from the synchronicity guidelines, the Editor may try to corral it. That could be acceptable. But if the Crazy Child heads out in earnest, the Editor and the Writer should let it go. Why do the practice, if your Crazy Child is on to bigger things — like building the Eiffel tower or digging the Grand Canyon?

Your Editor and Writer should learn when to let the Crazy Child direct everything. Your creative unconscious might want to continue the exercise, for instance, instead of doing the practice. If your Editor and Writer respect the Crazy Child, this decision is easy. When all three voices are working in harmony, the writing can proceed smoothly and easily.

## Synchronicity in Progress

For this practice, you could expand an existing piece in progress. Pretend you are one of your characters and do the synchronicity practice as that character. Go to the character's hangout, in real life or in your imagination, and write what your character would see, think, and hear. You will broaden your sense of that character a great deal. You might also deepen your sense of the piece's issue.

The bolder and wilder you are — in whichever alternative you choose — the more you are likely to learn. You may discover a new arena for your writing, or come up with fresh raw material, or attain a richer understanding of a piece in progress. It's a win-win situation: in any case, you will be flexing your Crazy Child muscles. This practice is for fun.

# Chapter 12
## Resolution

*I have never started a poem yet whose end I knew.*
*Writing a poem is discovering.*

ROBERT FROST

"Resolution" is the third and final element of plot. The hook snags our attention, and the issue — with all its complications — draws us through the piece. At last, in a definitive event, image, scene, or thought, the threads come together. This is the resolution.

Resolution comes toward the end of any writing — it may be the next-to-last event in a story or novel, the concluding stanza of a poem, the last scene of a play, or the end paragraphs of an essay. Resolution gives the plot its spin. When we read the resolution, we know what the point is.

The point can be obvious. If the author has a message, we find it written loud, clear, and tied with a bow. Or the point could be as subtle as an impression. The author might present a dilemma and therefore cannot tie a bow on one point, or a process, which does not have any fixed point.

But when we arrive at a resolution, we know we are there. If it's the triumph of good over evil, we get that; if it's the downfall of a beloved character, we get that too. If it's an impression of bouncing between two extremes, or a feeling of alienation, or a picture of the complicated workings of the mind, we get these also.

Resolution is the target of any piece; it is the iron bar that the plot's magnet is pulling us toward. We know the resolution has arrived when the magnet hits that target — it's like hitting a gong.

> ... [T]he china night-light ... outside is painted with a scene, which is one thing; then, when the lamp is lighted, through the porcelain sides a new picture comes out through the old, and they are seen as one. A lamp I knew of was a view of London till it was lit; but then it was the Great Fire of London. .... The lamp alight is the combination of internal and external, glowing at the imagination as one; and so is the good novel.
>
> EUDORA WELTY, *Place in Fiction*

## Surface and Undercurrent

Plot has two tiers, the "surface" and the "undercurrent." The surface is where the reader lands. It can be a physical place in the world, like Eudora Welty's unlit china lamp, or it can be an event or a narrator. Part of us stays on the surface all the way through to the resolution.

The undercurrent hovers underneath the surface. It is the haunting presence of that London fire, waiting to spring forth when the light is turned on. It is like a tide in the ocean or a current in a river, and it might be stronger than the surface current.

This two-tiered reality has a parallel in our persons. When you meet someone, you see the surface of that person, and that person sees you — your face, your dress, your gestures. This is your surface. Under your skin are your impulses, your desires, your history — your Crazy Child. This is the undercurrent. It informs what you say and do.

Creative writing works in the same way. At first we are aware of the surface, but there usually is a submerged issue. The creative unconscious will be in that submerged current, with all its explosive or subtle material. Roiling along underneath, that undercurrent gives the writing its twists and its turns — like a rip tide.

The "surface" is a veneer, as discussed on pages 154–155. You pretend no undercurrent exists when you write in a distanced manner, but the reader receives a chunk of emotion by the end of the piece. Other terms for the two tiers, like "message" and "meta-message" or "text" and "subtext," point to the same two-part dynamic. When the tiers come together at the resolution, they display the full result of the plot.

The tiers generally work as in this example. Suppose a story follows an athlete who recovers from an injury and reclaims a place on the basketball team. The athlete matures in the process, learning how to live and train within healthy limits. The steps taken to rejoin the team is the surface, and the maturing of the athlete is the undercurrent.

In Margaret Atwood's novel *Surfacing,* the protagonist discards her lover, hides from her friends, and discovers a sign her father may — or may not — have left. She does not ferret out the cause of his death, but she does develop a sense of self. "Will the woman discover her power?" is a summary of the undercurrent. We recognize it as the magnet.

Similarly, in Ernest Hemingway's novel *The Old Man and the Sea,* we wonder why the man does not give up and head for shore when the storm starts battering his small boat. Then we realize the man is fighting to assert his expertise, or, better, his dignity. The question becomes, "Will the old man maintain his dignity in his battle with the sea?"

We can state the surface and the undercurrent in two-part sentences. They identify the magnets that pull us toward the resolution. "Will the woman find the cause of her father's death, and in the process discover her own power?" "Will the old man bring in the marlin, and thereby maintain his dignity?"

## Crazy Child and Resolution

The goal of the Crazy Child is to express itself. This could mean saying something focused, or it could mean getting on stage and talking at random. But such random indulgence is tiring — it becomes far more satisfying to say something particular.

If you scratch gently, you will find your creative unconscious has something definite to say. Something tickles your Crazy Child, and scratching that itch will stimulate your creative powers. Your creative unconscious wants to praise something wonderful, or to raise a question, or to deliver a precise blow.

That precise blow could be the resolution of a piece — even if it is only displaying the interconnected workings of society or asking an unanswerable question. Or your creative unconscious might want something obvious: to come out of the forest, vanquish the evil knights, and ride off with the prince or princess.

The surface and the undercurrent are Crazy Child territory, too. An infant shows its expertise when it squeals and, at the same time, rubs a hungry belly — or caresses a scraped knee, or points to a butterfly. The dynamic is like that scout, on pages 126–128, who keeps the village focused, while explaining the dangers of an approaching tiger. The Crazy Child is practiced at holding the reader's attention and conveying the undercurrent — both.

Whatever its inclination, your creative unconscious' most satisfying goal is to express itself — with impact. It becomes known to the world with a statement: something to experience, to relish, or to ponder. In a resolution, your Crazy Child strokes the gong at the county fair.

## Resolution in Poems

The surface of Mariana Ruybalid's poem comes together with the undercurrent in the last stanza. The poet is painting and, at the same time, following a train of thought:

## Watercolor

Blue, the color of sky
I use small strokes.
Light, air, joy,
shared breakfasts,
chamomile tea.
I am gentle with
my nervous system.

Red, fire and anger,
boldness across the page.
A friend of a friend
commits suicide.
"She was disabled,
she just got tired."
I catch myself
holding my breath,
remembering despair.

Purple forms bridges
and clouds between
red and blue as colors
merge and run. Stability
is a continuous blending
that doesn't forget wounds.

For my forty-sixth birthday,
I ask for chocolate cake
and a trip to
Monterey Aquarium.

The poet conveys the flavor of stability in solid, vivid images — chocolate cake and a trip to the aquarium — so we can savor their strength. The images contain the message.

The undercurrent ripples with a dangerous sadness. Stanza two suggests that the poet's persona has visited despair, and barely survived. A sense of gratitude and of newfound control are poised against that despair. The healthy nurturing of the chocolate and the trip becomes more powerful.

Ruybalid may not have thought out the details of surface and undercurrent — more likely she simply followed a feeling. Most authors work in this fashion. An author will have a corner of the conclusion in advance, but usually not all of it. The feeling you chase as you write exists because your creative unconscious is busy with the two tiers. The Crazy Child writes them both, without the aid of conscious planning.

In the title poem for his book, Tom Quontamatteo stays carefully on the surface. The undercurrent is subtle, and may become clear after you live with the poem. The surface is a trail of details, one after another:

Emptiness That Plays So Rough

> The last moments of the day
> fall quietly on my shoulders
> like snow gathering
> on a hillside,
> a silent movie.
>
> In the afternoon hours
> the wind backs awkwardly
> up Dwight Way, and
> the dust curls oddly in the air.
> This, and the hot rush of the day
> catch the late sunlight
> leaving me trembling.
>
> The five o'clock traffic moves
> devotedly up the street, and
> a line of sweat gathers
> on my brow.
> The telephone rings
> a few times before I take notice of it.

The undercurrent is an aimlessness and loss of center, to the point where externals take over. The poet does not, at first, even recognize that the telephone is ringing.

The resolution is a complete picture of this state of mind. It is not presented as a character flaw, or as some tragedy, but as a natural condition. It is accepted without judgment — like electricity, or cement streets, or a virus.

## Resolution in Stories

Resolutions are just as obvious or just as challenging in prose as they are in poems. Lin Carlson's surreal piece seems to shift realities as it ends:

### Seiji

Peter runs away suddenly, sticking Ramona with his basset hound, Seiji. The dog has bad habits. Pees in the dining room. Slings slobber on everything; it dries white and stains. Ramona ignores the hound for days, hoping he too will vanish.

On Saturday she finds him sitting in Peter's big recliner, smoking Peter's pipe, reading Henry Miller. "Ah," the dog says, glancing her way, "You know, I can't fathom the Americans proclaiming Miller profane. In France and Japan he's revered. A literary — "

"Get down!" she shrieks, pointing to the floor. He jumps at the command. She slaps his flank. "You know you're not allowed on the furniture! What do you think you're doing?"

Seiji cowers. Whimpers. Rolls on his back to expose a downy, vulnerable belly. This softens her. Later she allows him into her bed and they curl together. His big neck and head mold over her middle, so warm. Palpable. Lying like puppies.

Ramona has to do without Peter, and she has to put up with his obnoxious dog — who then imitates his master. The turning point comes when Ramona yells and Seiji rolls on his back.

With the dog, Ramona gets a version of what she wanted with Peter. There is heavy irony in this resolution, however. On the surface, Seiji replaces Peter, but in the undercurrent, Ramona is slave to her wish to cuddle — to the point of becoming puppy-like with a dog. I come away with both a loving warmth and a defeated, hopeless feeling.

## Resolution in Plays

The audience wants to be involved, instantly, in a dramatic issue that works through the play like a machine or a clock — or a runaway truck. The playwright wants the audience wondering what is going to happen next, all the way through to the resolution.

Our understanding of what is happening needs to keep pace with the action. Timing is crucial. If the action goes too slowly, the audience gets bored. If the action goes too fast, the audience is left behind. If the pace is apt, the threads come together at the resolution and make resonating sense.

In my one-act drama *Spikes*, the sprinter CJ is disillusioned, but John pushes him to win at all costs. Martin, in contrast, has been playful and enthusiastic — like CJ's former self. The threads come together in the resolution:

*John:* What's wrong with you?

*CJ:* It's what's wrong with you. Your program sucks. And you turn your back.

*John:* Okay, CJ, for the last time. You've betrayed yourself. You're fighting the sprinter in you, and that's weak. Put on those spikes and everything will change. You've forgotten the one concept behind winning. The single important principle, in track and in life. No pain, no gain.

> *[Gives a triumphant smile and turns away.]*

*Martin [to CJ, teasingly]:* Yeah, you wimp.

> *[CJ looks at Martin, then rushes John and punches him in the*
> *face.]*

CJ's pain collides with John's rigidity. The spark is Martin's teasing accusation, which exposes the underpinning of their inter-actions — anyone who doesn't go with the program is a wimp. The play ends as Martin helps John off the track:

> *Martin [to CJ]:* You ever hear of live and let live? What you did
> was fucking childish.
>
> *[Martin helps John up and both exit.]*
> *CJ [shakes his hand, as if to shake out the pain of the blow]:* That
> hurts. And John won't get it. But at least I shut him up.
> For now. No pain, no gain.

When CJ repeats John's line, "no pain no gain," he has turned John's macho creed on its head. The fuller humanity that CJ strug-gles with throughout the play has won, if only temporarily — and with blood.

## Resolution in Essays

An essay is written so that it can be tracked by the conscious mind. We follow the surface logic, point by point, through to the resolu-tion. There may also be an undercurrent, carrying a ripple of emo-tion or irony or shock.

After he steps around the puddle, on pages 177–178, the pris-oner in George Orwell's "A Hanging" begins talking to his god. He chants, "Ram! Ram! Ram!" A bag is put over his head, but his chanting is still audible, and the entourage is uncomfortable. Finally the superintendent gives the order to hang. The piece comes to a climax when the noose jerks around the prisoner's neck.

Fear and shock have been building among the escort. After the man is dead, Francis, a soldier, tells how during another execution a doctor needed to hang on a prisoner's legs to finish him off, and how another prisoner needed six men to pull him out of his cell. They tried reasoning with him, to no avail: "Think of all the pain and trouble you are causing." Orwell continues:

I found that I was laughing quite loudly. Everyone was laughing. Even the superintendent grinned in a tolerant way. "You'd better all come out and have a drink," he said quite genially. "I've got a bottle of whisky in the car. We could do with it."

We went through the big double gates of the prison into the road. "Pulling at his legs!" exclaimed a Burmese magistrate suddenly, and burst into a loud chuckling. We all began laughing again. At that moment Francis' anecdote seemed extraordinarily funny. We all had a drink together, native and European alike, quite amicably. The dead man was a hundred yards away.

The hanging itself is the surface, and the shock in the undercurrent erupts as laughter. Orwell dwells in the scene long enough to give us its full impact, and he includes himself among those who are laughing. The last sentence ends the essay with a sobering punch.

## Premodern, Modern, Postmodern Resolutions

Resolutions come in three varieties. "Premodern" is displayed in writing before the twentieth century, "modern" in writing since World War I, and "postmodern" since the 1960s. Premodern writing is often called "traditional," but since all three varieties have traditions, the term is confusing.

English literature once had an automatic cultural or religious imperative. You couldn't write without expressing the value of the culture, or interpreting God's will — and the handprint of God was everywhere.

> *Premodernism: the mind expressing an ordered world.*
> *Modernism: the mind looking at an unfamiliar world.*
> *Postmodernism: the mind examining a suspect mind.*

Premodern resolutions have morals or sweeping, general

insights, as if all readers will agree. If we liken a short story to a black box that you go into and come out of changed — as story writer Raymond Carver does — then, in a premodern story, that box is wrapped with ribbon and tied in a bow.

With industrialization, Darwin, Freud, Einstein, and World War I, the structures of church, state, and heart lost their authority. Now we were largely on our own — instead of being part of a sensible creation. An issue could be approached only by a mind looking at an unfamiliar world.

The authority of modern resolutions comes from within the piece, not from God or the culture — or anywhere else. Modern resolutions are pragmatic, as in Ruybalid's poem "Watercolor." The black box of modern stories is wrapped with twine or strapping tape.

Postmodern resolutions show the influence of molecular biology, Heisenberg's uncertainty principle, cultural relativism, quantum mechanics, the atom bomb, and neurolinguistics. Fifty or sixty years later, events early in the twentieth century seeped to the personal level.

Now, every thought is suspect. Our thoughts might come from cultural history, or from our psychology, or from hormones. Perceptions are not what they seem. They may result form a language or process that operates beneath our minds and we know little about it — and underneath that language may be another language.

Postmodern resolutions, like that in Quontamatteo's poem "Emptiness That Plays So Rough," may not seem like resolutions at all. They may give a sense of the topic or only pose a question. Many of John Ashbery's poems ask how the mind conveys a sensation to consciousness — or whether it does. The postmodern story is a black box tied with virtual tape.

All three resolutions are common today. You do not have to be postmodern just because this is a postmodern era. You can write in any mode. Complete innocence is unlikely, though. Postmodernism often seeps into premodern or modern writing, simply because it's in the air. The resolution of Carlson's story "Seiji" has a postmodern tinge, for instance. It describes a process distant from Ramona's will.

## Steeped in the Issue

Whether your point is premodern, modern, or postmodern, it will come across if you are "steeped in the issue." This concept originates in the critical writing of Henry James, who recognized its importance in fiction. Your precise point is being delivered when you have dreamt so far into your issue that nothing else seems to exist.

"Steeped in the issue" is a guide for selecting what particulars to write. You have steeped your Crazy Child like a bag of tea, and the essence of the tea is everywhere. It's filtered into everything you see, everything you think, and everything you write.

How authors do this varies a lot. Some of us read about the issue, or write a few paragraphs about it, or talk about it with friends, or think about it late at night. Or we simply sit and scratch our faces. We get steeped in the issue by letting the feeling of the creative unconscious take over.

When it takes over, you write from the inside of your piece. Your creative unconscious is focused. You see only the details that contribute to your story, poem, play, or essay — and no others. You hear only the speeches that contribute, and only the thoughts that contribute.

Being "steeped in the narrator," as on pages 149–151, or being "steeped in the character," as on page 203, can result in being steeped in the issue. When you are steeped in the issue, you certainly will be steeped in the character. You will be steeped in the narrator too.

As you write, simply follow the Crazy Child feeling — in all its intensity. Become steeped in that feeling and run at your resolution, letting your creative unconscious handle the complexities. You are the clapper sailing easily up a track to that gong.

## EXERCISE

The first exercise is designed for a more thorough understanding of resolution, and the second is designed to bring clarity to the dynamic of the Editor, Writer, and Crazy Child. You will profit from both. If your time is limited, choose the one that seems most interesting.

### Freeze-Frame

In the first exercise, rewrite a dramatic scene by "freezing the frame." Choose the resolution of something you are rewriting, or, if you like, choose the final scene of a new piece, or an important scene from the middle of any exercise or practice. Write for a half hour.

Freeze the frame. Make time stop, so the scene becomes completely static. You can now roam around in it. Almost any place you land, you will be in the middle of an unfamiliar view. Describe it. Go into detail — more than you have in the rest of the writing — and use slow motion techniques.

Have your character look around the room and record thoughts from one instant to the next. Or write from a new place, such as the point of view of a minor character, or a chair, or the pistol, or the underwear, or the fly on the ceiling. You are indwelling in a new way.

Often the buildup to a resolution is fine, but at the crucial scene, or "set piece," the writer loses attention. We may see it in our minds so clearly we forget to show it to the reader. And it's in the resolution that we want the reader to dwell, and to experience the scene most fully — to feel all the implications. The resolution needs to arrive with flying flags and firing cannons.

As you write, include plenty of image detail, dialogue, a strong persona — all the aspects discussed in *Let the Crazy Child Write!* Even write the material you think is excessive. If your Crazy Child sends it up the pipeline, it's worth putting in ink.

You might want to keep what you write — every word — or you might not. Either way is fine; the writing does not have to be perfect. The goal is to gain a fuller understanding of the scene.

## Editor, Writer, Crazy Child Confrontation

In the second exercise, have the Editor, Writer, and Crazy Child talk to each other. Give one voice the floor and let it have its complete say, without interruption. You might begin with the Editor. The Editor will talk to the Crazy Child, and then to the Writer, one at a time, until it is done. Then go on to the next voice.

This exercise could become a brawl. The voices often have serious issues with each other, and they might begin shouting out of turn. Let them. They are showing you their dynamic — as they make insults and find fault.

The goal is to review the contract between the voices. What you write will display the contract currently in force. That contract determines the role each voice plays in your writing — who is in charge, whether the voices respect or condemn each other, how much the Crazy Child is honored.

When you began this book, you may have made a contract, for instance, to explore *Let the Crazy Child Write!* for as long as your Writer found it interesting. As you progressed, that contract probably changed. You can bring that contract into focus with this exercise. Then you can alter it however you wish.

After each voice has its say, let them speak again. They will talk differently the second time around. This indicates some readjustment, but you can ask for more. The Writer is the negotiating voice. Your Writer can pet, tug, barter, reason, compromise — whatever is necessary — to keep the Crazy Child central and to help the voices work together.

Any time you feel blocked, try this exercise. When the voices shout at each other, they are unstuck and mobile. The Editor or Writer might have been stepping on your creative unconscious. Get that boot off your Crazy Child's neck.

## WORKSHOP

You have a surrealism practice and the resolution exercises to workshop. The author often thinks the freeze-frame exercise is uninteresting, but the workshop is likely to be intrigued. Tell the author what phrases capture your interest.

In the Crazy Child-Editor-Writer jam session, the author might think the dialogue is so private — or so histrionic or so crass — that it is boring. But the workshop may identify with the dialogue, and this is valuable to the author. Those snarl-ups are likely to be similar from writer to writer.

### Say Just Enough

A workshop often recommends that a writer leave off a last line, or a last paragraph, or even a last page. The reader has the resolution and does not need to recapitulate. Notice the ending of Sharon Davies' poem:

The Rose

unfolds its crimson petals
to the rising sun,

surrenders its blossoming
to the heat of day.

In the cool of the afternoon,
its edges fold outward

and drop to the ground
as darkness takes the land.

We feel the seasons of life through the transformation of the rose. The poet gives us crisp, well-chosen images, and we fill in the gaps.

Originally, the poet added two lines at the end, "stirred by winds rising / from the sun's swift journey." The workshop decided those lines divert attention from the resolution. We get it without the last lines.

If the reader fashions the bow — or the twine or the virtual tape — that wraps the package, that may be the strongest possible ending. Of course, the writing must lead the reader to that point. But strong writing often does let the reader take the final step.

---

*The best craftsmanship always leaves holes and gaps in the works of the poem so that something that is not in the poem can creep, crawl, flash or thunder in.*

DYLAN THOMAS

---

## Bring the Issue Into the Foreground

A writer may discover what the issue is after the first draft is completed. This is true for the most accomplished authors. Authors commonly do not know — even after a second or third draft and much discussion — exactly what the issue is.

When you do know the issue, workshop comments are easily put to use. Will a change contribute to the issue, or not? Does this scene heighten the tension, or diminish it? The same can be asked of every line of dialogue and every bit of description.

Here is an example. One of my workshops was confused by these suggestive and bell-like lines at the resolution of a poem:

A man came upon her once.
He was lost
and she was found.
He stood silent.
He looked at her right hand
lying palm up.

The man and the woman seemed equally lost in the rest of the poem. The workshop could not understand why, at the end, one was lost and the other found.

Before she joined the syngenetic workshop, the poet thought she was a bad writer if people did not understand her work. She used to feel terrible. Now she understands that an unclear draft is part of the writing process, and she simply needs to take the next step.

She asked herself why the woman was found. Her creative unconscious gave her the answer later — she felt it rise through her body. The woman could be seen by someone who was as vulnerable as she was, and by no one else. The poet set up that ending by changing a few lines, and the poem was done.

The poet brought the issue into the foreground. The issue in prose, too, is commonly submerged in a wealth of not-quite-to-the point detail. It needs to be brought directly into the foreground — either as surface or as undercurrent — so the reader can feel it from the start.

## The Rake

The surrealism practice requires careful listening. The writing might be like a growth of wild green and purple plants — or maybe pink and metallic. The reader needs to get a definite feeling, so the images should all be flowing in the same direction toward a single target.

For instance, the narrator could have done many different things in Nancy Peterson's "Mud Pie," on page 220. The narrator might have put baubles on that pie or sugar frosting or a message spelled with chocolate chips. If you read the first paragraph now, you discover that she has only mud on the pie. She has raked out everything else.

You might go through your piece with a mental rake — like a garden rake. This concept is helpful in getting the issue into every word. It's useful when the workshop is not quite sure what the issue is, but has a feeling for it. You don't need to state the issue to know when a rake is necessary. In "Mud Pie," we know the mud is essential.

Pull a rake through your piece. Get all the words to line up in the same direction — so they point to the bull's eye.

## Move the Target to Hit the Arrow

This guideline, from the social-activist Highlanders School, elucidates an experience of Doris Lessing's. She had second thoughts about the chapter in her novel *A Proper Marriage* where a woman begins menstruating during a date at a classy restaurant. She telegraphed her agent to take out the chapter, but he refused. He said it was her best.

Lessing thought the novel veered off course with that chapter. But her creative unconscious knew what it was doing. What she first thought of the chapter did not reflect its true impact. She was learning to follow the course of the story, and to move the target.

The writer is like a boat following a river, and must go where the river goes. On one curve, the target may seem to be up in the hills, and on the return curve, the target appears to be on the near bank. But the target — after all the twists and turns — is the river's ultimate destination.

You will know when the issue you wrote agrees with the issue your workshop perceives. Your Crazy Child will automatically compare its feelings with the workshop's discussion. After zigzagging through the possibilities, you may have a growing excitement, or you may ring like a struck bell. It could happen in a few minutes, in a day, or in a few months.

In the Crazy Child paradigm, the conscious mind finds out about the unconscious mind by reading what the Crazy Child writes. This is why it is important, on one hand, to let your creative unconscious write as freely as possible, and, on the other hand, to give its writing careful attention. The Crazy Child informs us what our issue is.

While you are writing, you may have only the vaguest feeling what the piece is about. You may know what the next scene or stanza is — but that may be all. This is your Crazy Child shining a flashlight into the darkness. It's enough.

## Nitpicky Remarks

A nearly finished piece may provoke as much workshop discussion as a first draft. A full half-hour might be spent on which tiny parts contribute to the resolution, and which do not.

> *Murder your babies.*
>
> WILLIAM FAULKNER

Perhaps you need to change a word here or there, or twist the implication of several phrases, or alter a line of dialogue to keep it in character. These lines may be ones you love. You may have to "murder your babies" to get your piece to hit its target exactly.

But these comments are quite different from earlier ones, which might have questioned large chunks of the writing. These are picky. When you, the author, hear these nitpicky remarks, you know your piece is nearly done.

## PRACTICE

I'll describe a practice for understanding resolution, plus a general, five-step guide for creative writing used by Ron Schreiber at the University of Massachusetts.

### Writing in Reverse

Start with the ending of a new piece. The ending could be your freeze-frame exercise or any new ending you like. The piece needs middle parts that lead up to that ending, and it needs a beginning.

Write these in any order. Your Crazy Child can write "takes," like a jazz musician making a recording. A "take" is any paragraph or stanza or sentence that might fit somewhere in your piece. You can do them on the moves, so keep a small notebook handy. Your Crazy Child will present you with takes in class, at work, as you drive, or as you ride a bus. When it does, whip out that notebook.

> *It's a talent that I have, so that I can get out of the way and let something come through. The words are like a meal. You just serve them. I see my role as . . . a waiter. I bring the food out and take the plates away.*

The takes might come in haphazard order. Quite a few stories and poems are written in reverse, since the creative unconscious often starts with a scene from the middle or the end. The piece is constructed from there. You need to step aside, and let the Crazy Child proceed in its own way.

You will want all the parts, finally, to merge as a fluid trance into the resolution. You do not have to begin with that fluidity, however — you can attain it through rewriting. The flow needs to seem natural only to the reader.

## Five Steps of Creation

These five steps mimic the creative process. They are useful in rewriting and in writing from scratch. Choose a story or topic your Crazy Child feels some excitement for — naturally.

> Step 1: State the target of the piece, in one sentence, as con- cisely as you can. The target can be an intuition, or an event, or an idea.
>
> Step 2: Do "takes" on the material — whatever occurs to you, one line or one page or one paragraph at a time. The takes can include parts of your first draft, if you are rewriting.
>
> Step 3: Put the takes in order and number them.
>
> Step 4: Make an outline as you study the takes. The outline will indicate where there are gaps in the sequence, or where there are duplicate takes.
>
> Step 5: Repeat the steps.

Step 1 will become more precise the second time through. You are zeroing in on your target. Your piece will organize around that sentence as you repeat the steps. Your words will begin to aim straight at the target, like an arrow.

## Poetic License

Writers often "lie to make sense." A story may become more clear if a writer rearranges the facts. In life, for instance, the clothesline in John Tinloy's story "Malady in Madrid," on pages 129–130, might have been empty. By hanging out a half dozen chorizo sausages on that line, the writer gives the reader a vivid detail — and the ending has an odor.

*Life is stranger than fiction.*

Life is not only stranger than fiction, it is more complicated. A writer must sort out the threads, and present one or two on paper. The way something happened may not make an effective story, poem, play, or essay. You should alter reality to keep those essential threads in focus.

You can bend the facts on purpose. Plot will "mix and match," just as character does. Take from gossip, newspaper accounts, stories from childhood, myths, history — anything. Mix the facts until the resolution and the action fit. You are creating a world for the truth of your Crazy Child.

When do you change your target, and when do you keep the target and rearrange the facts? There is no easy answer. The experience you gain working with your Crazy Child will guide you, and you may take wrong turns a few times while you are learning. When you listen to your body, you may gain some important clues.

## Continuing Your Writing

*Let the Crazy Child Write!* has explored a wide range of writing, all powered and enlivened by the creative unconscious. Here are a few suggestions for continuing.

You could learn more about your Crazy Child by doing the exercises and practices again. There are enough alternatives in *Let the Crazy Child Write!* to go through the book a second time. If you started a workshop, and your workshop also wants to repeat the chapters, this will work well.

If you did not join a workshop, you might be confident enough now to begin one. Most people find that writing is too isolating to do completely on their own. This book discusses ways to begin a workshop on pages xvii-xix. Try, at a minimum, to find a writing partner or a friend to read your writing.

If you did join a workshop, and it was successful, take steps to keep it going. The pieces you find yourself writing can be shared and strengthened in your workshop. It is important to follow the syngenetic rules on pages 16–17 — even the most advanced workshops find them invaluable.

You may have discovered exactly what kind of writing is for you. Taking a class at a university or community college is an excellent way to continue. In any major bookstore, also, you will find inspirational books and guides to writing novels, stories, poems, plays, and essays. I recommend thumbing through these and picking one that seems attractive — for whatever reason. Most of the books are quite good; you almost cannot go wrong.

There is inspiration in your lives, too, as well as in personal reading and in public readings. Inspiration from your Crazy Child is free, limitless, and may be anywhere in this world. The creative unconscious is your source of ideas, feelings, and the drive to write. You know now, by experience, that it can give you great pleasure and satisfaction.

In *Let the Crazy Child Write!* you have been making a habit of bringing your creative unconscious out onto paper. By keeping in touch with your Crazy Child, you will be provided with the richness of a writing life. Plan your next step, and make it one that is exciting and challenging. Follow those twinges from your Crazy Child.

# Notes

## Preface
"Beginning my studies . . . in ecstatic songs."
— Walt Whitman, from "Beginning My Studies," *Leaves of Grass*, Modern Library, New York, following the 1891–2 edition, page 9.

## Chapter One
"Without . . . playing with fantasy . . . is incalculable."
— Carl Jung, *Psychological Types*, 1923, page 82.

"What is there . . . that give the likeness-to-life. . . ."
— Eudora Welty, *Place in Fiction*, 1957.

"Even if I could put down . . . not copy it."
— Georgia O'Keeffe, *Georgia O'Keeffe: Portrait of an Artist* by Laurie Lisle, 1980.

"It may be going too far . . . our confidence in him."
— Eudora Welty, *Place in Fiction*, 1957.

## Chapter Two
"Find out . . . what the action . . . person who reads it."
— Ernest Hemingway, in *Words of Wisdom*, William Safire and Leonard Safire, 1989.

(paraphrase) Journal writing improves the immune system.
— James Pennebaker, "Writing Your Wrongs," *American Health*, January/February 1991.

"In a poem the excitement . . . governed by gravity."
— Marianne Moore, in "Five Famous Poetesses" by Louis Untermeyer, *Ladies Home Journal*, May 1964.

## Chapter Three
"No tears for the writer . . . no surprise for the reader."

— Robert Frost, "The Figure a Poem Makes," preface to *Collected Poems*, 1939.

"I have been afraid. . . . I'm not lying."
— Barbara Kingsolver, *The Bean Trees*, Harper Perennial, New York, 1988.

"We read five words . . . and dream that dream again."
— John Gardner, *On Becoming a Novelist*, Harper and Row, New York, 1983, page 5.

"If the baffling . . . a second chance at enlightenment."
— Frederic Golden, "One Step Beyond Black Holes," *San Francisco Chronicle Review*, September 12, 1993.

"Art is a mystery . . . doesn't matter a very good God damn . . . "
— e.e.cummings, *six nonlectures*, Harvard University Press, 1953, page 68.

## Chapter Four
"I hold a beast . . . is their self-expression."
— Dylan Thomas, in *The Life of Dylan Thomas* by Constantine FitzGibbon, 1965.

"Everyone has talent . . . dark place where it leads."
— Erica Jong, *The Artist as Housewife*, 1972.

" . . . the brain in REM sleep . . . the vantage point of wakefulness."
— William Dement, M.D., in *The Sleepwatchers*, The Portable Stanford Series, Stanford, 1992.

"A child's attitude toward everything is an artist's attitude."
— Willa Cather, *Willa Cather on Writing*, 1949.

## Chapter Five
"There is, indeed, only . . . whatever form it may take. . . ."
— Mircea Eliade, in the forward of *The Forge and the Crucible*, translated by Stephen Corrin, 1962.

"I make all my decisions. . . . That is intellect."
— Ingmar Bergman, *Colorado Springs Gazette Telegraph*, March 9, 1981.

## Chapter Six
"The experience of art . . . its basic intractability. . . ."
— Aaron Copland, 1952, in *Copland on Music*, 1960.

"Innocence of heart and violence . . . exist without them."
— Louise Bogan, in *Achievement in American Poetry: 1900-50*, 1951.

## Chapter Seven
"In the writing process . . . even when you are at rest."
— Doris Lessing, in *Words of Wisdom*, William Safire and Leonard Safire, 1989.

"The laws you can lay . . . hour of creation arrives."
— Raoul Dufy in *The Taste of Our Time* by Albert Skira, 1954.

"In effect (writing a plot) . . . only as you move forward."
— Sue Grafton, in an interview on Pacifica Radio KPFA, May 12, 1992.

## Chapter Eight
"You have not grown old . . . life calmly gives out its own secret."
— Rainer Maria Rilke, from the poem "You see, I want a lot . . . " in *A Book for the Hours of Prayer*, translated by Robert Bly, 1981.

"Writing is rewriting"
— reported by Dorothy Bryant in *Writing a Novel*, Ata Books, Berkeley, 1978.

## Chapter Nine
"The intensity with which a subject . . . beauty in art."
— Paula Modersohn-Becker, 1905, in *Paula Modersohn-Becker: The Letters and Journals*, 1983.

"The dream of every cliché is to enter a great poem."
— Charles Simic, personal communication.

"Paint what's in your head . . . may be pretty exciting."
— Georgia O'Keeffe, in a speech given at Bryn Mawr College, 1971.

"Start wherever you can . . . leads to more rewriting."
— Dorothy Bryant, in *Writing a Novel*, Ata Books, Berkeley, 1978.

## Chapter Ten
"I always try to write . . . water for every part that shows."
— Ernest Hemingway, interview in the *Paris Review*, spring 1958.

"The chief use of the 'meaning' . . . meat for the house-dog."

— T.S. Eliot, *The Use of Poetry and the Use of Criticism*, 1933.

"The training of a poet . . . with the communal unconscious."
— Erica Jong, *The Artist as Housewife*, 1972.

## Chapter Eleven
"All good writing is swimming . . . holding your breath."
— F. Scott Fitzgerald, from an undated letter.

"When I walked down the corridor . . . with that brass snout."
— Stephen King, on *The Shining*, from a interview with Whoopie Goldberg, June 5, 1993, on PBS television.

"When we are dreaming . . . real because it is real."
— William Dement, M.D., in *The Sleepwatchers*, The Portable Stanford Series, Stanford, 1992.

"The idea of (inner) child . . . of conscious mind."
— Carl Jung, quoted in "Hidden Secrets of Childhood" by Suzanne Short, *Psychological Perspectives*, issue 21.

## Chapter Twelve
"I have never started . . . a poem is discovering."
— Robert Frost, *New York Times*, November 7, 1955.

"(T)he china night-light . . . and so is the good novel."
— Eudora Welty, *Place in Fiction*, House of Books, Ltd., New York, 1957, page 7.

"The best craftsmanship . . . crawl, flash or thunder in."
— Dylan Thomas, "Poetic Manifesto," *Texas Quarterly*, winter 1961.

"Murder your babies."
— William Faulkner, in his Nobel Prize speech.

"It's a talent . . . food out and take the plates away."
— Coleman Barks, in "Poetry as Path" by Katy Butler, *Common Boundary*, November/December 1991.

# Permissions Acknowledgments

Grateful acknowledgment is given to the following publishers and copyright holders for permission to reprint in *Let the Crazy Child Write!*:

Excerpt from *The Woman in the Dunes* by Kobo Abé, translated by E. Dale Saunders. Copyright © 1964 and renewed 1992 by Alfred A. Knopf, Inc. Reprinted by permission of the publisher and by permission of Secker & Warburg, London.

Excerpt from "Eric's Come to Live on the Farm" by Lillian Almeida. Reprinted by permission of Lillian Almeida.

Excerpt from "Vines and the Quarter Moon" by Jonathan Austin. Reprinted by permission of Jonathan Austin.

"Mom Was Cremated," copyright © 1984 Patricia Bentson. Reprinted by permission of Patricia Bentson.

"Mister Funky's Date" from *Under a Gibbous Moon: The Adventures of Mr. Funky* by Larry Beresford. Copyright © 1996 by Larry Beresford. Reprinted by permission of Larry Beresford and Broken Shadow Publications.

"Creation Myth" by Wendell Berry, from *A Part* copyright © 1980 by Wendell Berry. Reprinted by permission of North Point Press.

Excerpt from *Jane Eyre* by Charlotte Brontë. Copyright © 1961 by Dell Publishing Company. Reprinted by permission of Dell Publishing Company, New York.

"Seiji" by Lin Carlson. Reprinted by permission of Lin Carlson.

Excerpt from the first draft of Linda Cohen's novel. Reprinted by permission of Linda Cohen.

Excerpt from "The Emotional Con Meets a Virgin Ideal" copyright © 1990 by Wanda Coleman. Reprinted from *African Sleeping Sickness: Stories & Poems* with the permission of Black Sparrow Press.

Excerpt from "Ulysses" by P.A. Combs. Reprinted by permission of P.A. Combs.

Excerpt from *Jurassic Park* by Michael Crichton. Copyright © 1990 by Michael Crichton. Reprinted by permission of Alfred A. Knopf, Inc.

"The Rose" by Sharon Davies. Reprinted by permission of Sharon

Excerpt from "Tell Me a Riddle" from *Tell Me a Riddle* by Tillie Olsen. Introduction by John Leonard. Copyright © 1956, 1957, 1960, 1961 by Tillie Olsen. Introduction © 1994 by Dell Publishing. Used by permission of Delacorte Press/Seymour Lawrence, a division of Bantam Doubleday Dell Publishing Group, Inc.,and by permission of the ElaineMarkson Agency, New York.

Excerpts from "A Hanging" in *Shooting an Elephant and Other Essays* by George Orwell, copyright © 1950 by the Estate of Sonia B. Orwell, reprinted by permission of Harcourt Brace & Company., and by permission of A. M. Heath & Company, Ltd., London.

Excerpt from "The Ticket" by Mark Peterson. Reprinted by permission of Mark Peterson.

"Mud Pie" by Nancy Peterson. Reprinted by permission of Nancy Peterson.

Excerpt from "What is permitted" by Marge Piercy. Copyright © 1977, 1978 by Marge Piercy and Middlemarch, Inc. From *The Twelve-Spoked Wheel Flashing* published by Alfred A. Knopf, Inc. Used by permission of the Wallace Literary Agency, Inc., New York.

Excerpt from "The window of the woman burning," from *Circles on the Water* by Marge Piercy. Copyright © 1982 by Marge Piercy. Reprinted by permission of Alfred A. Knopf, Inc., and by permission of Wallace Literary Agency, Inc., New York.

"Emptiness That Plays So Rough" by Tom Quontamatteo, from *Emptiness That Plays So Rough* copyright © 1995 by Tom Quontamatteo. Reprinted by permission of Tom Quontamatteo and Broken Shadow Publications.

Excerpt from *Still Life With Woodpecker* by Tom Robbins. Copyright © 1980 by Tom Robbins. Reprinted by permission of Bantam Books, Inc., New York.

"Great Poets" by Christopher Russell. Reprinted by permission of Christopher Russell.

"Watercolor" by Mariana Ruybalid. Reprinted by permission of Mariana Ruybalid.

"My Childhood" and "K's Childhood" from *Dreams Are Another Set of Muscles* by David Shaddock, copyright © 1987 by David Shaddock. Reprinted by permission of In Between Books, Sausalito, California.

Excerpts from "Buried Child" by Sam Shepard, copyright © 1979 by Sam Shepard. From *Seven Plays* by Sam Shepard. Reprinted by permission of Bantam Books.

## About the Author

Clive Matson enjoys writing poems, stories, plays, and essays. His avocations are playing table tennis, growing organic vegetables, and collecting minerals in the field. He lives in Oakland with poet Gail Ford — his wife — their son Ezra, and three cats.

He is published in numerous anthologies, and his six books of poetry include *Mainline to the Heart* (Poets Press, New York, 1966), *Equal in Desire* (ManRoot, South San Francisco, 1983), and *Hourglass* (Seagull Press, Oakland, 1988); his Crazy Child poems will appear in *Squish Boots* (Broken Shadow Publications, Oakland, 1999).

In the 1960s he was protegee to the Beat Generation; in the 1970s he worked with the Berkeley Poets Cooperative and with Josephine Miles; in the 1980s with the National Organization of Changing Men and with Robert Bly; he won a fellowship to Columbia University where, in 1989, he earned an M.F.A. in poetry.

Since 1978 he has taught hundreds of writing workshops, to thousands of students, nationwide. He gives one-day workshops, three-day seminars, and teaches 10-week courses, including one for the University of California Extension in Berkeley. *Let the Crazy Child Write!* is the distillation of his unusually broad writing and workshop experience.

His reading and teaching schedule can be found at http://matson-ford.com.